EXISTENCE, IDENTITY AND MOBILIZATION

The Cotton Millworkers of Bombay, 1890-1919

Existence, Identity and Mobilization

The Cotton Millworkers of Bombay, 1890-1919

SHASHI BHUSHAN UPADHYAY

MANOHAR
2004

First published 2004

ISBN 81-7304-529-1

Published by
Ajay Kumar Jain for
Manohar Publishers & Distributors
4753/23 Ansari Road, Daryaganj
New Delhi 110002

Typeset by
FineCurve Computers,
Meerut 250002

Printed at
Lordson Publishers Pvt. Ltd.
Delhi 110007

To
My Uncle, Dr. Shyam Narain Chaturvedi
and
My Parents

Contents

Acknowledgements

In the course of writing this book, which has developed from my doctoral thesis, I have incurred many debts.

I am especially thankful to my supervisor, Professor Sabyasachi Bhattacharya for providing academic inspiration and personal encouragement. I would also like to thank Professor Bipan Chandra who found time from his busy schedule to read my dissertation and offer suggestions.

My friends, Salil, Basant, Vijayshree, Sharmishtha, Khurshid and Meenakshi, have been a source of constant encouragement and support. I am indebted to all of them. I am doubly thankful to Salil for reading my manuscript and giving suggestions.

At academic level, I have benefited a lot from my interaction with the colleagues at Indira Gandhi National Open University. I am thankful to all of them, particularly Khan Saheb, Swaraj, Abha and Ajay. I am particularly grateful to my senior colleague, Professor Kapil Kumar for encouraging me to finalize the manuscript.

Discussions with another colleague and friend, Professor J.M. Parakh, even though he does not belong to the discipline of history, has always been intellectually stimulating. I am grateful to him.

I must also thank my erstwhile colleagues at Centre for Social Studies, Surat for their support during my one-year stay there.

I am very grateful to the extremely cooperative staff of the Maharashtra State Archives, Mumbai, where I collected the major part of my source material. I am also thankful to the staffs of Nehru Memorial Museum & Library, National Archives of India, the Central Secretariat Library, the JNU Library, the ICHR Library and the IGNOU Library.

Parts of the book in earlier versions have been published in two issues of *Economic and Political Weekly*, on 29 July 1989 and 28 July 1990, and in *Contemporary India*, vol. 1, no. 2, April-June 2002.

Conventionally, one's biggest gratitude is reserved for the end, and the same is the case here. It is for Vijaya, my wife, whose suggestions, comments, support and encouragement have made it possible for me to complete this book.

The responsibility for any error, however, remains entirely mine.

SHASHI BHUSHAN UPADHYAY

Abbreviations

AFR	*Annual Report on the Working of the Indian Factories Act in the Bombay Presidency*
ARMC	*Annual Administration Report of the Municipal Commissioner of Bombay*
BC	*Bombay Chronicle*
BG	*Bombay Gazette*
BIT	Bombay Improvement Trust
BMOA	Bombay Millowners' Association
BTLU	Bombay Textile Labour Union
FC	Factory Commission
GOB	Government of Bombay
GOI	Government of India
EPW	*Economic and Political Weekly*
IDC	Industrial Disputes Committee
IESHR	*Indian Economic and Social History Review*
IFC	Indian Factory Commission
IFLC	Indian Factory Labour Commission
IIC	Indian Industrial Commission
ITB	Indian Tariff Board
ITJ	*Indian Textile Journal*
JD	Judicial Department
LMI	Labour Movement in India: Documents
MAS	*Modern Asian Studies*
MSA	Maharashtra State Archives, Bombay
NAI	National Archives of India, Delhi
RCL	Royal Commission on Labour in India
RNP	*Report on Native Newspapers*, Bombay Presidency
TFLC	Textile Factories Labour Committee
TLIC	Textile Labour Inquiry Committee
TOI	*Times of India*

Introduction

THE PRESENT STUDY is concerned with the early phase of the labour history in the Bombay cotton textile industry. It mainly covers the period from the early 1890s, when the industry faced its first serious crisis after a long span of prosperity since its inception, to 1919, a few years before another long era of crisis began to trouble this premier manufacturing enterprise in the early 1920s. The beginning of this period witnessed the first serious occurrences of workers' protests, expressed in the form of small-scale but frequent strikes, which continued with varying intensity over the years with several ups and downs. This phase ended with the first general industrial strike over economic issues in 1919, which the workers' accumulated experiences and the generalized miseries of the War years brought about. After this another phase began for both the industry and its workers, in which the employers tried to effect intensification of work in the form of rationalization while the workers resisted these attempts of intensification and retrenchment by resorting to many general strikes and other forms of protest. The period under study, therefore, covers a particular phase when the industry, despite its prosperity, was trying to come to terms with the adverse effects of colonial policies, and increasing international competition, while workers' solidarity had not sufficiently matured for unity at the industrial level on economic demands.

There are a few important studies dealing with the Bombay textile workers and their protests by, among others, M.D. Morris, Richard Newman, S. Bhattacharya, Dick Kooiman and Rajnarayan Chandavarkar.[1] While Morris is mainly concerned with the formation of the workforce and the questions related to the supply of labour and industrial discipline, the others mainly deal with the inter-War period, only marginally touching the early years.

The cotton millworkers in Bombay have been noted for their militancy, particularly in the inter-War period. However, the pre-War period, though comparatively quiet, was not uneventful. The growth of the textile industry, along with the railway workshops, dockyards and other trades, was remarkable. The concentration of a large number of workers in a relatively small area and the emergence of distinct mill-districts could always provide great mobilizational potential around a melange of identities which the social and political movements in the city spawned. Some of these identities relating to caste, language, region and religion could form parts of the inherited consciousness of the workers which they could easily comprehend while others, such as class, communal and national identities, could be induced in the city through modern social and political ideas and movements. Even the relatively older identities could be reinforced, modernized and widened in the urban setting.

The late nineteenth and early twentieth centuries also witnessed the initiation and intensification of a variety of social and political movements in the Bombay city and Presidency whose votaries at times attempted to bring the working classes under their influence. The workers also sometimes initiated certain social and political activities with or without this bearing on their work in the mills. Thus the urban working classes, like other groups, were possessors of a variety of identities which, depending on specific conjunctures, tended to generate both sectarian and unitarian mobilizations.

The Indian labour history until quite late had been chiefly concerned with the workers as economic beings for whom strikes constituted the only form of mobilization and class was the only available identity. Even the formation of the workers as a class was assumed rather than elaborated. The presence of many other complimentary or competing identities was ignored. Although these studies were significant in the sense of creating the tradition of labour history in India, they presented a rather one-sided picture of the workers and ignored the plurality of their existence.[2]

Dipesh Chakrabarty, in a major study of the jute millworkers of Calcutta, has justifiably reacted against the 'economistic' portrayal of the workers. But he has shifted to the other extreme and offered a culturalist explanation of their existence and activities. In this view, entire domains of working-class lives and mentalities are sought to be explained by their moorings in a 'prebourgeois culture'. Here the culture becomes the sole determinant of the entire range of behaviours and relationships where the 'political-economic analysis' has no role to play. From the nature of the industry and the behaviour of the employers through the attitudes and organizational initiatives of the workers' leaders to the protests and movements of the workers themselves, all are explained in terms of a monolithic and ahistorical concept called 'prebourgeois culture'.[3]

Reactions to such an extreme view were to be expected. Many historians have criticized this approach and tried to restore the primary role of the economic and political factors, particularly the sordid lives of the workers and their struggle to survive in the urban situation and the part which the colonial state and colonialist ideas played.[4] Here, however, the emphasis is basically on the economic and political, with an almost complete exclusion of the cultural. Even writers like Dilip Simeon, who are aware that 'The places whence the workers came were rich in symbolic co-ordinates',[5] think that 'the world of industrial labour is one whose basic coordinates are created by capital'.[6]

It is difficult to believe that the centuries' old tribal and peasant societies had no bearing on the minds and attitudes of the workers, whereas a few years of patchy, tardy capitalist industrialization could change their mentalities and behaviour in a space of a few months or years. This is to imbue capital with magical qualities capable of subduing the traditional societies with their age-old values and norms with effortless ease.

There are some specific area studies that have brought out the presence of several identities which sometimes hindered the formation of a broader class identity and restricted the extent of mobilization. These studies explored the possibilities of workers' mobilization around caste, communal and nationalist identities, besides that of class.[7]

Our basic thesis here is that although the grim conditions of their existence and the consequent struggle for adjustment and survival shaped their consciousness, the workers, at any given moment, possessed not one but several identities. Some of these might be their cultural inheritance from the villages, while others would be engendered and acquired in the city through a variety of political and social ideas and activities. The earlier identities were nurtured and widened in the city both due to the workers' attempts to survive in the new atmosphere and because of the general political activism sometimes induced by the colonial policies. The completely new identities relating to class, religious community and nation were often based on and around the previously existing consciousness of religion, caste and region. They constantly intermingled and determined the behaviour-pattern of the workers.

The book is divided into two parts each consisting of three chapters. Part I deals with the composition of the workforce and the working and living conditions of the workers. Part II is concerned about the formation of certain broad identities in the modern, colonial and urban context and which related to religious community, nationalism and class. All these were generated as a result of modern political ideas and movements, sometimes based on certain pre-modern identities and resulted in three of the biggest mobilizations during this period—a communal riot in 1893, a nationalist mobilization in 1908 and the protests and small mobilizations around economic issues which culminated in the general industrial strike of 1919. The study endeavours to explore how far these identities were ingrained in the consciousness of the workers.

Our attempt here is to take the workers' point of view into account. But any such endeavour has its limitations because of the nature of the sources. The workers during this period were mostly illiterates and had not left any written records of their own. Their voices reach us through double mediation—of some educated middle-class persons or the colonial officials and of an alien language. The problems and prejudices inherent in such accounts leave a large gap in our knowledge about workers' existence and activities. Even though we can find the trends, the accuracy is often impossible to achieve. With these limitations, this study attempts to narrate and analyse certain aspects of the workers' existence, identity and mobilization.

NOTES

1. M.D. Morris, *The Emergence of an Industrial Labour Force in India: A Study of the Bombay Cotton Mills, 1854-1947* (Berkeley and Los Angeles, 1965); Richard Newman, *Workers and Unions in Bombay, 1918-29: A Study of Organization in the Cotton Mills* (Canberra, 1981); S. Bhattacharya, 'Capital and Labour in Bombay City, 1928-29', *EPW*, XVI, 42 and 43 (1981) pp. PE36-PE44, 'The Colonial State, Capital and Labour: Bombay, 1919-31', in S. Bhattacharya and Romila Thapar, eds., *Situating Indian History* (Delhi, 1986), pp. 171-93, and 'Swaraj and the Kamgar: The Indian National Congress and the Bombay Working Class, 1919-31', in R. Sisson and S. Wolpert, eds., *Congress and Indian Nationalism: The Pre-Independence Phase* (Berkeley and Los Angeles, 1988), pp. 223-49. Dick Kooiman, *Bombay Textile Labour: Managers, Trade Unionists and Officials, 1918-1939* (Delhi, 1989); Rajnarayan Chandavarkar, 'Workers' Politics and Mill Districts in Bombay between the Wars', *MAS*, XV, 3 (1981), pp. 603-47, and *The Origins of Industrial Capitalism in India: Business Strategies and Working Classes in Bombay, 1900-1940* (Cambridge, 1994).
2. Most of the all-India studies of the workers face this problem. See, for example, V.B. Karnik, *Strikes in India* (Bombay, 1967) and Sukomal Sen, *The Working Class of India: History of Emergence and Movement* (Calcutta, 1977).
3. See Dipesh Chakrabarty, *Rethinking Working-Class History: Bengal, 1890-1940* (Delhi, 1989). Later on, in a paper, he appears to concede that he has

over-emphasized culture to the exclusion of other ingredients in human lives and movements. See Dipesh Chakrabarty, 'Culture in Working Class History: A Discussion', Working Paper no. 3, V.V. Giri National Labour Institute, Nov. 1998.

4. See A.K. Bagchi, 'Working Class Consciousness', *EPW,* XXV, 30 (28 July 1990), and 'Workers and the Historians' Burden', in K.N. Panikkar, T.J. Byers and Utsa Patnaik, *The Making of History: Essays Presented to Irfan Habib* (Delhi, 2000); Parimal Ghosh, 'Communalism and Colonial Labour: Experience of Calcutta Jute Mill Workers, 1880-1930', *EPW,* XXV, 30 (July 28 1990); R. Chandavarkar, *The Origins of Industrial Capitalism in India* (Cambridge, 1994).
5. Dilip Simeon, *The Politics of Labour under Late Colonialism: Workers, Unions and the State in Chota Nagpur, 1928-1939* (Delhi, 1995), p. 2.
6. Dilip Simeon, 'Work and Resistance in Jharia Coalfield', in Parry, et al., eds., *Contributions to Indian Sociology,* vol. 33, nos. 1 and 2 (January-August 1999), p. 44.
7. See E.D Murphy, 'Class and Community in India: The Madras Labour Union, 1918-21', *IESHR,* IV, 3 (July-September 1977) and *Unions in Conflict: A Comparative Study of Four South Indian Textile Centres, 1918-1939* (Delhi, 1981); Richard Newman, *Workers and Unions in Bombay*; S. Bhattacharya, 'Capital and Labour in Bombay City', and 'Swaraj and the Kamgar'; Chitra Joshi, 'Bonds of Community, Ties of Religion: Kanpur Textile Workers in the Early Twentieth Century', *IESHR,* XXII, 3 (1985); Janaki Nair, 'Production Regimes, Cultural Processes: Industrial Labour in Mysore', *IESHR,* XXX, 3 (July- September 1993), and *Miners and Millhands: Work, Culture and Politics in Princely Mysore* (Delhi, 1998).

PART I

HOME AND THE MILL

CHAPTER 1

City, Industry and Workforce

THE CITY OF Bombay derived its name from Mumbai which, in turn, was derived from Mumba Devi, the patron goddess of the original Koli inhabitants of the island.[1] The Portuguese acquired the island in 1534 from the king of Gujarat, Sultan Bahadur. The island changed hands again in 1661 when it was offered as dowry in the marriage of a Portuguese princess to an English prince. In 1668, the island, seemingly considered as worthless possession, was given to the East India Company by the British crown on an annual rent of ten pounds in gold.[2]

The Portuguese period in the history of Bombay had been one of religious intolerance and witnessed the flight of people from there. On its transfer to the English, the population of the island stood at 10,000. English rule, largely defined by religious non-interference, coupled with measures of economic improvement undertaken by Gerald Aungier (1669-77) and aided by the arrival of some traders and merchants from Surat due to the turbulent political atmosphere there, saw a rapid increase in population. In 1673, only a few years after its takeover by the English, the population of the island was said to have increased to 50,000-60,000.[3]

For the next hundred years the growth of Bombay was slow and fraught with vicissitudes. The decline of Surat was not yet final, nor was the British rule over India yet in sight. Maratha power was formidable and at its zenith in the eighteenth century and the French were also significant, sometimes dangerous, rivals. Cholera and the plague were other enemies that the rulers and the people of the island were to face and in the later part of the seventeenth century it was the general belief that 'two monsoons were the life of a man' in the island.[4]

In the late eighteenth century, through a series of treaties and conquests, the British were able to occupy territories in western India, and in 1818, the final defeat of the Maratha power led to the firm establishment of the British rule in the region and 'transformed Bombay from a trading town into the capital of a large province'.[5] From then onwards there was steady economic and demographic development in Bombay. In 1770, trade with China had started. It continued to grow over the years. The important road to Poona, the Bhor Ghat, was opened in 1830; pack animals were subsequently substituted by bullock carts thereby reducing freight charges and facilitating the movement of goods. Bombay also provided increasing port facilities for ocean traffic. The building of steamships commenced in 1829. The first railway lines were laid between Bombay and Thana in 1853.

Nineteenth-century Bombay witnessed rapid growth in international commerce. While in 1801-2, the total foreign trade in goods moving through Bombay was estimated to be of Rs. 15.2 million, in 1859-60 it rose to Rs. 145.6 million and ten years later, owing mainly to the Cotton Boom, it rose to Rs. 381.1 million.[6] All these commercial and construction activities led to a rapid increase in population (Table 1.1).

It was in this environment of general commercial activities that the cotton mills also had their origins. The persons who established the first mills had been engaged in trade, both in Indian and Chinese goods, but mostly in subordinate positions to the European commercial firms. C.N. Davar, the pioneer, had been a broker for English firms. Others like Petits, Wadias, Tatas, Sassoons, Nathubhais had all been involved in the China trade. Although they earned a lot of money, their subordinate position *vis-á-vis* the European, mainly English, firms, combined with fluctuations in trade, forced them to look for other opportunities to invest their capital. The cotton mills provided them this opportunity. However, it entailed a lot of investment and risk.[7] All the machinery, managerial personnel and skilled people needed for the erection of mills had to be imported. The only advantages 'lay in the availability of the basic raw material on the spot, cheaper wages' and the availability of a market, albeit limited, at home.[8]

Table 1.1: Population in Bombay, 1661-1846

Year	Population
1661	10,000
1673	50,000
1744	70,000
1780	113,726
1814	180,000
1836	136,000
1846	566,119

SOURCE: *Imperial Gazetteer of India*, 1908, p. 410.

The first mill started production in 1856. It faced several difficulties, the most important being the lack of trained workers. But these difficulties were soon overcome and, by the end of 1858, it registered 'a sizable profit'.[9] Even earlier, however, the prospects were sufficiently promising for C.N. Davar, the first millowner, to establish another mill which began production in 1859.[10] Other entrepreneurs were also attracted towards this enterprise. Maneckji Nuserwanji Petit, the father of the more famous Dinshaw Maneckji Petit, floated his Oriental Spinning and Weaving Company in 1855 which started operations in 1858. The success of this mill prompted the son, D.M. Petit, to found the Maneckji Petit Mills in 1860.[11] From 1860 to 1865, there was a significant growth in this sector and in 1865 there were 10 mills in Bombay with 250,000 spindles and 3,400 looms.[12]

The Cotton Boom due to the American civil war halted the progress of the industry as it diverted capital to other investments, particularly trade in raw cotton. The collapse following the boom had even more disastrous consequences. No mill was erected between 1865 and 1871 and it was only after that year that the industry showed recovery. From 1871 to 1892, the industry's growth was phenomenal. Two factors were mainly responsible for this. The opening of the Suez Canal reduced the distance between India and England thereby substantially reducing the cost of freight for importing machinery. Another important development was the increasing availability of the Chinese market for yarn. So, while in 1871 there were 10 mills with 305,896 spindles and 4,290 looms and 8,553 workers, in 1892 there were 68 mills with 19,34,716 spindles and 14,900 looms and 65,087 workers.[13]

During the 1890s, the industry faced a series of crises. The currency crisis, created by the colonial government in 1893, disrupted the China market for quite some time. The development of cotton industry in China and Japan further curtailed the scope for Bombay yarn in China's market. The communal riots of 1893 also disrupted commercial activities in the city for a brief period. In 1896, instead of helping the industry in the face of competition, the colonial government imposed a countervailing excise duty on the clothes manufactured in the Indian mills. The Plague, which entered Bombay in 1896 and ravaged it for many years disrupted the labour market considerably, particularly during 1897-8. The famines of the closing years of the century in Maharashtra led to further shrinking of the market for Bombay cloth and yarn. Talking about the depressed conditions of the industry in the mid-1920s, the Bombay Millowners' Association (BMOA) complained before the

Indian Tariff Board (ITB) that it was 'during the closing decade of the last century that seeds were sown for the serious condition of the cotton mill industry which we are witnessing today'.[14]

The industry recovered from these crises by 1901, but remained vulnerable to many ups and downs until 1914. The beginning of the century saw an increase in the export of yarn to China. In 1904, however, the steep rise in the prices of raw cotton led to the closing of many spinning mills. But it did not lead to any general recession. Later the enthusiasm of the Swadeshi movement combined with the lowering of cotton prices and the Russo-Japanese war (which lessened the Japanese competition in the Chinese market) soon revived the industry which again enjoyed a few years of prosperity till 1907. From 1908 to 1913, however, a series of factors affected the recovery. Crop failure, malaria and shrinking of the Chinese market affected the sales in 1908; the rise of cotton prices in 1909 and the enhancement of duty on silver in 1910 and the crisis in Indian banking in 1913 created problems for the industry.[15]

Despite these setbacks the industry on the whole made a gross profit of about 27.1 per cent between 1905 and 1914. The outbreak of the First World War made the home market more available to Indian mills by decreasing the import of cloth and yarn from Britain and other European countries. There were some initial problems but they were soon overcome and from 1915 to 1922 there was a period of great prosperity for the industry. The average gross profits were 75.6 per cent and touched a very high figure of 102.7 per cent in 1920.[16] This boom petered out in 1922 and a long era of depression beset the industry and its negative effects were felt both on the industry and its labour.

The history of the development of the cotton textile industry in Bombay has to be viewed in the colonial context. Almost all the early entrepreneurs were involved in trade in a subordinate position to British expatriate capital. They invested in the industry in an effort to break free from their subordination.[17] But the risks were high and capital was difficult to mobilize initially. There was no help from the colonial government and the home market was occupied by the imported British goods. The allurement of trade still remained and was startlingly evident during the Cotton Boom of the mid-1860s when capital was almost totally diverted to trade in cotton and to financial speculation. Even after the boom ended, the reach to the home market remained tenuous and uncertain. In such a situation, some amount of 'tariff protection would have made all the difference, because then the mills could have tried out new counts of yarn and new varieties of piece-goods on a wider scale'.[18] But that was not to happen. In 1878, under pressure from the Lancashire, the duties on the import of 'certain coarser kinds of cotton goods were remitted' and, in 1879, certain other cotton goods were exempted. Finally, in 1882, the Indian market was completely thrown open for all cotton goods. From then until 1894 'India was virtually without any tariff duties, and conformed more nearly to the principles of Free Trade than any other country. Even ports of Britain were less free than those of India'.[19] In 1894, due to financial exigencies, the Government of India (GOI) had to impose 5 per cent duties on imported cotton goods but, at the same time, under pressure from the Lanacashire lobby, it imposed 5 per cent countervailing duties on the products of the Indian cotton textile industry to offset any advantage it might have otherwise derived from the limited tariff protection.[20]

Confronted with a limited home market and an indifferent government the Bombay mills encountered many problems in the initial years. The opening of the Chinese market for yarns provided a big boost to this fledgling industry. But it also engendered a lopsided growth and made the industry dependent on the vagaries of a foreign market. Most of the mills established during the 1870s and 1880s were spinning units only. In 1894, 41 out of 69 mills in Bombay were exclusively spinning units and even the composite units used their looms mainly as safeguards against the slump in the Chinese yarn market.[21] The crisis which the industry faced in the 1890s, particularly with respect to the relatively decreased availability of the Chinese market, forced it to make certain adjustments, the most important being the move towards the installation and expansion of weaving capacity. The number of mills with a weaving section was 33 in 1905; in 1931 this number increased to 63.[22] The expansion in the spinning section between 1905 and 1921 was minimal. In fact, the average number of spindles installed declined between 1911 and 1921. On the other hand, the average number of looms installed increased from 700 in 1905 to 917 in 1921. Between 1911 and 1921 most of the investment in the industry occurred in installation and expansion of the weaving section.[23]

But the problem was that, before the First World War, the domestic market was already occupied by the British imported goods and, to some extent, by those of the textile mills of other cities like Ahmedabad. It was, therefore, not easy for the Bombay mills to secure a safe place in the domestic market and the industry remained crisis-prone in the 1890s and occasionally in the early decades of the twentieth century, except for the War period and its immediate aftermath. There were certain periods of prosperity requiring intense activities and heightened demand for labour and capital. This added to the uncertainties and induced the industrialists to devise mechanisms for quick mobilization of labour and capital. The managing agents and the jobbers were the two instruments which the owners employed to tide over this problem and for procuring and managing capital and labour respectively.

As the industry remained perpetually uncertain about its position, there was no attempt on the part of the millowners to create a stable workforce. In fact, faced with constant fluctuations, they resorted to variable working hours and differing strengths of the workforce. It was accomplished by relying on the jobbers for recruitment and control and by maintaining a semi-permanent workforce which could be hired and fired at will. It is true that there were some exceptions like the Tatas who thought otherwise and sought to create a more stable workforce but the majority of the millowners were happy to resort to flexible labour time and to maintain a partly disposable labourforce to maximize their short-term profits. This short-sightedness on the part of the millowners added to the woes of the industry and its workers. Interestingly, it is the workers who tried to fight against this temporariness, uncertainty and irregular hours which were the hallmarks of the industrial system in Bombay.[24]

The growth of the cotton mills, the railways, the dockyards, the construction and several other commercial activities attracted people from various regions and many walks of life to Bombay. The *Gazetteer* reported in 1885:

> Hardly any city in the world presents a greater variety of national types than Bombay. The Hindu and the Muhammadan, of course, predominate in numbers, but in the busy streets the characteristic dress of every Oriental people may be seen. The green and gold turban of the Musalman, the large red or white head-dress peculiar to the Maratha, the pointed red turban of the Guzerathi Baniya, and the black or brown brimless hat of the Parsi lend colour and variety to the scene.[25]

The most important source of migration to the city was from the Ratnagiri district. In 1881, the number of people from Ratnagiri stood at 126,190. This number kept increasing over the years and in 1921 it had swelled to 235,566.[26] Other important streams of migration were from the districts of Poona, Satara, Cutch, Kathiawar and Surat. The people from the United Provinces were initially less in number but by 1921 they had significantly increased in number to 70,911.[27]

The immigrants from Ratnagiri constituted about half of the cotton textile workforce in 1911, but their proportion had declined by 1921 to about 35.53 per cent. Meanwhile, the share of the workers from the United Provinces in the total workforce increased from 3.05 per cent in 1911 to 9.42 per cent in 1921.[28]

The migrant population remained predominant in the city. Most of the denizens did not have homes there and the rural areas provided the source of supply as well as the final resort for the tired and retired working people of the city. As the population of the city increased, it increasingly became a city of migrants. The number of people born in Bombay remained low and even declined over the years from 31.1 per cent of the total population in 1872 to only 16.0 per cent in 1921 (Table 1.2). The migrant character of the population was further evident when we consider the proportion of the city's female population in comparison to the male one (Table 1.3). This proportion increasingly declined over the years. Among the textile workers also we notice that the number of those born in Bombay was much less than those born outside, although the trend here was towards an increase in the proportion of the Bombay-born (Table 1.4).

Most of the immigrant workers were male single migrants who had left behind not only their relatives and members of the joint family at home in the village but also their wives and children. In 1921 the millworkers came chiefly from the regions given in Table 1.5.

The proportion of women in each of these streams of migrants was quite low (Table 1.6). Among the immigrant population of Ratnagiri, U.P. and Satara which contributed about 50 per cent to the total

Table 1.2: Percentage of people born in Bombay to the total population (1872-1921)

1872	1881	1891	1901	1911	1921
31.1	27.8	25.0	23.4	19.6	16.0

SOURCE: *Census of India, 1921*, vol. IX, part I, p. 16.

Table 1.3: Females per 1000 males in Bombay (1872-1921)

1872	1881	1891	1901	1911	1921
612	664	586	617	530	525

SOURCE: *Census of India, 1921*, vol. IX, I, p. 26.

Table 1.4: Percentage of the Bombay-born cotton millworkers to the total

1911	1921
10.92	18.87

SOURCE: Morris, *Industrial Labour Force*, p. 65.

labourforce, the number of women was extremely low, reaching as low as 167 per thousand males in the case of U.P. immigrants who were the second largest regional group in the textile workforce in 1921. This shows that the large majority of workers were single male migrants.

Other important evidence which shows the rural connections of the workers as well as that of the city's population in general is that in the districts of the Bombay Presidency from which these workers were mainly drawn, the relative number of women increased over the years (Table 1.7).

Table 1.5: Proportion of workers from different areas in the workforce

Area	Percentage to the total millworkers
Ratnagiri	35.53
United Provinces	9.42
Satara	6.63
Poona	6.18
Kolaba	4.47
Ahmednagar	2.99

SOURCE: Morris, *Industrial Labour Force*, p. 63.

Table 1.6: Number of females per thousand males in each stream of migrants

Area	Number of females/thousand males
Ratnagiri	35.53
United Provinces	9.42
Satara	6.63
Poona	6.18
Kolaba	4.47
Ahmednagar	2.99

SOURCE: *Census of India, 1921*, vol. IX, part II, p. 19.

Table 1.7: Number of females per thousand males

District	1872	1881	1891	1901	1911	1921
Ratnagiri	1,075	1,108	1,153	1,133	1,175	1,198
Satara	966	995	997	1,015	1,006	1,007
Poona	936	979	957	980	973	952
Kolaba	968	988	998	989	1,013	1,012
Ahmednagar	955	969	967	1,005	985	978
Total British territory in Bombay Presidency	911	939	931	938	921	903

SOURCE: *Census of India, 1921*, vol. VIII, part I, p. 65; *Census of India, 1901*, vol. IX, part I, p. 102; *Census of India, 1931*, vol. VIII, part I, p. 118.

Table 1.8: Distribution of people between the age of 15 to 40 years per thousand of population in 1921

Age Group	Presidency	Bombay City
15-20	72	94
20-25	80	141
25-30	92	156
30-35	88	138
35-40	64	90

SOURCE: *Census of India, 1921*, vol. IX, part I, p. 23.

The city's population, on the other hand, consisted mostly of young adults. In Bombay, 62 per cent of the population comprised of people between the age group of 15 to 40 years, while in the case of the Presidency the figure for this group was only 40 per cent (Table 1.8). It appears, therefore, that the city was not a hospitable place for either the very young or old people and the people of advanced age went back to their villages after working in the city for a few years.

The Marathi-speakers formed the largest proportion of the total population. The next were the Gujaratis, while the Hindi-speakers also represented a significant section (Table 1.9).

If we take the religious composition of Bombay's population, the Hindus and Muslims from various areas and linguistic backgrounds predominated. The Parsis and Christians, though significant, formed very small minorities; and Jews, Jains, Buddhists and Sikhs were numerically insignificant (Table 1.10). Except for the Parsis, single male migrants dominated the population of these religious groups. This is again evident by the lower proportion of females to the males among the people of these religious groups (Table 1.11).

The distribution of these groups was not even across the city. There were localities in which a particular group was numerically dominant.

Table 1.9: The percentages of the main languages to the total population of the city

Language	Percentage	
	1911	1921
Marathi	50.9	51.4
Gujarati	20.9	20.1
Hindi	14.8	14.8
Kacchi	4.2	3.4
Konkani	2.0	2.8

SOURCE: Ibid., p. 29.

Table 1.10: Religious Composition of the Bombay population (percentage to the total), 1872-1921

Religious Group	1872	1881	1891	1901	1911	1921
Hindu	63.3	65.2	66.1	65.5	67.8	71.2
Muslim	21.6	20.5	18.9	20.1	18.3	15.7
Christian	5.4	5.5	5.5	5.8	5.8	5.8
Parsi	6.8	6.2	5.8	6.0	5.2	4.5
Jain	2.3	2.2	3.1	1.8	2.1	2.0
Jew	0.5	0.4	0.6	0.8	0.7	0.6
Others	0.1	–	–	–	0.1	0.2

SOURCE: *Census of India, 1921*, vol. IX, part I, p. 14.

Table 1.11: Number of females per thousand males in each religious group, 1872-1921

Religious Group	1872	1881	1891	1901	1911	1921
Hindu	608	664	571	610	521	531
Muslim	634	679	633	617	507	452
Christian	461	521	493	521	486	480
Parsi	909	931	910	904	903	864
Jain	246	341	311	381	329	357
Jew	–	–	–	–	883	870

SOURCE: Ibid., p. 15.

For example, the Muslim population was preponderant in four sections —Chakla, Umarkhadi, Khara Talao and Second Nagpada—where they formed more than 60 per cent of the population. There was further concentration within each section, hence the emergence of some Muslim *mohollas*.[29] Most of the Christian population lived in Upper Colaba and the North Fort, while the majority of the Parsis were to be found in the North Fort and Dhobi Talao where they constituted 43 and 32 per cent of the total population of the respective areas.[30] Similarly, even though the Hindus formed the majority in most of the localities in the city, except in the above-mentioned sections, their proportion in Dongri, Kumbharwada, Girgaum, Parel, Sewri and Worli was from 80 to 90 per cent of the total population of the areas.[31]

Because of the concentration in other areas the proportion of Muslims to the total population in the mill areas was about 10 per cent which was lower than their overall city average (Table 1.12). Though small, even these figures were more than the relative proportion of Muslims in the total workforce in this period. In 1881, Muslims constituted 8.13 per cent of the total number of cotton millworkers; by 1921, their proportion had gone down to 5.15 per cent (Table 1.13).

Table 1.12: The percentage of Muslims to the total population in the mill areas (1881-1921)

Section	1881	1901	1911	1921
Byculla	14.2	20.7	21.9	20.9
Tadwadi	10.4	12.2	10.8	10.7
Mazagaon	14.1	13.9	15.2	13.5
Parel	7.5	5.7	4.8	5.4
Sewri	4.2	4.3	5.2	5.8
Sion	12.6	7.9	7.8	7.4
Mahim	12.6	8.5	11.8	11.7
Worli	3.1	6.0	5.4	5.2
Average in the mill areas	9.8	9.9	10.4	10.1

SOURCE: *Censuses*, various years (comparable figures for 1891 are not available).

Table 1.13: Hindu-Muslim composition of the cotton textile workforce, 1881-1921

Year	Total Number of workers	Total number of Hindu workers	Percentage to the total	Total number of Muslim workers	Percentage to the total
1881	25,241	22,821	90.41	2,053	8.13
1911	118,512	104,400	88.09	12,575	10.60
1921	117,110	110,065	93.98	6,032	5.15

SOURCE: *Censuses*, various years (comparable figures for 1891 and 1901 are not available).

Table 1.14: Approximate percentage of the workers from various castes in the total population of the cotton millworkers

Caste	Percentage Share
Maratha	44.16
Mahar	8.79
Sheikh	3.78
Kunbi	4.49
Chambhar	3.59
Bhandari	3.05

SOURCE: Calculated from the *Census of India, 1921*, vol. IX, part II, Table VI, given in Newman, *Workers and Unions*, p. 52.

While the proportion of the Muslims in the labourforce declined during this period, that of the Dalit castes like Mahars and Chambhars showed a significant increase. From an insignificant 1.0 per cent in 1872, their proportion rose to 12.0 per cent in 1921.[32] The Census of 1921 gives the castes of the mill workers. If we take some major castes, the share of the Marathas, along with the Kunbis, was almost half in the total workforce, while that of the Dalit castes such as Mahars and Chambhars was more than 12 per cent (Table 1.14). According to a survey done by the BMOA in 1940, the Marathas (including Kunbis) formed about 51.8 per cent of all male workers, Hindu immigrants from U.P. (called *Bhaiyas*) 13.8 per cent, the Dalit castes 11.9 per cent and the Muslims 5.2 per cent.[33] These figures corresponded closely to the Census figures for 1921. There seems to be a surprising consistency in the employment pattern of various groups over the years.

There was also a tendency for some groups to congregate in particular departments of the mills. The BMOA survey showed that 53.8 per cent of Hindu migrant workers from U.P. were in the 'mixing to speed frame' and formed about 46.8 per cent of the total workers in that department; 72.5 per cent of the Dalit castes were employed in the ring-spinning department and made up 39.5 per cent of all male workers; 52.2 per cent of all Muslim workers were employed in the weaving department where they formed 6.9 per cent of all the weavers.[34] Contemporary observers attested to this trend of particularistic concentration. Burnett-Hurst wrote: 'The Mohammedan Julaha generally works in the weaving department only, his women folk as a rule employed in the colour-winding branch of the reeling room. On the other hand, the Hindu from the U.P. . . . is found in the carding departments of the cotton mills.'[35]

In 1921, out of all the weavers, 61.7 per cent were Marathas, 21.9 per cent from the backward castes and 11.4 per cent were Muslims.[36] We find that both the Marathas and Muslims were over-represented in this department in comparison with their industrial average, which was 52 per cent for the former and 5.15 for the latter. Morris suggests that there might have occurred a 'shift of "clean" castes from spinning into weaving sheds' thereby making the spinning department 'more easily accessible to untouchables'.[37]

There was a bias against employment of low-caste people in certain departments, particularly the weaving sheds where the yarn had to be sucked by the workers into their mouths to put it on the shuttle thereby constituting a danger of ritual defilement for the upper castes. It was due to this discrimination against them that the proportion of the lower castes in the weaving departments was just 0.6 per cent.[38]

In the earlier period, this practice seemed to prevail in the industry as a whole. J. Helm, the manager of the Bombay United Mill, said before the Factory Commission of 1875 that 'the operatives in my mill are almost all Hindus. There are a few Mahomedans and about half a dozen Parsees. No low-caste operatives are allowed to be employed in my mill.'[39] In 1908, Saklatvala, the manager of the Petit Mill, stated that 'There were no low-caste men in the weaving shed. . . . When a man applied for work his caste was enquired into. Caste, in fact, was a great consideration.'[40] These problems persisted and, in 1928, one employer commented that 'In our mills we have got people who go into various departments according to castes.'[41]

The holidays given to the workers also followed the same pattern. The mills were closed mostly on Hindu holidays. One mill manager said that 'on Parsee and Mahomedan holidays we never stop the work. It is only on Hindu holidays that we do so.'[42] Another manager confirmed that they stopped the mill on 12 holidays in a year and 'they are all Hindu holidays'.[43]

These caste-based practices were quite common among the workers. Maya, a low-caste girl, told the Factory Commission of 1885: 'I belong to Mochee caste, consequently I cannot mix with the higher castes in the reeling room.' She wanted to work in the reeling department but could not do so.[44]

The statement given by Sakoo, the female overseer of the reeling department, confirmed this: 'There are different castes and the food would be defiled by the different castes and it would be practically impossible to do it. There are Mochees, Mahomedans and other castes and if any of them touched us or our food we should be defiled. . . . What is caste made for if it is not to be maintained?'[45]

In 1922, one of the first grievances raised by the workers before the Tata Committee was 'the lack of separate water taps for untouchables'.[46] Even where the Muslims and the Hindus worked in the same department there were separate arrangements for them for drinking water.[47] In the mills with facilities for providing tea for the workers, there were generally two separate rooms for the Hindus and the Muslims. In cases of single room and a single fire-place, two cooks belonging to both the religions were employed to make separate tea.[48] The Chief Inspector of Factories, T.W. Johnstone, testifying before the RCL, said that the construction of a common dining shed might create 'caste difficulty in the mills'. He supported his statement by his experience of one mill in Ahmedabad: 'Some years ago . . . I happened to visit a mill and I found about 70 or 80 people fighting with rods they use in the blow room; half a dozen of them were laid out. They were all low caste people, wagris and dheds. The trouble arose through a wagri touching a dhed's food.'[49]

The observation of caste rules among the workers as among other groups was a very strong sentiment and had its bearing on the composition of the workforce and its distribution in various departments.

The fluctuating demands of the industry had a bearing on the supply of labour. There were contradictory contemporary accounts regarding the adequacy of labour supply. Morris had tried to show that there were no problems in procuring labour on demand.[50] There are also some contemporary statements in support of this point. But the complaints about labour shortage were too numerous to be ignored. Although there was no problem in the availability of labour in general, it was not always possible to procure it in particular circumstances. The employers adopted a policy of recruiting and dismissing the workers at will. Moreover, even during the regular working of the mills the workers could not expect a fixed time all the year round because when there was a need to work long hours in times of boom the employers compelled the workers to stay longer in the mills without breaks, leaves or holidays. But, in times of depression, they resorted to short-time working or laying off the workers. The latter, therefore, could never be sure how much their wages were going to be in a particular month or when they would be relieved of their work without any notice or compensation. The large employment of casual labour, which the Labour Officer put at 28 per cent of the total workforce in the mid-1930s[51] (and which was much larger in the earlier period), enabled the industry to maintain flexibility in employment of labour but made the workers uncertain about their jobs. In addition to this, the employers did not invest in housing, health and general well-being of the workers. In times of sickness or other needs the workers were forced to either go to their villages or seek the help of their friends and relatives in the city. The industry, therefore, transferred the cost of reproduction of labour on to the countryside or to the other formal or informal networks of the workers. However, once the employers absolved themselves of the responsibility of creating a stable labourforce, they could not expect a stable supply of labour as the workers had to cater to the economic and social demands of their rural and urban networks. To keep their contacts and relations alive the workers had to leave their work at odd times to attend to marriages, funerals or other social and religious ceremonies, or to sustain their economic base at home for times of need or simply to recover from illness. Therefore, the usual supply of labour would not be available to the industry when it was needed.

The numerous economic and social contacts which the workers had to forge and nurture to tide over the adverse circumstances also had their regular and irregular demands on their time and resources. As there was no security or regularity of earnings or employment provided by the industry, the workers did not hesitate to leave their work and go off to their villages or to cater to other demands of their networks. This is not to say that otherwise their rural links would have snapped completely. But the workers' dependence on them would have lessened and these links would have weakened over time and the regular and irregular absenteeism would have declined, if not vanished altogether, if the industry had offered them sustenance in times of need. But the short-term policies adopted by the employers generated instability in the labourforce. The frequent complaints by the owners and managers about the shortage of labour, about the ineptitude of the workers to learn and about the lack of a formed workforce owed basically to the shortsighted policies of the employers in the given colonial situation.

The *jobbers* were the product of these circumstances. The extreme reluctance of the employers to invest in the creation of a stable labourforce and their imperative of having a disposable one to suit the short-term needs of the industry gave rise to the phenomenon of jobbery. From the diverse mass of people the workers for the textile mills as well as for other concerns in the city were to be recruited, trained and disciplined. The jobber was the means through which this problem was solved and the process of recruitment and control was set in motion. The institution of the jobber was almost universal in the Indian context. The jobber was known as *mukaddam* (the male jobber) or the *naikin* (the female jobber) in Bombay, the *sardar* in Calcutta, the *mistri* in Kanpur. In all these places his/her job was to recruit, train and supervise the workers in their particular situation of work. In Bombay's context, Morris claims that the jobbers 'were intended to play the role of a middle management cadre from the beginning'.[52] According to him, 'the evidence is quite clear that the jobber's basic responsibility was the overseeing of the labor in his section. . . . His recruitment function was only an incidental aspect of his foreman's role.'[53]

However, it seems that although the role of the jobbers was also to train and discipline the workers, their main job was conceived to be procurement of labour. The jobber in the Bombay mills was basically a worker who had put in a number of years in the mills. But this was not the only attribute which qualified him for the position. He also needed to have sufficient influence over the workers to bring enough of them to particular departments in the mills. His failure to procure workers in times of need would make him liable to dismissal. Although he was also supposed to give training to the raw recruits and maintain discipline, the principal function he had to perform was to get the required number of workers as per the needs of his department. As John Wallace, the editor of the ITJ, pointed out that 'it seems to be the practice here to move a jobber from one mill to another, not because of his efficiency in work, but primarily because he can bring so many "hands"'.[54]

The jobber's role in procuring labour was considered so important that even by the late 1920s the representative of the BMOA considered it very difficult to get labour through any other system of recruitment: 'How are you to get your labour?' said H.P. Mody, the BMOA's Deputy Chairman, 'We think the jobbers are the men most competent to do that under the present circumstances.'[55]

Despite the acknowledgement that jobbery was a system full of corruption and detrimental both for the industry and the labourers, the employers could think of no alternative:

> 'We think,' H.P.Mody asserted, 'that it would be more satisfactory to get our labour through jobbers for the reason that I do not think otherwise we can fill up the places of our absentees or keep all the machinery going. These jobbers are in touch with the men. The assistants are not in touch with the men as much as the jobbers and naturally therefore the recruitment is being done through jobbers.'[56]

This point was repeatedly emphasized by the BMOA representatives before the ITB. If there was no lack of labour in the city, why were the employers pleading such helplessness in procuring it? Saklatwala explained the problem: 'In Tata mills we employ over 4,000 people. At the gates we do not get a thousand people. Fifty or 60 come. Of course that makes a large crowd at the gate. But it does not mean that the spinning master can fill his requirements merely from that'.[57]

The role of any centralized recruiting office was also discounted:

> 'We have 90 mills in Bombay,' N.N. Wadia stated, 'and if each wanted 50 men in a day you would want about 4,500 men. You cannot get them out of your recruiting office. You have got to sort them out, and you have to send them to the different mills. The time taken to send them from the recruiting office to the mills should be considered. In practice here there are a certain number of men waiting outside and there are jobbers to recruit them.'[58]

The jobbers, therefore, had to cultivate their constituency in the neighbourhood by supporting the workers in times of joblessness, by securing credits and other facilities for them. There were numerous charges that he took *dasturi* from the workers whom he provided employment,[59] and it was also alleged that a portion of this payment reached even the middle-level managers.[60] Morris states that 'much of labour was hired not on the basis of experience and efficiency but on the size of the payment the worker was willing to give'.[61] It seems, however, that the payment of *dasturi* was not such an important issue in the relationship between the jobbers and workers. It was a symbiotic association which tended to benefit both the parties. As the jobber's most important assignment was to arrange the optimum number of workers for his department, and his 'failure to do so may result in his dismissal. Accordingly he endeavours to acquire an influence over his friends and acquaintances who live in the same or in neighbouring chawls. He lends them money, advises them in family affairs and arbitrates in disputes. When labour is required, he uses the influence so gained and is generally successful in procuring hands.'[62]

Thus by allowing jobbers to recruit freely the employers gave them the licence to select persons from their own regional, caste and religious backgrounds. In fact, the distribution of the jobbers along caste lines closely corresponded to that of the workers. For example, in 1921, 59.9 per cent of jobbers were from Maratha and allied castes, 22.2 per cent from the backward castes and 9.1 per cent were Muslims.[63] In 1921, there were 3,919 (head, line and assistant) jobbers.[64] So, on an average, each mill had 45 jobbers and one jobber to every 37 workers. For the ordinary workers the managers, the managing agents and the owners remained alien figures. It was through the jobber that the workers got their jobs and it was through him that they could hope to retain them. The loyalties to the jobbers not only maintained these caste and other divisions but also, by creating small units of influence and control, tended to prevent the creation of a stable and unified workforce.

NOTES

1. *Imperial Gazetteer of India, 1908*, vol. VIII, new edn (Oxford, 1908), pp. 402-3. An earlier Gazetteer mentions that the name Mumbai was derived from Mahima, the Great Mother. *Imperial Gazetteer of India, 1885*, vol. 3, 2nd edn (London, 1885), p. 74.
2. *Imperial Gazetteer, 1885*, vol. 3, p. 74.
3. Ibid., p. 74. Also, *Imperial Gazetteer, 1908*, vol. VIII, p. 404.
4. *Imperial Gazetteer, 1908*, vol. VIII, p. 404.
5. Ibid., p. 407.
6. Morris, *Industrial Labour Force*, pp. 14-15.
7. M.D. Morris, 'The Growth of Large-Scale Industry', in Dharma Kumar, ed., *The Cambridge Economic History of India* (CEHI), vol. II, p. 579, fn. 1.

According to Morris, the 'cost of erecting a spinning mill in Bombay, including spindles and fitting up, was about three times the cost in Lancashire'.

8. S.D. Mehta, *The Cotton Mills of India, 1854 to 1954* (Bombay, 1954), p. 5. Also Morris, *Industrial Labour Force*, p. 24 and R. Chandavarkar, *Industrial Capitalism in India*, p. 65.
9. Mehta, *Cotton Mills*, p. 17.
10. Morris, *Industrial Labour Force*, p. 24.
11. *Indian Tariff Board (Cotton Textile Industry Enquiry)*, 1927 (hereafter ITB), vol. II, Bombay Millowners' Association (hereafter BMOA), written statement, p. 13.
12. Ibid., p. 13.
13. Ibid., p. 69, Table 1. Also see Appendix I.
14. ITB, II, p. 15.
15. Mehta, *Cotton Mills*, p. 86. Also ITB, II, p. 18.
16. Morris, *Industrial Labour Force*, p. 29. Also Mehta, *Cotton Mills*, pp. 146-8.
17. For a detailed discussion of this point, see Chandavarkar, *Industrial Capitalism in India*, pp. 60-5.
18. A.K. Bagchi, *Private Investments in India, 1900-1939* (New Delhi, 1980; London, 1972), p. 11.
19. Bipan Chandra, *The Rise and Growth of Economic Nationalism in India: Economic Policies of Indian National Leadership, 1880-1905* (Delhi, 1966, 1991), p. 221.
20. Ibid., p. 236.
21. Chandavarkar, *Industrial Capitalism in India*, p. 247.
22. M.M. Mehta, *Structure of Cotton Mill Industry in India* (Allahabad, 1949), p. 41
23. Ibid., pp. 69-70.
24. See Chapter 6, Section I.
25. *Imperial Gazetteer, 1885*, vol. 3, p. 80.
26. *Census of India, 1921*, vol. IX, part I, p. 18.
27. Ibid.
28. Morris, *Industrial Labour Force*, p. 63.
29. Jim Masselos, 'Power in the Bombay "Mohollas", 1904-1915: An Initial Exploration into the World of the Indian Urban Muslim', *South Asia*, 1976, vol. VI, p. 77: 'Three of the nine circles in Chakla in 1901, for example, had very low Muslim percentages of 7.8, 16.2, 23.0, while the other six had very high percentages ranging from 99.8, 98.0, 93.2, 87.8, 68.1 down to 63.6. Even allowing for probable inaccuracies in census data, there were thus extremely heavy concentrations in these four sections which, combined with circles 3 and 9 of Mandvi and circles 4 and 5 of Bhuleshwar, may be said to constitute the Muslim quarter of the city.'

30. *Census of India, 1921*, vol. XI, part V, Report, p. 21.
31. Ibid., p. 22.
32. Morris, *Industrial Labour Force*, p. 74.
33. Ibid., p. 75.
34. Ibid.
35. A.R. Burnett-Hurst, *Labour and Housing in Bombay: A Study in the Economic Condition of the Wage-Earning Classes of Bombay* (London, 1925), p. 13.
36. R. Newman, *Workers and Unions*, p. 42.
37. Morris, *Industrial Labour Force*, p. 82.
38. Ibid., p. 76.
39. Factory Commission (hereafter FC), 1875, p. 23.
40. Indian Factory Labour Commission, 1908 (hereafter IFLC), p. 82.
41. *Bombay Strike Enquiry Committee*, 1928-9, Proceedings, p. 674; quoted in Newman, *Workers and Unions*, p. 51.
42. FC, 1875, p. 21.
43. Ibid., p. 28.
44. FC, 1885, evidence of Maya.
45. Ibid., evidence of Sakoo.
46. Newman, *Workers and Unions*, p. 279.
47. J.H. Kelman, *Labour in India: A Study in the Conditions of Indian Women in Modern Industry* (London, New York, 1923), p. 134.
48. Ibid., p. 136.
49. Royal Commission on Indian Labour (hereafter RCL), 1929, vol. I, part 2, Oral Evidence, p. 241.
50. See Morris, *Industrial Labour Force*, pp. 39-83.
51. Given in Chandavarkar, Industrial Capitalism in India, p. 296.
52. Morris, *Industrial Labour Force*, p. 131.
53. Morris, *Industrial Labour Force*, p. 133, fn. 10.
54. Indian Industrial Commission, 1916-18 (hereafter IIC), IV, p. 341.
55. ITB, II, p. 347.
56. Ibid., p. 347.
57. Ibid., p. 348.
58. Ibid., p. 351.
59. See, for example, RCL, 1929, Report, p. 24.
60. ITB, III, p. 547, evidence of N.M. Joshi.
61. Morris, *Industrial Labour Force*, p. 135.
62. Burnett-Hurst, *Labour and Housing*, pp. 46-7.
63. Newman, *Workers and Unions*, p. 53.
64. *Report on an Enquiry into the Wages and Hours of Labour in the Cotton Mill Industry*, by G. Findlay Shirras (hereafter *Wages and Hours*), 1921, p. 11.

CHAPTER 2

Conditions of Work and Life

WORK IN THE mills introduced many changes in the lives of the workers. Coming mainly from the ranks of the peasantry, the first change they experienced was the relatively busy and fast-paced city life. Then there was a disruption of the family and social life. There was also a change in the nature of their work from open fields with simple tools to the closed, ill-ventilated mills with vast, alien, awe-inspiring and overpowering machinery. Moreover, now there was a distinction between work-time and leisure-time.

Long hours in the mills exhausted them both physically and mentally. The environment in and around their homes was no better and did not provide them with much relief after the hard day's work. Neglected by the authorities and exploited by the private builders, the workers lived in ill-ventilated, ill-lighted dens in largely undeveloped, undrained areas. In most cases, their rooms were overcrowded and many slept on the streets. To find solace from this hard life of labour the workers often resorted to drinking alcohol. The regular intake of alcohol, coupled with their hard work in the mills and polluted atmosphere both at home and in the mills weakened their resistance and made them easy prey to various diseases. In this chapter we will discuss the conditions of their existence both in the mills and in their homes.

HOURS OF WORK

One of the most contested and enduring issues in the history of industrial relations in the Bombay cotton mills related to the length of the working time. It became a matter of contradictory assessments and varying interpretations by the people involved. Although other issues related to the working of the mills also came up for discussion but nothing aroused so much feeling and generated so much heat as the hours-of-work. It evolved into the parameter by which compassion and sympathy for the workers, profits and competitiveness of the mills and their owners and the commitment to the cause of the nation were defined. It also became the touchstone on which the workers' commitment to the industrial system was tested. It served, even more than the wages and housing, as the defining point of the industrial system in Bombay.

The initial couple of decades witnessed a perfect system of *laissez-faire* in the working of the mills. There were no restrictions of any kind except those imposed by the nature, social pressure, and the technicalities of working in the mills. The operatives could be employed for as long as the daylight permitted without any holiday, except on the occasions of religious festivals. Women, except those in the reeling and winding departments, had to work as long as men and children of any age could be employed for as long as the employers wished.

The appointment of the first commission to enquire into the working conditions in the Bombay factories was done under pressure from the Lancashire lobby and some philanthropists in Britain. Questions were raised in the British parliament about 'ill-treatment of little children in the growing cotton industry of India'.[1] But there was another angle to the concern so felt. It was stated in clear terms by the Earl of Shaftesbury later on:

> There is also a commercial view to this question. We must bear in mind that India has the raw material and cheap labour; and if we allow the manu facturers there to work their operatives 16 or 17 hours and put them under no restrictions, we are giving them a very unfair advantage over the manufacturers of our own country, and we might be undersold, even in Manchester itself, by manufactured goods imported from the East.[2]

The Secretary of State for India, although wary about such pressures, wrote to the Government of India (GOI) conveying the concerns of the British lobbies and a commission to look into the conditions of the Bombay factory workers was appointed in March 1875.

The appointment and the working of the commission met with stout opposition from a majority of the vocal opinion in India. The recently formed Bombay Millowners' Association (BMOA) considered any legislative interference in the working of the mills as 'most injurious to the manufacturing interests of India', particularly in the background of the Indian Tariff Act of 1875 which was prejudiced against the Indian industry, and warned of 'strongest opposition' to any such measure.[3] The nationalist reaction was even more strident and talked openly of a colonial conspiracy to stifle the fledgling mill industry of India.[4] The Secretary of State summarized these reactions in the following words:

generally this proposal to limit the hours of factory labour is looked upon as a great conspiracy for the purpose of promoting the interests of Manchester manufacturers. There is no subject more commonly discussed, and writers in the native journals dwell on the wickedness of the English who are trying to stifle the native manufacturers in India under the guise of philanthropy.[5]

These reactions and the opposition from among the ranks of the Commission itself which had six out of nine members with interests in the textile industry induced the Commission to be extremely modest in its recommendations. The Indian Factories Act of 1881, which was based upon these recommendations, concerned itself basically with child labour. The employment of children below the age of 7 was prohibited and those between the ages of 7 and 12 years could be employed only for 9 hours with an hour of rest and were to be given one holiday in a week.[7]

What did the workers think? The persons with ownership or other interests in the industry asserted that 'the factory operatives never . . . complained of the working hours or other arrangements in the factories'.[8] It appears at first sight that the workers did not find the working hours excessive as none of them complained about it before the first Factory Commission. But many witnesses, including some workers, albeit in a subdued voice, spoke about the long hours of work. Asked by the Commission whether they found the hours too long, the six women witnesses replied, 'yes'.[9] The Health Officer to the Bombay Municipality commented that 'the hours for work were too long'.[10] Even one mill manager thought that 'it was too much for people to work . . . from daylight till dark daily, including Sundays'.[11] And another said that the 'work-people are obliged to rise at 3 o'clock in the morning to cook their meals before going to work in the Mill'.[12] About the children there was an almost unanimous opinion that they were overworked.[13]

So why were the workers reticent about admitting that the working time was too long? One reason might have been their initial hesitation and the fear of the employers. But an even more important reason seemed to be the association of the working hours with wages. In the answer to the question about getting four holidays, a boy, aged 13, replied:

'If I take four holidays, how am I to fill my belly?'

Another boy, aged 12, when queried, said:

Q. Would you like to work half day and attend school for the other half?
A. Yes.

Q. But you would not get your half day's wages then.
A. If so, what am I to eat?[14]

Children interviewed by the Commission at the Girgaum Spinning Mill:

Q. Would four holidays in a month be better?
A. Yes.
Q. But would you like to get four holidays if you were to get reduced pay?
A. No, then we would not like any holiday.[15]

The six women witnesses, when asked, 'Would you like your hours of work to be reduced?' replied, 'Any diminution of working hours, as it would be attended with loss of income, would not be satisfactory.'[16] The workers, therefore, would have liked to work shorter hours but not when it aggravated their already penurious condition.

However, this situation did not continue for long. As the workers were feeling the pressure of long working hours, some of them voiced their grievances. In 1879, some workers submitted two memorials to the government asking for legislation in restricting the hours of labour in the mills.[17] Again in 1884, when the appointment of another commission of enquiry was announced, some workers held a meeting and presented a petition to the Commission listing their grievances.[18]

The new Commission was appointed in 1884, again under pressure from the various manufacturing and trading lobbies in England. Some workers registered their complaint about long hours before it. Genoo Babaji, the Head Mule Jobber in Alexandria Mill, said: 'some have to get up at three and some at 4 o'clock in the morning to go to the mill'. He added: 'I have worked in the mills for 28 years. I was 10 or 11 years of age when I commenced working in mills. I am all sick and all my limbs are aching. I am altogether broken to pieces and I shall soon die.'[19]

Another worker-witness said that he had to leave his house at 4-30 in the morning to reach the mill.[20] Despite this, the FC concluded: 'Male adults have always been considered to be outside the principle of protection afforded by factory law. They are supposed to be able to take care of themselves; and experience has clearly shown in England that they have done so and managed to diminish their hours of work more effectually than any Act of parliament could have done.'[21]

These hours of labour were rendered even longer by the uncertainty of the working time. At one place, we find that the longest days of work are about 12.5 to 13 hours and the shortest from 11 to 11.5 hours.[22] At another place it is stated that 'some mills are at work as long as daylight lasts, or 13 to 13.5 hours, while other mills work 12 and 12.5 hours'.[23] In 1898, to take an example, the number of days on which some of the mills worked more than 12.5 hours are vastly different (Table 2.1).

The working hours varied not only with mills under different managements but also in mills under the same management. Thus the Indian Manufacturing Co. Ltd. and the New Kaiser-i-Hind Mill, both managed by Manmohandas Ramji, worked for more than 12.5 hours for 88 days and 17 days respectively in 1897 and 106 and 57 days respectively in 1898.[24] Similarly, David Sassoon's two mills, David Mill No. 1 and David Mill No. 2 worked over 12.5 hours for 299 days and 180 days respectively in 1899.[25] Many more examples can be found in the IFLC which shows the variation in the hours of work from one mill to another.

In principle, the mills worked from sunrise to sunset, but as the time of sunrise kept changing and as the decision regarding the opening of the mills varied with individual mills,[26] the workers were in great difficulty. The IFC, 1890, remarked:

> The use of the steam whistle being prohibited by the Municipality, and there being no public clocks in the quarter of the town occupied by operatives, they are unable to tell the time, or to guess how long it is from daylight. In this uncertainty and to avoid being late, they often find themselves arriving at the mill long before it begins work. Those operatives who are early may . . . be found lying about the approaches to the mill sleeping.[27]

They could not afford to be late because if they reached even 20 minutes late to the mill one-fourth of their day's wages were cut.[28]

Another problem was the mid-day recess. Although some of the mill representatives claimed that they gave half-hour rest to the workers,[29] the workers were almost unanimous in asserting that they got only about 10-15 minutes in the middle of the day.[30] The workers' statements were supported by many non-worker witnesses as well. Jones, the Inspector of Factories in Bombay, said that 'very frequently the time allowed for rest

Table 2.1: Number of days exceeding 12.5 hours in 1898

Name of the Mill	Number of days
1. The Indian Manufacturing Co. Ltd.	106
2. New Kaiser-i-Hind Mill	57
3. The Ebrahim Pabney Mill Co. Ltd.	117
4. Standard Mill	309
5. Dinshaw Petit Mill	91

SOURCE: IFLC, 1908, II, pp. 64-82.

is only 15 to 20 minutes'.[31] The ITJ wrote that that 'although the midday interval for rest is believed to be full 30 minutes, many concerns start their engines about 10 minutes earlier'.[32] Even one mill manager, Hormasji Sorabji, admitted that 'sometimes we give less than half-an-hour'.[33] Thus the IFC, 1890, concluded:

> Most of the Bombay mills profess to give half an hour in their rules; but in many cases, either from selfish motives or for the purpose of getting their operatives upto their work in time, the gong or whistle for recommencing work is sounded 10 or 15 minutes before the full half-hour has expired. The half-hour recess allowed by the rules thus becomes one of 15 or 20 minutes only. The operatives naturally feel aggrieved at this, and they ask in their petition that the Government should interfere and fix a recess of half an hour by law.[34]

The problem of long hours was further aggravated by the fact that the workers got very few holidays. A report on Bombay mills by John Robertson stated that the 'number of holidays during the year which give occasion for stopping do not amount to more than twelve'.[35] According to the Factory Commission of 1875 the total number of holidays, including the festivals, was about 26 in the whole year.[36] Even this seemed to be an overestimate, as one mill manager clearly said: 'There are no regular holidays except the Hindu holidays in his Mill, and it is only on those holidays that they stop work. They do not allow more than 10 holidays in the year.'[37]

One worker complained that 'in a month we do not get even one day's rest. Our mill stopped at Dussera, and it stopped one day last month. Sometimes we stop once, sometimes twice, and if there is a holiday sometimes three times in a month'.[38] Even those holidays so grudgingly given by the employers were not entirely at workers' disposal. They had to come to clean the machinery for two-three hours on these holidays.

Almost all the workers giving evidence before the IFC expressed the desire for a weekly holiday.[39] On this, they were even willing to get less pay. One worker firmly stated that 'If we had the holidays for which we ask and our pay was cut in proportion we would not object'.[40] It was because, as another worker clarified, 'we get ill for want of rest, and as for the loss of wages it is of greater benefit that we should have more comfort for the body'.[41] It made perfect economic sense because for one day's absence two days' wages were cut. Besides, they had to spend on medicines and doctors if they fell ill.

The IFC, although recommending for a weekly holiday and certain other things, refused to limit the general hours of work stating that 'there is nothing in the conditions under which Indian operatives work which calls for any legislative restrictions as to the hours an adult male may choose to work. Nor can we conceive any conditions which can ever call for state interference in this matter'.[42]

The Indian Factories Act of 1891 raised the minimum and maximum ages of the employable children to 9 and 14 respectively and restricted their hours of work to 7 hours in a day with half-an-hour of rest after every 6 hours of continuous work. For women it was this Act which first restricted the working hours to eleven in any one day with the interval of rest for an-hour-and-half. It did not make any change in the working hours of adult males, but it did give them one holiday in a week, preferably on Sunday, if no other holiday was given during that week. It also made half-hour rest compulsory at midday. In addition it asked the millowners not to call the workers to clean machinery on a holiday, but the workers were to do the cleaning on the evening preceding a holiday once in a fortnight without payment.

The BMOA accepted these legislations without much protest stating that 'These alternatives do not go beyond the views which the members of this Association have always favoured, and there has therefore been no necessity for assuming an antagonistic position with regard to the discussion in the Bill.'[43]

Its earlier opposition to the recommendations of the commissions had not been so much on their scope as on the interference they were supposed to cause. In his note of dissent as the representative of the BMOA on the Factory Commission 1875, Munguldass Nathoobhoy said that the basic point was not the recommendations of the Commission as they were not very restrictive but the fact that the millowners wanted 'to avoid as much as possible direct contact with Government and its executive officers and, consequently, they would rather keep aloof from these undertakings in which they apprehend interference and annoyance from this quarter'.[44]

The provisions of this Act did not make much difference as they were systematically evaded by the employers in collusion with the jobbers. The children were surreptitiously employed overtime and the women never enjoyed the statutory one-and-half-hour of rest. For women, in any case, the restriction of hours did not make much difference as most of them were usually not employed for more than 11 hours. The workers were also called on holidays to clean the machinery. The *Din Bandhu* complained:

Indian Factory Act as worked in Bombay Presidency is simply a sham, the proprietors of factories openly violating its provisions. The present system of inspection of the factories is extremely faulty, because the Inspectors give previous notice of their visit. The paper challenges the Factory Inspectors to disprove . . . that mill-hands are asked to attend the mills on holidays, when repairs to the machinery are executed, that a separate register is kept of such attendance and extra wages given for it, and that the mill hands who refuse to attend on holidays are discharged.[45]

A more sinister development, however, was taking place with the introduction of electric lights in the mills. As early as 1893 the BMOA talked about a report that some millowners were thinking of working longer hours with 'the aid of electric light'. The BMOA also received 'a long communication from the Collector of Bombay' about night work. But it flatly denied that any 'such movement was in contemplation'.[46]

By 1895, the Factory Inspector noted that a couple of mills were putting up electric lights but he took this lightly because they seemed to him 'to lack the sufficiency of natural light in their lower stories'. It also came to his notice that some newly built mills who have sufficient natural light were also 'furnished with an electric light installation'. On this, he innocently queried: 'It is not therefore understood for what purpose the installation will be used.'[47] In 1896, the number of mills which were reported to be working with electric lights was five.[48] The Collector again wrote to the BMOA that 'an attempt was being made to extend working hours beyond the close of the day by the aid of electric and other artificial light'. But the BMOA again flatly denied 'any probability of a general resort to night labour in the Bombay mills'.[49] The outbreak of the Plague slowed the pace of this development but did not stop it because in 1898 the Factory Inspector reported that there were 13 mills fitted with electric light and feared that in future this number might increase.[50] All these mills were working about 14 to 15 hours a day. The situation was worsening and the BMOA was forced to pass a resolution on 7 March 1899 discouraging those putting up electric installations: 'In the opinion of the BMOA it is undesirable under any circumstances, to work the mills with the same set of hands for more than 13 hours per day, inclusive of the necessary stoppages for meals.'[51]

But the resolution was a dead letter even before it was passed. Even those who had proposed and seconded it did not believe in it and never tried to enforce it afterwards. The mill agents who were given a percentage of production were in a hurry to raise the working hours by any means possible. The market condition was becoming good but the machinery remained more or less the same. So to prolong the working hours was considered the only solution. As the market remained unstable, only short-term adjustments were sought. Mill after mill went on fitting the electric light installations and the hours of work kept on increasing. By 1905, the number of mills with such facilities had increased to 39 out of which 32 were working from 5 a.m. to 8 p.m., that is, 15 hours a day.[52] The data provided by the millowners themselves to the IFLC showed that the number of days on which the mills worked for more than 12½ hours was sharply increasing over the years (Table 2.2).

Public protest against this was long in coming, but it came at last. In fact, it first came from the ranks of the millowners themselves, from those who were farsighted. H.E.E. Proctor, the Vice-chairman of the Bombay Chamber of Commerce, severely chided the millowners on this issue: 'To swell your profits you are ready to sink all feelings of humanity and to sweat your mill hands to any extent. You know this is so. It is not a question of competition from Lancashire or Japan, but it is a question of increasing your profits which are already anything between 20 per cent and 50 per cent.'[53]

Bomanji Dinshaw Petit also condemned his colleagues in no uncertain terms:

> I deliberately assert that every additional pound of production got by making them work longer than twelve hours a day is wrung out of their aching limbs.... strong efforts will be made to bring the matter to the notice of the Government and to make it interfere in the matter, and to bring to an immediate end this degrading and disgraceful spectacle of cold-blooded humanity.[54]

Table 2.2: Number of working days exceeding 12.5 hours

Year	Currimbhoy Co. Ltd.	David Mill No. 2	Century Mill
1897	102		
1898	111		
1899	150	180	
1900	105	280	2
1901	264	306	74
1902	279	309	105
1903	284	312	104
1904	269	312	111
1905	215	311	118
1906	286	311	212
1907		267	241

SOURCE: IFLC, 1908, II.

The *TOI*, which was earlier thanked by the BMOA for its support to the Indian mill industry against any restrictive legislation,[55] published an article by its editor, Lovat Frazer, which accused the millowners of crushing the 'vitality' of the workers and demanded that 'there should be no delay in dealing with the matter'.[56] The *ITJ* had earlier criticized the Lancashire lobby for their attempts to impose legislation on the Indian industries and had asserted that 'any attempt to draw a parallel line with English legislation means the crippling of our manufacturers'.[57] But the horror of the situation was such that by 1905, it had made a *volte-face* and condemned the greedy millowners for whom the operatives were 'so many additional machines, that may be hired instead of being bought, and which may be scrapped without any pecuniary loss as they lose in efficiency'. It further added that the 'mill *cooly* to them is of less account than a bullock, for which they have paid the market price'. It demanded the 'severest penalties' for such people and thought that the government interference was 'absolutely necessary'.[58] Many other papers joined hands in this condemnation. Even those who tried to defend the 'native industry' could not overlook 'certain well-known defects in the present-day management of the cotton mills'.[59] But the nationalists in general were definitely opposed to any sort of legislative interference.[60]

What did the workers think? As has been shown earlier, most of them wanted reduced hours. There were not many public forums where they could express their opinions, but whenever they got a chance, they spoke against such inordinately long hours of work. The *TOI* representatives collected a 'large crowd' of workers on their way to work and asked their views on this. It reported, though a little hastily, that 'a whole forest of hands went up in favour of shorter hours even with smaller wages. There was not a single man who was not prepared to sacrifice his extra earnings for shorter hours'. The experiment was repeated and 'the result was identical'. Some of these correspondents went to long-hour mills and interviewed the workers and, even in front of the mill officials, the workers were said to express the same opinions. Thus the paper concluded: 'If the attitude of the millhands is so emphatically against the excessive hours, and violates all precedents by disregarding even the additional wages earned, is not this the strongest proof of the terrible strain imposed upon them?'[61]

Another paper, the *Oriental Review*, conducted similar interviews and reported that the operatives were against the long working hours. One worker pathetically said: 'We leave our homes so early for work and return there so late that our children do not see us. On Sundays and holidays when they see us, they look upon us as strangers.'[62]

When the members of the IFLC visited the workers' chawls and interviewed them, most of them demanded shorter hours.[63] On the basis of their investigation the Report of the IFLC concluded that 'while many of the workers were undoubtedly in favour of the long-hour day, a very large number were strongly opposed to it'.[64]

On 24 September 1905, a massively attended meeting of the workers was held at Chinchpoogly where a memorandum to the government was adopted demanding restriction of working hours to twelve a day.[65] And on 8 October 1905, many of the millworkers protested violently, stoning the mills and causing strikes in some mills.

Faced with unfavourable, sometimes hostile, public opinion and rioting workers, the BMOA passed a resolution asking the constituent mills to work not more than 13 hours, inclusive of the rest time.[66] But, like many BMOA resolutions, it was not observed and the Secretary of the Association complained in a letter about 'the gradual dereliction of rules regarding hours of labour which had by general consent been fixed at 13 hours a day'. The letter ended with a frantic appeal to the millowners 'to combine in self-defence and loyally abide' by the resolution, because the 'individual and collective interests of the members, as well as the good name of the Association, are at stake'.[67] Finally, due to pressure from various quarters, the situation improved a little. The IFLC's investigations into the matter arrived at the conclusion that by 1908, most of the mills followed basically two systems: either they worked by natural light or they worked for 13 to 13½ hours a day throughout the year.[68]

In 1911, a revised Factory Act was passed which restricted the working hours of adult males to 12 in any one day. The amended Act of 1922 further reduced the working hours to eleven. But by then the Bombay mills were already working a 10-hour day as a concession to resolve the general strike of 1920.

VENTILATION

There were many who believed that the deterioration in the health of the workers was 'due more to the want of good ventilation and other sanitary requirements . . . than to the much abused long hours'.[69]

There was some force in this argument. In fact, the ventilation in some departments of the mills was so bad that one witness said that the working 'child will get fresh air in the gutter, which is unfortunately often more than can be said for the mills'.[70]

Although the mills, particularly the new ones, were fitted with sufficient number of windows for ventilation, they were never opened for fear that the draught would break the cotton threads thereby slowing the pace of work. To facilitate the work the temperature was kept high and sometimes it reached as high as 100° F. With such high temperature and the closed windows the workers were virtually boiled inside. One witness associated with the management of the Alliance Spinning Co. pointed out that the 'inside of the Mill is very hot. He cannot stop there for more than a quarter of an hour at a time'. But he asserted that the windows could not be opened as it would interfere with the working: 'the windows of the mill are intended for giving light and not to ventilate the mill'.[71] Another witness thought that 'the temperature of 98° was too high for the operatives to work in for long hours'.[72] One mill secretary commented that it was 'very hot' inside the mill and the heat in the sizing room was 'particularly oppressive'.[73] And a mill manager stated that the 'atmosphere in the blow room is dusty and unhealthy, but it cannot be helped', that the 'grinding room has the largest quantity of dust' and the workers there were compelled to tie clothes on their mouths and noses to protect themselves.[74]

The FC, 1875, which paid more attention to the managerial and millowners' viewpoints, cautiously pointed out the 'evidence on this subject shows that, while there are abundant means of ventilation in all the mills, they cannot be used in consequence of the interruption of the work by draughts'. A little later it admitted that the 'temperature is injuriously high, and that the operatives have to submit to the inconvenience and danger of a fluffy and tainted atmosphere'.[75]

The Factory Commission of 1885 gave a separate report on the ventilation in different rooms of a cotton mill by T.G. Hewlett, the Deputy Surgeon-General, Sanitary Commissioner. It stated that in the mixing room 'much dust is necessarily given off', that the blow rooms 'are, as a rule, insufficiently ventilated', that the carding room is filled 'with much fluff and dust and this is generally recognised as the most unhealthy room in a mill', that in the grinding room 'the windows are rarely opened' and 'the air in the room is therefore contaminated by the breath of the operatives, by cotton fibres floating in it, by particles of iron given off in the grinding of the permanent cylinders', that in the mule and throstle room 'there is an absence of fresh air and much fluff and dust accumulates below each mule and throstle machine', that the reeling and winding rooms, if they were placed above the mule and throstle rooms, suffered from 'the hot and vitiated air' from these rooms below and 'baked by the hot sun' from above, that in some of the sizing rooms 'the steam was found to be acrid and to cause a smarting sensation of the eyes', that in the weaving rooms the 'windows are almost invariably found to be shut' and 'much fluff accumulates below each loom, together with dust consisting of China clay & c'.[76]

The situation was such that it called for immediate attention because working long hours in such a vitiated atmosphere most certainly impaired the health of the operatives, made them susceptible not only to lung diseases but also weakened their resistance and made them prematurely old. But the history of ventilation in the Bombay cotton mills is one of managerial callousness and governmental indifference. The owners were obviously not interested in investing even small amounts in such improvements which would not lead to any increase in their profits. The pusillanimous attitude of the colonial state was explained by the fact that it was not interested in labour conditions unless it became a law-and-order problem or unless it was pressurized by the manufacturing interests at home.

The Factory Act of 1881 did not concern itself with any improvement in the ventilation and sanitation inside the mills. This absence was noted by the Factory Commission of 1885 which considered some legislation necessary to improve the situation.[77] The Factory Act of 1891 contained a provision on this issue. The matter engaged the attention of the Factory Inspectors appointed to monitor the working to the Factory Acts. On 6 June 1894, an Inspector of Factories, A. Shore, wrote to the Chief Inspector of Factories stating that many departments in the cotton mills were fluffy, dusty and hot. The Chief Inspector, in turn, wrote to the Collector, Land Revenue, Customs and Opium, pointing out that the Rule 5 of the Factory Act of 1891 stated that: 'No factory shall be considered ventilated unless openings are provided in the proportion of 10 square feet for each person employed in any room, the openings being such as to admit of a continued supply of fresh air.'

He, however, said that the '10 square feet of lateral opening . . . is to be found in scarcely any of the factories' and added that 'even when it exists in the shape of window space, no benefit is derived therefrom owing to the practice of keeping the windows closed for various reasons'.[78]

On 5 April 1895, the Collector wrote to the Committee of the BMOA putting forward two separate schemes for ventilation. But the BMOA, in its reply asserted that 'the cotton spinning and weaving mills in Bombay, as a whole, fairly fulfilled all requirements of good ventilation'.[79] The Chief Inspector did not accept it and said that 'it was directly contrary to the evidence of senses, the surest test in questions of this nature'.[80]

The correspondence went on and, after some time, two mills, the Bombay Cotton Mill and the Khatau Makanji Mill, announced that they had initiated some experiments in the direction of improvement in ventilation.[81] But, by the end of 1896, the new Factory Inspector was 'unable to report the substantial progress which my predecessor expected' in these two mills. In the Bombay Cotton Mill, only one side of a room bore the marks of the experiment. When the work started on the other side of the room, the rains came and after that the plague. So the experiment remained incomplete. In the Khatau Makanji Mill, even lesser enthusiasm was displayed in conducting the experiment. A few windows were put but the draught was found to be too strong and gunny bags were put on them.[82]

By the end of 1897, 'the futility of the experiments' was clear. Since the year was one of plague and depression the officials did not press the matter. Meanwhile, another millowner claimed to have 'perfected and patented the design for a window' for better ventilation. But the Factory Inspector seriously doubted 'the efficacy of this window as a means of supplying air to the half-stifled workpeople'.[83]

Experiments were tried again,[84] the subject was further discussed,[85] but nothing was done. In 1893, the *ITJ* reported that the:

> subject of ventilation in cotton mills of India appears to have had less attention given to it than any other part of the business of manufacture. The millowners were indifferent to it because they seemed to be making their money without scientific study, and the authorities appointed by the Government to inspect factories have shirked it because they did not understand it.[86]

On 27 February 1903, the Collector wrote to the Secretary to the GOB that the 'question of ventilation in Bombay mills has been the subject of protracted discussion dating as far back as 1894, between the Factory Inspector's Office and Millowners' Association'. He felt that no solution could be found due 'to the absence of any scientifically established standard of ventilation'.[87] The problem was further complicated by the absence of any generally agreed method to test the purity of air and by the reluctance of the millworkers themselves to open the windows as it would have interfered with their work leading to loss of wages.[88]

To assist in this process a new apparatus, devised by Haldane, was brought from England. Samples of air in the mills were tested. On this basis the Chemical Analyser to the Government decided that since in Bombay the temperature, humidity and other related things were so different the results were 'inconsistent and unsatisfactory' and could not form the basis for legislation.[89] Samples of air were taken again and the results were again 'not satisfactory'.[90] A new scheme for taking samples was devised but because of 'frequent changes . . . in the inspecting staff' the experiments were 'temporarily discontinued'. By the end of 1906, a few tests of the air were again taken and it was found that 'the carbon dioxide was present in one room to the extent of 18.5 [vols.] in 10,000 vols. of air, in another 16.5 and in other cases the standard fixed in England at 9 per 10,000 vols. was considerably exceeded'.[91] But no measures were taken and the Factory Inspector was complaining that the 'rule 5 of the Act is unworkable and has been practically ignored'. He added that the 'authorities in the majority of the mills take little interest in the question of ventilation'.[92] By the end of 1907, he regretted that he was 'unable to report any improvement',[93] and by the end of 1908, he was hoping that after the passage of the new Factory Act it would be 'possible for this department to enforce any improvements'.[94]

In 1907-8, before the IFLC, one witness talked about the 'suffocating, impure and artificial atmosphere in the Factory',[95] while another confirmed that 'at present ventilation in the mills was very defective'.[96] One mill manager admitted the requirement of improvement in ventilation,[97] while another said that the 'bad atmosphere made the work very exhausting, and if a man only sat on a chair for the same number of hours he would be quite exhausted'.[98]

The matter came to a head in 1909 when on 12 October, W. Whitaker, an Inspector of Factories, visited the Textile Manufacturing Co. Ltd. and found that the ventilation was unsatisfactory. He wrote in the Inspection Book: 'There should be a fan in use to take out the foul air. Four weeks allowed in which to improve the means of ventilation.' On 14 October, the manager of the mill wrote to the Chief Inspector of Factories protesting the order and blatantly declaring that the 'Rule 5 has been a dead letter since it was made'. In another letter to the Collector on 22 October, the mill agents asserted that the Inspector had 'no authority to give order to the Manager of the Mill'. The Chief Inspector visited the mill and found that 'the present means of ventilation are not sufficient'. He demanded 'an early improvement' in the situation and warned that 'if proper action is not taken within four weeks from this date, steps must be taken to enforce compliance with the law'. Now the agents wrote to the BMOA complaining about the supposedly rigid stance taken by the Chief Inspector and asked the Association to register 'a strong protest against this arbitrary conduct'.

On 9 November, however, in a letter to the Chief Inspector, the mill agents agreed to put up a fan. But, on 17 November, they sent a report to him which claimed that the air did not contain carbon dioxide beyond 9 vols., which was the standard of purity fixed in Britain, and asserted that any improvements therefore were 'entirely unnecessary and unreasonable'. The Chief Inspector did not agree with this point of view but thought it proper not to 'take any further steps until the new Act is passed'. The agents did not feel satisfied. They again wrote to the BMOA demanding that it should lodge a complaint with the Government about the 'arbitrary actions on the part of the Inspectors'. The Secretary of the BMOA, on 15 December 1909, wrote to the Collector that no rule should be promulgated 'without first making inquiry through a special commission'. Finally, the Collector assured the BMOA that no rules regarding ventilation would be promulgated 'until due enquiry has been made and the proposed Rules referred to your Association for opinion'.[99]

The matter rested there. A new committee was appointed in 1911 to look into the matters related to ventilation and air purity in the textile mills.[100] But by the end of 1911, the Factory Report mentioned that 'satisfactory ventilation is still the exception and not the rule in most spinning and weaving factories'.[101]

In 1912, it was still talking of 'dust nuisance'[102] and in 1913, of 'excessive humidification' about which the owners remained 'stolidly indifferent'. It placidly commented that 'nothing short of legislation will effect a general improvement'.[103] The situation remained much the same by the end of this period.

ACCIDENTS

Most of the workers joined mills without any sort of previous training. There they had to work inordinately long hours in a hot and suffocating atmosphere which heavily worked upon their bodies and nerves. This not only caused fatigue but also made their senses dull. To this were added the noisy and big machinery. So the possibilities of accidents became quite marked. The figures do not say much because not many accidents were reported and the minor cases and those involving the daily casual workers were, in many cases, hushed up. Furthermore, the Factory Inspector's system of reporting was also not very efficient. All these leave a large gap in our knowledge about the actual number of the accidents.[104] The Factory Commission of 1875 mostly collected evidence from mill managers and mill agents and many of them agreed that accidents did occur in the mills, but individually they said that such instances were negligible in their own mills. The commission concluded that in the Bombay mills the 'average number of serious cases involving skillful and careful treatment or amputations and other operations are four monthly, while the trivial ones amount, in the same period, to 14 or 15'.[105] The Factory Commission of 1890 gathered the evidences from the workers and almost all of them complained about accidents. The annual reports of the Factory Inspector corroborate these evidences. The only problem was about where to lay the blame for it. When enquired about the fencing of their machinery, all the mill representatives said that they were well-protected in their mills, but they were not so sure about the other mills.[106] But there was an almost total unanimity among the mill representatives in attributing the accidents 'to the negligence and carelessness of the workpeople themselves instead of to preventable causes'.[107] This view was so prevalent that even the Factory Inspector was of the opinion that the accidents occurred due to the 'absent mindedness of the ordinary native mill hands'[108] and to the 'perverse determination on the part of the boys to creep under the machine by whatever access was left open to them'.[109]

He could not or did not want to understand that such 'absent-mindedness' arose due to fatigue and the 'perverse determination' of the boys was due to their desire to take out the remaining cotton from under the machinery to increase their piece-rate wages even at the risk of their lives. He did, however, think that such arguments could not always be advanced 'against guarding the rollers' and the ring-frames which caused many fatal accidents.[110] He further remarked that 'accidents of this nature appear to be too numerous for such a contention to be accepted'.[111] And wherever the machinery were fenced the number of such accidents declined.[112] Dr Joseph Anderson, the House Surgeon of the J.J. Hospital, pinpointed the problem when he said: 'Nearly all these accidents arise from unprotected machinery, but are attributed to the fault of the sufferers themselves.'[113]

Whether the negligence was on the part of the millowners or the workers, the fact which made the accidents even more serious was that there was no provision for compensation to the victims in any case.

There were no laws regarding this and everything depended on the goodwill of the millowners and the managers who in most cases refrained from providing any help to the victims or their families. All that was done sometimes was not to cut the wages while the sufferer was recovering.[114]

EARNINGS

The two most crucial features about the wages in the cotton mills were:

(i) there were wide variations in the wages across the industry even for the same category of workers and jobs; and
(ii) the wages remained at subsistence level till at least 1918.

Initially, most of the workers were employed on piece-rates. A report on the Bombay mills by John Robertson of Glasgow pointed out that 'from the scutching-house to the baling room, every hand, old and young, skilled and unskilled is made to depend more or less for his wages on the amount of production'.[115] The BMOA confirmed it that 'in nearly every instance, old and young, skilled and unskilled, are paid by a piece rate, that is to say, according to the amount of production'.[116] One of the mill managers testifying before the Factory Commission of 1875 said that 'all the hands are paid according to piece-work'.[117] But another mill official referred to some workers getting 'monthly wages'.[118] Yet another commented that 'Three-fourths of the people are employed on piece-work, while probably less than one-fourth are salaried.'[119] What was meant by people on monthly salary is a little doubtful; whether this meant the workers or the clerks and some supervisory staff as well. But it was certain that a great majority of the workers were on piece-rates.

The FC, 1885, recorded the evidence of one jobber who said that he was a 'fixed salary man', although all the 150 men working under him were on piece wages,[120] while another jobber said that he received piece wages.[121] Many witnesses before the IFLC in 1908 confirmed that the majority of the workers were on piece-rates.[122]

By the early 1920s, the situation seemed to have changed as more than half of the workers were reported to be on time-wages (see Tables 2.3 and 2.4). It appears that with the extension of ring spinning, where mostly the big lads were employed who were paid time-rates, the proportion of the time-workers increased over the years. But the time-workers were paid on the basis of the days they attended the mills,

Table 2.3: Number of time and piece rated workers

Grade of Workers	Total Number	Percentage of Total Workforce	Number of Time-Rated Workers	Number of Piece-Rated Workers
Jobber	3,919	2.95	1,812	2,107
Weavers	30,777	23.22	–	30,777
Spinners	6,370	4.80	6,005	365
Piecers	15,867	11.97	14,179	1,688
Reelers	9,555	7.20	354	9,201
Winders	7,514	5.67	286	7,228
Frame-tenters	9,714	7.33	3,410	6,304

SOURCE: *Wages and Hours*, 1921.

Table 2.4: Percentage of time and piece workers to the total workforce

Year	Men		Women		Big Lads		All Workers	
	Time	Piece	Time	Piece	Time	Piece	Time	Piece
1921	51.5	48.5	36.6	63.4	96.3	3.7	54.0	46.0
1923	53.2	46.8	33.1	66.9	97.1	2.9	52.8	47.2

SOURCES: *Wages and Hours*, 1921 and 1923.

which came to around 26 or 27 days in a month; while the piece workers could not come later or go earlier than the rest. Thus, at least in the early years, the basic working conditions of all the workers in a mill remained almost the same even though their wages differed widely. Most of the time-workers were to be found in the ring spinning, carding, sizing, mixing and blow rooms. Piece rate was applied universally to the weavers but also to the reelers, warpers, most of the frame tenters and winders. The piece-rates, although theoretically paid by the amount of production, were determined by so many factors, such as the quality of the yarn, nature of the design, efficiency of the equipment, etc., that nobody was sure how much a worker was going to get at the end of the month. He/she was kept guessing about his/her wages which were, in any case, paid about a month and sometimes a month-and-a-half later. This also allowed for manipulations in the amount of wages to be paid. The worker concerned could not plan his/her expenditure and it had quite an unsettling effect.

Another distinguishing feature about wages was the variations in their rates in different mills. There was no general scale, nor was there any central control. Each mill had its own scale of wages and there were substantial differences between mills. If we construct a table of wages paid in certain mills on the basis of the evidence given before the Factory Commission of 1875, we get the following picture (Table 2.5). These were

Table 2.5: Variation of monthly wages in different mills (*in Rs.*)

Mill	Men	Women	Children	Skilled	Jobbers/ Overseers
Fleming Spg. & Wvg. Mill	15-20	–	–	–	–
The Bombay United Spg. & Wvg. Mill	10-15	7.5-8	5-7	50-60	50-60
Frere and Mazagaon Spg. & Wvg. Co. Ltd.	7-20	7.5	4-10	30-50	40-60
Alliance Spg. Co.	6-15	7	2.5-4	20-40	–
Morarhi Goculdass Spg. & Wvg. Mill	7-10	7.5	4.5-8	15-50	–
Alliance Spg. & Wvg. Mill	10-12	7	2-3.5	–	–

SOURCE: FC, 1875, pp. 75, 121-7.

important variations by the standards of the times for all categories of workers, except women.

The BMOA also made frequent complaints about the different rates of wages which hindered its purpose of 'encouraging friendly feeling and unanimity among mil-owners and users of steam and water-power, on all subjects involving their common good'.[123] In 1891, it regretted that:

it seems . . . doubtful whether anything like a general movement can be advantageously adopted with respect to the scale of wages. The condition of labour at different mills are so extremely various that it would be a work of extreme difficulty to attempt to reconcile them or provide for them . . . any fixed system, and ultimately it will probably be found that the (wage-structure) will have to adjust itself as hitherto by the usual operation of supply and demand.[124]

When asked about wages in 1893 by the Chief Inspector of Factories, the BMOA's reply was: 'Rates of wages are very various, depending upon the situation of the mill, the class of material operated upon, and the general regulations under which the mills are worked. . . . The Association has no record of the scales of wages paid.'[125]

In 1897, when the plague epidemic had disorganized the labour market, the attempts of the BMOA to regulate the payment of wages failed completely as the individual millowners tried their own ways to settle with their workers.[126] This remained a constant source of trouble for the BMOA which tried to introduce uniformity in the scales of wages. As late as 1922, it was reported that the 'employers' associations have not yet evolved any standard scales of wages and individual employers are usually ignorant of how their rates compare with the wages given by others. . . . The attempts made to standardise wages on a definitive principle have hitherto been largely ineffective.'[127]

Each mill followed its own policies and even in mills under the same management the rates of pay varied. For example, between the Rachel Sassoon Mill and Alexandria Mill the monthly earnings of a weaver varied by about 21 per cent.[128]

In the earlier period the wage variation was one of the reasons for a high turnover of the labour. The workers, whenever opportunities offered, moved to a mill where rates of payments were better. But this movement had its own limitations. There could not always be chances of getting a new job. So, in the later stages, the workers started striking work for more wages which were already being paid in the neighbouring mills. The Industrial Disputes Committee observed that 'the un-corelated raising of wages in one factory is almost invariably seized upon in other factories of the same class, and instances of strikes caused in this way are within the memory of all'.[129]

Many contemporary observers believed that the levels of wages in the cotton mills of Bombay were higher than the wages in agriculture, in other forms of manual work, or in other textile centres. The *ITJ* remarked in 1893 that while a worker might earn two annas a day from agricultural work, the average daily wages in the mills were 6 to 8 annas. It further stated that a family in the factory could save about 33 per cent of its earnings.[130] The IFLC also concluded in its report that the 'wages of the operatives in textile factories vary from place to place, but are everywhere considerably higher than those earned by the same class of men in other employments'.[131] The IIC commented that wages were higher in Bombay than in Calcutta.[132] S.M. Rutnagar wrote that 'Prior to 1909 their earnings in the field amounted to 2 to 3 annas per day, while in the mill a man was worth 6 to 8 annas.'[133] The representatives of the BMOA, in the evidence before the Indian Tariff Board, repeatedly complained about the wages being very high, particularly after the war.[134] According to them, the cost of labour was 37.8 per cent of the total cost of manufacture in 1914, while in 1924, it was 40 per cent.[135]

We find that the real wages remained more or less at the same level till about 1918. Between 1882 and 1918 the percentage increase in the money wages was 64.7.[136] The increase in the real wages between 1900 and 1918 have been calculated to be only about 14 per cent, while the increase in the money wages was 71 per cent in the same period.[137] The wages had not increased much during the War years. The increase in the money wages between 1914 and 1918 was 28.3 per cent, while real wages had actually declined by about 12.5 per cent.[138] And, according to the *Prices Enquiry Report*, real wages had actually declined by 8 points between 1895 and 1912.[139]

Between 1918 and 1921, however, the wages, both money and real, registered very significant increases. While money wages increased by 45.5 per cent, real wages increased by 24.5 per cent.[140] It was the massive agitations launched by workers in the form of two general strikes in 1919 and 1920 as well as many small strikes during this period that were responsible for this increase.

Even though the trend might show an increase over the years, it is difficult to get any reliable figures for the actual average wages in the Bombay industries. The series given in *Prices and Wages* is based on the figures supplied by a single factory in Bombay. The millowners, on their part, tried to overstate the wages paid. The Bombay Labour Textile Union questioned the figures supplied by the BMOA to the ITB because 'the salaries of the assistant carding, spinning and weaving masters, the head jobbers of all the mill departments, store-keepers, factory clerks, etc., are included in them and are, therefore, calculated in arriving at the "average" monthly wages of the textile workers'.[141] Therefore, according to the BTLU, the wage bills of the workers were said to be inflated and the actual wages of the workers were 'appreciably less'[142] and did not form more than one-tenth of the total cost of production.[143]

If the actual wages were less than the stated ones, the realized wages became even more meagre due to several deductions prevalent in the mills. The most important deduction was in the form of fines.[144] Fines were imposed quite frequently on the workers on several counts. If a worker was absent for one day without leave (which was in any case not easy to get), he/she lost wages for two days. If the workers were late even for fifteen minutes, they had to lose one-fourth of their daily wages. Apart from this, workers were penalized monetarily for spoiling the clothes or not obeying the jobbers or other superiors. Another method of inflicting fines, particularly on the weavers, was to force them to take the spoilt clothes and to deduct its assumed price from their wages. This practice was adopted in almost all mills in Bombay and the annual amount of such fines per mill varied from Rs. 700 to Rs. 7,000.[145]

Another problem was that the wages were paid to the workers about a month or one-and-a-half month after they were due. This was done to discipline the workers, to check the instability of the workforce, and finally to keep the wages in hand so that deductions could be conveniently made on any ground. This practice caused great hardship to the workers who had to borrow from various quarters until they got their wages. Four to six weeks were a rather long period for withholding the wages. There were many instances in which workers had to either leave for their villages or fell ill in the intervening period and were consequently dismissed by the mill management. In many such cases their wages for the period were not paid to them. The Kamgar Hitwardhak Sabha, in a memorial to the Secretary of State, claimed that the total amount of such 'unclaimed and forfeited wages' would come to at least Rs. 2,000 per mill.[146] Thus what the workers got was less than the nominal wages given in the various documents. Even the rise in wages in the mills were not so much as those of skilled workers in other occupations in the city. The ITB, on the basis of the figures supplied by the Bombay Labour Office concluded that 'the wages in 1925 of all skilled labour in urban areas in Bombay Presidency had risen since 1914 by a considerably higher percentage than they had in the cotton mill industry'.[147]

The cost of living in Bombay was also higher than in other Indian cities as well as in rural areas. It was reported in 1918 that the 'average expenses of a family without tea and liquor are Rs 19-8-0 per month'.[148] The average monthly earnings of the millworkers in Bombay was stated to be Rs. 16-6-3 in 1914.[149] Even if we assume that there was an increase in the wages to some extent by 1918, it was really difficult for a family to survive on one person's earnings. Now if we go back to the earlier cited instance by the ITJ about the working-class family being able to save or spend 33 per cent of its earnings in 1893, we find that this calculation was based upon those situations where other family members were also working and contributing their whole earnings to the kitty:

> A man in Bombay will earn on an average Rs 14 per month, a woman from Rs 7 to 8 and children from Rs 6 to 7. A family of a man, a woman and two children, may earn Rs 32 per month. The food of the family will cost Rs 18, and the rent Rs 3; there is thus a surplus of Rs 11 per month for a family that is disposed to work steadily.

Apart from all the members earning, this calculation also relies upon their steadiness and not taking any leaves for illness or any other cause. It, moreover, takes only the food and rent into account, leaving aside other expenditures, such as the interests on debts, expenditure on social or religious ceremonies, or expenses involved for treatment for illness. And this is not all. The *ITJ*, besides assuming an extremely frugal life for the workers, also includes occasional reliance on charity.

> Charity is so universal, and food so cheap in India. . . . A Bombay cooly with bare head and a simple waistcloth is fully dressed for work in or out of doors; he

never needs fire or warmth or shelter, except from the rain. Alms are given daily at mosques, temples, and at hundreds of private houses, and begging is an honoured profession that supports many thousands of the people. . . .[150]

Thus a working-class family had to resort to all these forms of 'earnings' and frugal living for survival in most of the period before 1919. After that, however, the struggles by the workers led to significant increase in wages in 1919 and 1920 which, combined with declining prices in the early 1920s, registered an improvement in their standard of living.

DRINKING

One witness complained before the IFLC in 1908 that 'taking them as a class, they (the workers) were not so good as 20 years ago. Years ago it was rare to see an operative drunk, but of recent years they had contracted the vice of drinking'.[151] For the initial years there are contradictory evidences with regard to alcohol-consumption among the workers. In 1875, one mill manager said that drunkenness was 'almost unknown among them'.[152] But S.M. Edwardes, tracing the 'growth of intemperance' goes back to 1866-7 and describes the year 1876 as one in which this habit had increased enormously including among the 'Indian women of the lower classes'. He attributed this trend to 'the rapid expansion of the textile industry and the growth of the industrial population which, in the absence of facilities for decent recreation and in consequence of scandalous house-conditions, was prone to drown its discomforts by resort to the nearest liquor-shops.'[153]

According to the Census of 1881, there were many liquor and toddy shops in the mill areas,[154] and one observer said in 1908 that 'there were 14 grog shops within a small area in the mill district at Parel'.[155]

In any case, by the first decade of the twentieth century, the reports about the instances of drinking among the workers became very frequent. In 1905, we hear of 'great increase in spirit-drinking'.[156] The IFLC was flooded with a barrage of complaints in this regard. Many witnesses, coming from various walks of life, stated that the workers were greatly in the habit of drinking. It was said that 'the majority of the men spent one and half annas a day in drink'.[157] Another witness confirmed that 90 per cent of the millworkers indulged in drinking so much that 'twenty per cent of their pay was spent in drink'.[158] On the basis of much evidence the IFLC concluded that 'The consumption of liquor among the factory workers is . . . undoubtedly greater than among the men of the same rank in life engaged in other occupations.'[159] The findings of the Liquor Committee came to the same point that 'the mill hands spend more money in liquor than on food or clothes'.[160]

Bhiwa Ramji Nare, a former weaving master and a leading member of the Kamgar Hitwardhak Sabha, went to the extent of saying that the physical deterioration of the workers was less due to the long hours of work than 'due to their habits of drinking, to keeping late hours, visiting theatres and to such other vices'.[161] In fact, in 1905, at the height of the controversy related to the extremely long working hours, V.A. Talcherkar, another leader of the Kamgar Hitwardhak Sabha, claimed that the long hours were beneficial to the workers as it ensured 'enforced immunity from the temptation of drinking and gambling'.[162]

The liquor shops proliferated even more as time advanced. The Excise Committee noted in the early 1920s that 'the number of (liquor) shops in certain labouring localities and mill centres is provokingly large'.[163] These shops served both country as well as foreign-made liquor. They were often quite approachable and spacious and the liquor was served along with mutton, rice, *bhaji* and *pav.* Some of them also provided these things on credit.[164] All these led to increased consumption and it was reported that in Bombay city per capita liquor consumption was the highest (34.2 drams) in the whole of Bombay Presidency.[165]

This was considered a big moral issue and also a great hindrance in creating a model working class. The 'evil of drink' was supposed to incite criminal activities and to have 'an adverse effect on the output of work'.[166] S.H. Jhabvala of Central Labour Board asserted that the 'drink evil does promote crime'. He further added that it 'reduces output and efficiency and is the chief cause of absenteeism'.[167] S.D. Saklatwala, speaking for BMOA, complained that the drinking habit among workers 'affects production'.[168] There were some, like the Municipal Councillor, B.N. Motivala, who thought that this habit caused 'irregularity, inefficiency and accidents in industry'. He also held it 'largely responsible for the unreasoning attitude adopted by labour against capital in industrial disputes'. And finally, he asserted that it was 'the primary cause of pauperism in the world'.[169]

Various explanations were advanced for this habit among the workers. Tilak thought that it was an evil design of the government to extract more revenue by promoting intemperance.[170] According to Nare, however, the reason for this was the availability of ready money in the 'hands of uneducated and thoughtless persons'.[171] Later, the BMOA reached the same conclusion that 'owing to the general increase in their pay the millhands have started to consume foreign spirits'.[172] Another person attributed this to illiteracy among the workers and suggested that it was only through total prohibition that this temptation can be contained.[173]

None of these explanations appreciated that the roots of 'intemperance' lay in the lives of the workers, the exhausting nature of their work, the crowded and dirty surroundings and, in many cases, their solitary existence without spouse or family. There were some contemporaries who realized that the blame for this lay with the bad working and living conditions of the workers. Keluskar, the Secretary of the Maratha Aikyechhoo Sabha, maintained that 'the nature of mill work was such that the men were bound to take a stimulant'.[174] When the workers returned from their long and exhausting day's work, the prospect of going to stinking, crowded dens or equally uninviting streets which passed for their homes did not seem very attractive. Besides, there were often no families to give them emotional support. To have a stimulant in the form of liquor was one alternative. And once it started, it continued and became a habit with them, and, for some others, a means of amassing money and wielding power and influence. These liquor shops were owned by influential persons, jobbers, landlords and the like. They tried to hinder any temperance movement among the workers by harassing those who propagated this.[175] And, in any case, the workers themselves were not prepared to renounce whatever enjoyment they could derive by drinking.

DEBTS

The problem of debt was a very old one for the workers. Low wages, coupled with irregularity of payments and fines on many pretexts, along with high cost of living created a tightrope from which even the slightest deviation in the form of expenditure on marriage, festivals, drinking or illness plunged them into debt-traps from which it was very difficult to emerge. About 90 per cent of the workers were reported to be in debt.[176] The occasions which necessitated borrowing were many. One contemporary, on the basis of his survey among the millworkers, stated: '20% of the employees contract debt by marriage, 7% for funeral expenses, 28% for occasional extra expenditure such as journeys to their native place, etc., 7% for expenses at commencement of service, 14% for medical help and illness in the family, and 3% for famine at native place.'[177]

The rate of interest was exorbitant. The local grain-dealers and

Marwaris charged 48 to 96 per cent per annum. If the workers failed to get credits from the Marwaris they went to the Pathans who charged 150 per cent per annum and if the interest was not paid in time, the workers were 'molested and maltreated by these tall, powerful men who, armed with a heavy stick, settle their accounts with their debtors and collect their dues by brute force'.[178] Another problem added to the heavy rates of interest was that in many cases the workers were cheated. As they were illiterate they could not read the amount of money on the paper on which they put their thumb impressions. Even when some of them could read, they, in some cases, were forced to sign on blank papers under compulsion.[179] All these made their burdens even heavier and their debts perpetual.

A contemporary observer related the debt-burden to the poverty: 'Hopeless poverty engenders recklessness. Living from hand to mouth creates despair of ordered domestic economy; and the alleged extravagance and carelessness of the factory employee is less the proof of a spendthrift tendency than the evidence of the extreme difficulty of prudent expenditure.'[180]

Poverty, of course, was the most important reason of the indebtedness. But if we look at the comparative amounts of debts, we find that this amount increased with the increased earnings of the workers (Table 2.6). One reason could be that the number of dependents increased with the increased earnings of the family; but then the number of earners also increased.[181] It seems, therefore, that although for those in the lower income groups the cause for debts was meagre earnings, for

Table 2.6: Incidence of indebtedness in Bombay

Income Group	Average Monthly Income of a Working Class Family			Average Indebedness per Indebted Family		
	Rs.	anna	pie	Rs.	anna	pie
Below Rs. 20 and from Rs. 20 to Rs. 30	25	3	8	122	1	10
Rs. 30 to Rs. 40	34	3	3	136	6	6
Rs. 40 to Rs. 50	43	4	3	153	1	1
Rs. 50 to Rs. 60	53	3	5	173	0	8
Rs. 60 to Rs. 70	63	1	8	216	6	6
Rs. 70 to Rs. 80	73	3	4	283	12	6
Rs. 80 to Rs. 90	82	15	8	281	4	10
Rs. 90 and over	114	9	4	295	5	0
All Incomes	50	1	7	174	9	2

SOURCE: TLIC, 1937-8, vol. II, p. 294.

those in the higher income groups the reason for the higher debt figures with the rising incomes was social rather than economic. As the earnings became more the social pressure to spend more increased. It led to an increase in the number of dependents as well as the increased expenditures on social and religious occasions such as marriages, deaths, festivals, etc.

HOUSING

In the Cotton Boom of the early 1860s, a lot of people desirous of finding work came to Bombay. They lived temporarily in whichever place they could find. The boom had created temporary employment opportunities, the emigrants were new to the place and large in number and the city was not prepared to house them. All these factors led to a horrible overcrowding. It was reported that in a nine-feet wide lane,

> the houses on each side were of two or three floors, and the various lanes were densely peopled, and the floors of the verandas were fully occupied, while to eke out accommodation in some of the verandas there were *charpaees* or cots slung up and screened with old matting to form second tier of sleeping place for labourers that were employed in daytime at the Railway terminus or elsewhere.[182]

When the boom was over and the workers could not find any alternative employment as company after company collapsed, many of them returned to their villages. The expansion of economic activities after that, though significant, could not compare with the earlier period. That accounts for the abrupt fall in the city's population from 816,562 in 1864 to 644,405 in 1872, that is a decrease of about 21 per cent.[183] By 1881, the population had shown an increase which pointed towards steady economic growth. It kept increasing except when the plague was at its heights between 1897 and 1901. The population in 1901 registered a decline as many people had fled the city. This, however, was only a temporary phenomenon and as the epidemic subsided, many came back. During this period, the mill industry was showing a significant growth. In 1872, the number of the cotton mills in Bombay city was 11; in 1881, it was 32 and by 1911 it had reached 87. Apart from cotton mills there were railways, dockyards and construction activities that attracted people to the city. The population of the city increased by 82.5 per cent between 1872 and 1921 (Table 2.7).

As the population increased, the Bombay mainland was found to be inadequate to contain it and there occurred, over the period, a major shift in the population to the northern areas of the city which were still

Table 2.7: Population of Bombay city, 1872-1921

Year	Population
1872	644,405
1881	773,196
1891	821,764
1901	776,006
1906	977,822
1911	979,445
1921	1,175,914
Percentage Change	82.5%

SOURCE: *Census of India, 1921*, vol. IX, part I, p. 10.

rural in the beginning. The shift occurred due to rising rents and overcrowding in the central areas, on the one hand, and the rapid development of mill, factories and railway workshops in the northern areas, on the other. The eight sections of the city which roughly formed the mill districts later on were Byculla, Tadwadi, Mazagaon, Parel, Sewri, Sion, Mahim and Worli. Among these, the millworkers were most numerous in Byculla, Parel and Worli.[184] The workers, therefore, moved to the less densely inhabited and low-rent areas. Even by 1881, many people had moved northwards and it was reported that 'the population following Industrial pursuits were most numerous in Parel and Byculla'.[185] By 1891, the movement of population was very noticeable and the Census of 1891 reported:

In some of the most densely crowded parts of the Native Town—Umarkhadi, Dhobi Talao, Fanaswadi and Khara Talao—the total female population has decreased while the number of those born in Bombay has increased. This may easily be explained, as the emigrant women were chiefly employed now in the parts of Bombay north of Bellasis Road; and with the extension of house building there, they have moved nearer their work leaving more rooms for their Bombay-bred sisters in the more central portions of the island.[186]

Even in 1881, Chakla had 726, Umarkhadi 526, Market 558, Kumbharwada 778 and Khara Talao 700 persons per acre.[187] On the other hand, the northern sections were much less densely populated.[188] By 1901, in comparison to 1872, out of 33 sections of the city, 15 sections showed a decline while 18 showed an increase; the city, as a whole, registered an increase of 20.42 per cent. Out of the 18 sections showing increase, Byculla, Parel, Sewri, Sion, Mahim and Worli were on the top. The Census Report of 1901 offered the following explanation:

As regards Parel, Worli and Byculla, we should be inclined to ascribe this result mainly to the growth of mills and factories and to the consequent immigration of an Industrial population; and . . . Sewri, Sion and Mahim, on the other hand, are 'sections of refuge' and offer accommodation to the fugitive population of the central portions of the island.[189]

The population in certain sections, despite new births, showed a decline, while that of certain other sections registered a phenomenal increase which was several times higher than the average increase of the city as a whole. While the increase in the total population of the city was 82.5 per cent, the increase in the mill districts were much more (Table 2.8). The people who came to live in these areas were mainly the working classes, the cotton mill workers among them. In 1872, the number of mill workers enumerated was 5,175[190] out of which only 266, that is, 5.1 per cent of the total, lived in the places that later came to be known as 'mill districts'. By 1906, this percentage had increased to 82.1(Table 2.9). It must have increased in the later years but we do not have comparable figures for that period. We know, however, that by the end of our period about 90 per cent of the mill workers lived within 15 minute walk from their mills.[191]

The number of millworkers in proportion to the total population of these eight Sections increased from insignificance to a substantial presence. While in 1872 they had formed just 0.22 per cent of the population of this area, by 1906 their proportion had gone up to 26.01 per cent (Table 2.10).

Despite the fact that there was a very large labouring population in

Table 2.8: Growth of population in the mill areas

Section	Percentage Increase (1872-1921)
Byculla	225.6
Tadwadi	295.8
Mazagaon	53.0
Parel	332.3
Sewri	508.2
Sion	357.3
Mahim	229.6
Worli	1075.5

SOURCE: *Censuses*, various issues. Also see Appendix III.

Table 2.9: Percentage of mill districts (Byculla to Worli—8 sections) to the total population of the cotton mill workers in Bombay

1872	1881	1901	1906
5.1	49.4	76.8	82.1

SOURCE: *Censuses*, various issues.

Table 2.10: Percentage of the cotton mill workers to the total population of the sections (1872-1906)

Section	1872	1881	1901	1906
Byculla	0.03	12.64	19.60	23.20
Tadwadi		11.80	14.97	19.27
Mazagaon	026	7.93	15.10	19.90
Parel	0.59	17.38	39.80	42.80
Sewri		4.30	26.60	30.40
Sion	0.03	5.05	12.24	21.60
Mahim	0.83	2.54	8.94	10.20
Worli		2.55	37.60	40.70
Total Average	0.22	8.02	21.85	26.01

SOURCE: *Censuses*, various issues. Also see Appendix V.

the city, not much was done to provide them with habitable surroundings. In the late 1860s, many people were horrified to watch 'the wretched rows of cadjan huts occupied by human beings, but only raised by a few inches above the fetid mud of the flats'.[192] Even when the population had decreased in 1872, the Health Officer to the Municipal Commissioner wrote that 'the filthy dens in which the labouring classes of the city live are among the chief causes of the very high death-rate'.[193] By 1881, the population shift had started but no change was noticeable in the 'suburban sections which are more or less rural still as a whole; they are Parel, Sewri, Sion and Worlee; and as in these sections there has been a great change in population since 1972, there has been a corresponding augmentation of the density of this population around inhabited centres—the village clusters'.[194]

During the 1880s,. the government became somewhat interested in the development of these areas. Municipality was engaged in widening the streets and the Fergusson Road from Worli to Parel was built by 1884. But the construction of living quarters was left entirely to the private entrepreneurs. Innumerable buildings were constructed, but owing to the haphazard and unsystematic development, they did not provide better accommodation to the people and overcrowding continued.[195] In 1901, the mill districts had 15,082 houses, in 1911, 22,566 houses and in 1921, 27,227 houses. Out of these, 79.8, 79.3 and 81.2 per cent of the total number of buildings in 1901, 1911 and 1921 respectively consisted only of ground floors.[196] And these were mostly 'small tiled huts used as dwellings'.[197] In G Ward, an area mostly inhabited by working classes, there lived the poor people 'whose thatched, cadjan dwelling huts are more than two thousand in number'. And 'this last factor is in some degree responsible for a greater ground floor population in G Ward than in others. . . . In Wards G, F, and E the ground-floor population is most numerous.'[198]

This feverish construction activity resulted in the construction of every variety of insanitary dwelling. Burnett-Hurst, in his study on the housing problem of the working classes, divides the buildings in which the wage-earners lived into three types. The first were the '*Zavli*' sheds whose main occupants were the Ghati carters but sometimes the mill-workers might also be residing in them with their friends or relatives. These sheds were built of dry leaves from the date or coconut trees. The inhabitants often kept the domestic animals with them and the surroundings were extremely insanitary.[199]

The second type of dwelling consisted of corrugated iron, empty kerosene tins, etc. These sheds were inhabited mostly by municipal employees or by tenants evicted from other places by the Improvement Trust. Some of these sheds were built by Improvement Trust and the rest by private enterprises. There was no ventilation or light inside the rooms. Burnett-Hurst describes them:

> Entering the shed and passing down a dark narrow passage—so narrow that two persons could scarcely pass one another—one had to grope one's way to the doorways of the rooms. Upon peering into these, it was impossible to ascertain whether they were occupied or not. Not a ray of light penetrated them, and this at noon on a bright, sunny day. It was only on striking a match that the rooms were found to be inhabited.[200]

To these must be added the small huts, scattered in a large part of the mill areas, made 'mostly of clay and roofed with *cadjan*, a mat made of the palmyra or coconut tree plaited together. Some of these huts are so small that they only admit of the man sitting upright in them and barely shelter his feet when he lies down.'[201]

The most important abodes of the millworkers were the chawls built near the mills. By the turn of the century most of the workers were living in these chawls. They were built mainly by three agencies—the mill-owners, the government and the overwhelming majority of them by private enterprises.

The millowners or the government did not pay any attention to the problem of housing the workers in the nineteenth century. The work-people kept on living in mud huts, in tin sheds, in any type of building, even on the streets. The *ITJ* commented in its editorial in 1897: 'For many years the Indian millowner remained completely indifferent to the social condition of the operatives. They were so many human machines whose labour was to be purchased at the lowest possible price, but whose welfare was of no consequence.'[202]

However, in the wake of the Plague which devastated Bombay from 1896 onwards, this complacency was broken and some efforts were made for a little more organized development. One millowner, N.N. Wadia, built about 300 rooms for his workers.[203]

In 1898, the Bombay Improvement Trust (BIT) was formed by the government to provide sanitary houses to the poor. On 19 September 1900, the Trust wrote to the BMOA stating that 'very little has been done by the employers of labour to house their workpeople'.[204] It implored the millowners to cooperate financially with the Trust 'in an effort to improve the housing of millhands in Bombay'.[205] It proposed to build the chawls and then lease them to the owners of the mills for housing their workers. The millowners would have to pay back the cost of construction along with the interest over a period of time. The BMOA, on its part, tried to shrug off the responsibility by saying that 'suitable accommodation provided by many millowners in Bombay . . . has not been availed of to the extent they anticipated',[206] and thus they felt reluctant to cooperate in 'further efforts of the same kind'.[207] The BIT pursued the matter further by proposing a scheme in which the Trust and the millowners could fruitfully cooperate. To this the BMOA reciprocated by putting forward several conditions, including that the cost per room should not exceed Rs. 350 and that in case a mill ceased working the owner should be 'free to let the rooms to persons other than his own hands'.[208] Initially, the BIT agreed to the proposals but later, on calculation, it found impossible to keep the cost of construction within the limits proposed by the BMOA.[209] The matter rested there and the BIT also kept quiet due to its own problems.

From the millowners' point of view, the construction of houses for the millworkers was part of the larger task of 'relieving overcrowding in the city' and, therefore, should be undertaken by the government. As the 'workmen's chawls are not likely to prove profitable in the immediate future to the millowners', they did not feel actively inclined towards providing them.[210] In 1908, the IFLC observed that 'little has been done by the mills in this direction and operatives as a rule herd together, for the sake of economy, into large, many-storeyed, barrack-like building called chawls, which are provided by private enterprises'.[211] But, surprisingly, in the BMOA's annual meeting of 1908, its chairman vociferated eloquently on the need to provide their workers with proper housing facilities. He lamented that 'Long weary years have been wasted in talking of the provision of sanitary chawls while the poor are dying.' He poured scorn on the 'filthy slums' which were 'veritable death-traps and the haunts of plague and other epidemic diseases' and in which the workers had to pay heavy rents 'entirely disproportionate to their income'. He warned that any 'delay in the solution of this urgent matter is suicidal' and called for an improved collaboration between the millowners and the BIT.[212]

In 1909, after an interval of six years, the dialogue was resumed between the Trust and the BMOA, the former asking the latter for any suggestions 'on this matter, with a view to determining what chawls should be erected next year in pursuance of the scheme'. To this, the BMOA put the query 'whether the arrangement arrived at in 1903 would be the basis on which the cooperation of millowners is invited'. It also clearly communicated that the construction of the chawls was the primary responsibility of the Trust and not the millowners. The BIT comforted the millowners by agreeing to the 1903 scheme except that the period of payment should be 28 years instead of 37 years. On this, the BMOA expressed general agreement putting forward certain amendments.[213] On the whole, 23 mills seemed willing to collaborate with the BIT under this scheme. But, even by 1913, only two mills had entered into an agreement 'to avail themselves of the facilities offered by the Improvement Trust'.[214] In 1904, the 'housing problem still seems to hang fire'.[215] And, in 1915, the BMOA was expressing its 'deep regret that in spite of special facilities given to the mill industry for the erection of labourers' chawls by way of the compulsory acquisition of land and the advance of loans on easy terms, sufficient advantage has not been taken of this opportunity'.[216]

By 1916, under this arrangement, one set of chawls was in the process of being constructed. In all, eight chawls were to be built consisting of 504 rooms to house 2,016 workers.[217] This obviously was a very small portion of the total population of the millworkers. Even by 1929, only 22 out of 76 mills provided 'partial housing' for their workers. The total number of workers in these 22 mills was 64,270, out of which only 12,149, i.e. 20 per cent could be accommodated in these buildings.[218] By 1937, it was reported that 21 out of 58 mills provided partial accommodation for their workers, the total number of tenements being 4,301.[219]

The millowners, of course, were not much interested in investing in the houses for their workers as it might not have brought returns on its own. But the apprehensions expressed by them about their workers not availing the accommodation so provided was also not unfounded. The roots of workers' aversion in living in these houses lay in their relationship to the mills. As there was no security of employment and dismissals were quite common, the mill houses were a risky proposition for the workers because they would be evicted as soon as they lost employment with their mills or if the latter were stopped due to strikes or for any other reasons. Moreover, while they could dodge the rent collectors in the private chawls and delay or avoid paying rents by shifting their accommodations, in the mill houses the rents would be deducted from the wages. Many contemporaries observed the workers' reluctance to occupy the lodging provided by their own mills. The Indian Industrial Commission (IIC) talked about cases where 'only 57% of persons using the accommodation provided by the mills worked in those mills'.[220] It, therefore, concluded that 'there are objections, from labourers' own point of view, to the creation of a general system of landlord-employers, which would tend to keep labour too dependent on the latter'.[221] The Industrial Disputes Committee (IDC) also reached the same conclusion:

> The employer is not the ideal house builder . . . because it makes his employee doubly dependent on him—dependent on him for his wage and for his home; in case of dismissal he loses both. If therefore equally good accommodation is provided by an outside agency like the Development Directorate on equally easy terms, the operative will prefer to be housed in a building which is not owned by his employer; he wants what has been described as a "strike free" house. If ever there is a surplus of houses, the mill chawl is the one which will be first emptied.[222]

This observation was supported by the labour representatives as well. The BTLU, in its evidence before the ITB, stated: 'the workers do not like to occupy the chawls built by their employers because they feel that by their so doing, they come more under the grip of their masters. In times of strike there is always a danger of the workers being ejected. They, therefore, prefer to stay in private chawls, howsoever bad they may be.'[223]

The Girni Kamgar Mahamandal, another body representing the workers before the ITB, affirmed that the greatest problem with the houses provided by the mills was that 'the worker is left entirely at mercy of the millowners and repeated experience has shown that these houses have been used by the owners as a great instrument in putting down any strike agitation by threats of immediate ejection. No wonder then the labour fights shy of taking advantage of these rooms.'[224]

In fact, F.J. Ginwala, a labour leader of some standing, asserted that 'Even if the houses were built (by the millowners) it is better for the operatives not to live in them, because it gives the millowners an undue hold on them.'[225] Therefore, the ITB, in order to make the mill houses acceptable to the workers, proposed that the chawls should be 'taken over and administered either by a group of mills or by the Millowners' Association as a body'.[226]

While the much-debated cooperation between the BIT and the millowners proved to be a failure due to the reluctance of the millowners to invest in the houses and the unwillingness of the workers to live in them, the Trust's own attempts at construction of houses for the poor was no more successful. In fact, it dishoused more people than it housed. It evicted about 72,000 persons by demolishing the old chawls, but could provide housing to only about 18,247 persons in the chawls built by it.[227] By the end of 1915, the number of tenements provided to the working classes by all the public bodies in Bombay such as the BIT, the Bombay Municipality, the Port Trust, the BB & CI Railway Co and the GIP Railway Co, was only 8,223 which accommodated 28,843 persons.[228]

In 1920 the Government of Bombay embarked on an ambitious programme, through its Development Department, of constructing 50,000 tenements for the working classes. It imposed a duty of one rupee per bale of cotton on all the cotton coming into Bombay. This way the cotton mill industry had to indirectly contribute about Rs. 9.7 lakh annually towards the housing project. But the Development Department could build only 16,544 tenements and, by 1926, about 69 per cent of these rooms were empty.[229] By 1929, there was little improvement in the occupancy figures and it was reported that only about 50 per cent of the rooms were occupied.[230] Even by 1937, the occupancy was only about 52 per cent.[231] While the BMOA termed the scheme as 'a conspicuous and expensive failure',[232] the BTLU criticized 'the ruinous working of the Development Department'.[233] The problems with these chawls were that they were made of concrete which got hot in the summers and cold in the winters. In addition to this, the rents were high and the chawls were located a little far from the mills from where easy conveyance was not available. The situation was reported to have improved owing to the alterations done in these chawls in 1938 and the occupancy improved markedly in 1939 to 81 per cent.[234] But these chawls were not necessarily occupied by the millworkers and, according to an estimate by the BTLU, the houses provided by millowners, the BIT, and the Development Department all together accounted only for about 12 per cent of the millworkers.[235] The rest of the millworkers resided in the chawls built by the private entrepreneurs.

These private houses as well as their surroundings were extremely unhealthy owing both to the negligence of the authorities and the insanitary habits of the lodgers. There were no statutory provisions against the construction of such insanitary buildings. All that the owners of these buildings were interested in was in making easy money. The situation in the private chawls was so bad that one official wrote: 'In the drained districts there are dwellings on damp ground; in the undrained districts there are dwellings on sewage.'[236] And the mill districts were largely undrained. Byculla, Mazagaon, Parel, Mahim, Worli, etc., were almost completely undrained areas.[237] In fact, the pace of the construction of the buildings had been so fast that the municipality proved to be very sluggish and 'it has not been practicable to carry out works for the removal of the sewage and rain-water as quickly as the buildings have been constructed'.[238] The report for the year 1898-9 complained:

> Where but a few years ago there were solitary buildings in swamps, there are now towns or densely populated habitations, amidst which there are serious nuisances caused by pools of water and sewage in the rains. In some localities these nuisances cannot be removed through the system of drainage for the reason that the buildings and the nuisances in the midst of them are on grounds lower than the sewer.[239]

Many of the buildings were erected without connecting them to the sewers even in those areas where it was possible. In Lalwady (at Parel) the municipal authorities sent summons to many owners of the buildings to connect their buildings to the sewer. The Municipal Commissioner, however, complained: 'the proceedings in the Police Court will take a long time and the nuisances will continue . . . for another six months. The nuisances around buildings in Lalwady are very loathsome. The sewage which cannot be absorbed by the earth flows down the public road and through a hole in the street wall falls into a mill tank.'[240]

Such nuisance was quite common in many areas. The filth of the Government distillery at Dadar could not be drained and it accumulated and stank;[241] the water flowing from the houses could not be properly channeled and it flooded the streets and accumulated in the ditches and became a breeding ground for mosquitoes; sometimes the sewage of one mill overflowed into the water tank of another and many workers, who drank this water, fell ill;[242] there were open drains in the narrow lanes between two chawls sometimes occupying the entire space and seeping into the foundations of the buildings.[243]

On such grounds stood the chawls whose rooms were 'dark, unwholesome dens, into which the light of day never penetrates, and which must of necessity breed disease and pestilence'.[244] There were no proper latrines in these chawls. The children always defecated in the narrow lanes separating two chawls from each other. The houses were fitted with basket privies. Though the municipality employed labourers called *halalkhors* to remove the contents of these privies, they often did not perform their duties either by shirking work or for want of sufficient number of carts to carry the excreta. The contents of the privies kept overflowing either on the lanes or into the open drains thereby fouling the whole atmosphere. Sometimes the cesspits also overflowed and choked the drains. Many times, the *halalkhors*, who were supposed to remove the excreta daily and convey it to the night-soil depots, emptied the baskets into the open drains. These all together created such foul stench that the windows of the rooms had to be kept closed and the passers-by had to hurry on.[245] In most of these chawls no *nahani* or bathing place or sink was provided in the rooms and the 'approaches to the chawls are therefore as a rule filthy with pools of undrained and stagnant sullage dotting the place and breeding mosquitoes'.[246]

Even in the better constructed Improvement Trust's chawls, the insanitary habits of the workers were responsible for uncleanness. Spitting of *pan* or betelnut juice on the stairs, depositing the sweepings of the rooms in the corridors or throwing the rubbish in the lanes kept the place always dirty.[247] Moreover, the verandahs provided in these buildings were often used for bathing and since they were visible from the surrounding chawls they were enclosed with mats or sacks making free ventilation difficult.[248] Added to all these was the problem of overcrowding. Rents were high and ranged from Rs. 3 to Rs. 7. One individual or even the whole family found it hard to pay it on its own. So, the taking-in of additional lodgers was the usual practice.[249]

The mill districts were otherwise reported to be not very densely populated. Even though there was a manifold increase in the population of these areas, the total number of persons per acre was much less than in many other areas of the city.[250] But most of the space in the mill areas was occupied by the mills; this, combined with the haphazard development and the poverty of the people, led to a situation of overcrowding.

In 1901, 284,244 people, or about 36.6 per cent of the total population of the city, were living in rooms each occupied by 6 to 20 or more persons.[251] In 1920, about 36 per cent of the population was living in rooms each occupied by more than 6 persons.[252] For mill areas, the overcrowding was reported to be even more—47.4 per cent lived in rooms occupied by more than 6 persons in 1901, 36.0 per cent in 1911, and 42.6 per cent in 1921.[253] This clearly shows that although the city itself was quite overcrowded, the mill areas, along with certain sections, were even more so.[254]

In 1917-18, 97 per cent of the working-class households in Parel were living in single rooms.[255] There were many cases of 'three families occupying a single room and numerous indications of the presence of single adult lodgers in rooms occupied by one or two families'.[256] Some other sources reported that in many instances in one room 'two or three families are huddled together, generally numbering 10 to 15 persons excluding children'.[257] According to the Census of 1921, there were at least 135 instances in Bombay in which a single room was occupied by six families or more. The lady doctor appointed by the Government of Bombay to investigate the conditions of the women workers reported about the conditions of one such room:

> In the outside chawls I have several times verified the overcrowding of rooms. In one room, on the second floor of a chawl, measuring some 15' x 12', I found six families living. Six separate ovens on the floor proved this statement. On enquiry, I ascertained that the actual number of adults and children living in this room was 30. Bamboos hung from the ceiling, over which, at night, clothes and sackings were hung, helped to partition each family allotment. Three out of six of the women who lived in this room were shortly expecting to be delivered. All three said they would have deliveries in Bombay. When I questioned the District Nurse, who accompanied me, as to how she would arrange for privacy in this room, I was shown a small space some 3' x 4' which was usually screened for the purpose. The atmosphere at night of that room, filled with smoke from the six ovens, and other impurities, would certainly physically handicap any woman and infant, both before and after delivery. This was one of the many such rooms I saw.[258]

This was an extreme case. But in the workers' quarters, even when not so crowded, the situation was much the same. The room served for all purposes. Bathing, cooking, dining, sleeping—all were done there.[259] The whole situation was so bad that it forced the *Times of India* to say that 'our city has quite another side—a side reeking of poverty and filth, of misery squalor and disease'.[260]

Thus the workers lived in one of the most unhealthy parts of the city where, after the setting of the sun, 'mephitic exhalations arise from the adjacent swamps and pools',[261] where most of the areas were undrained and whatever drainage existed, it was open and the sewage often overflowed on the streets, where the human excreta choked the open drains and littered the lanes, where the houses were ill-lit, ill-ventilated and overcrowded and the constitution of the people, already weakened by their hard work in ill-ventilated, hot mills, was put to further strain in the neighbourhood. This was an ideal ground for diseases. And they came.

DISEASES AND MORTALITY

While there has been a decrease in deaths from cholera, there has been an enhanced mortality from small pox since 1865. In the four years from 1866 to 1869, 4,982 deaths were registered. . . . Towards the latter end of 1873 Rinderpest appeared. The disease was first noticed in November, and it existed up to October 1875. Towards the latter end of 1874, measles assumed epidemic proportions and increased up to March 1875 and then began to abate. In February 1875, Foot and Mouth Disease was noticed, and it did not disappear till October.[262]

Thus ran the Municipal Commissioner's Report for the city of Bombay in 1875. And those early years were no exception. The diseases and deaths continued. There was again 'cholera epidemic' in 1883; fever and dysentery in 1886; measles and diseases of respiratory system in 1888; and many similar and other diseases in the later years until the plague took over in 1896 and pulverized the city's population for the next two decades.

The death figures given[263] tell only a part of the story because most of the cases were not registered for two main reasons: (a). many people went back to their home villages either to recuperate or to die; and (b). even when deaths occurred in the city, many of them were not registered or even reported because the afflicted kinfolk and friends felt little obliged to observe legal niceties.Thus one person in the knowledge of the affairs said before the IFLC that he 'did not think that the death statistics of the city would be of any material use, for only about 45 per cent were properly certified'.[264]

But even these grossly understated figures tell a story which is frightening. The average death rate per thousand of population for 30 years between 1890 and 1919 was 46.36,[265] and this sometimes reached as high as 96.76 as in 1900, keeping in mind that this was less than half of the deaths that had actually occurred. The death rates always exceeded the birth rates by a substantial margin.[266]

If we compare the average death rate of Bombay City for the 30 years between 1890 and 1919 with that of Bombay Presidency for the same period, we find that for the latter it was 35.75 per thousand, while for the former it was 46.36.[267] This shows that although the conditions were sufficiently bad in the Presidency (with famines occurring several times from 1896 to 1901 as well as in 1906-7),[268] those in Bombay City were much worse. Moreover, while in the Presidency the birth rates generally exceeded the death rates, in Bombay the opposite was the case. The infant mortality rate was also much higher in the city than in the Presidency as a whole. There were times when Bombay almost became a city of death.[269]

Technically speaking, there were two broad categories of diseases which afflicted the cotton textile workers. First were the ones contracted through the hard work in the stuffy and hot atmosphere of the mills. They were broadly referred to as occupational disease. Phthisis was the main among these.[270] The second category of diseases was common to the whole population in the poor and insanitary sections, the millworkers among them. These were malaria, fevers, plague, cholera, influenza, tuberculosis, phthisis, etc.

The hot, suffocating atmosphere in which the millworkers had to work for about 12-15 hours daily impaired their physique so much that they became even more susceptible to other diseases apart from the occupational ones. One observer said: 'Stout and sprightly youths become gradually emaciated and lean as they continue working in the mills, and as years roll by, their stamina gives way, and they suffer from general debility and slow fever which sometimes become so unbearable that they have to quit work and go to their native place to recruit their health.'[271]

Almost all the witnesses before the Factory Commission of 1885 agreed that the dock labourers were in better physical health than the millworkers.[272] Similarly, in 1908, there were many who thought that the same class of workers in foundries had better physique.[273] Another witness said that 'there is no doubt that the general healthiness of the Bombay operatives is less than that of the non-factory population'.[274] The IFLC found in 1908 that the average weight of the jail population, between the age of 20 and 50 years, was about 8 to 10 pounds more than the average weight of the mill workers of that age.[275] The RCL in 1929 arrived at the same conclusion.[276] Even those who did not think that the millworkers were physically worse than others conceded that 'where the heat and dust in the rooms are excessive, factory operatives must suffer from the effects of chills and irritation of respiratory passages'.[277]

The devitalizing effects of the factory work was so clear even as early as 1887 that the Health officer to the Municipal Commissioner wrote that:

> the young people especially cannot continue working in factories without losing their health and strength. . . . To judge of the effect of factory life, compare the appearance of men and women engaged in hard, outdoor work, such as quarrying, with the appearance of factory labourers. I have been struck with the difference in appearance of the two classes of labourers walking side by side at the end of a day's work—the mill labourers, feeble, weak and having a pallid look; the quarrymen and women with active, springy gait and of cheerful look after hard work under the sun.

He went on to conclude: 'At any rate, there is growing up in our population a class which can be distinguished from their own class, from their own race engaged in other work, and from every other class, by a pallid look which may be called a "factory countenance".'[278]

The statistics on mortality for the millworkers is absolutely unreliable. This is evident from the Appendix VIII where we find that the deaths from phthisis alone exceeded the total deaths for some years. There were two main reasons for this misrecording. The first was that many workers went home when they fell ill. But this fact was a common one for all the workers. The second factor was more important. Most of the millworkers were out of work after falling ill. And by the time they went to the hospital, they had remained out of job for quite some time. So, when asked about their occupation, they registered themselves as 'general labourers'.[279] Furthermore, the casual workers, in many cases, would be describing themselves as general labourers. But, if other evidences were to be taken into account, the death rate among the millworkers would be the same as in the other classes of workers.

INFANT MORTALITY

Infant mortality was very high in Bombay. The Presidency rates, which were already quite high, were only one-third of the city's figures.[280] Even in normal times it was clear to many that 'one out of every two infants born has to die before reaching the age of twelve months'.[281] During troubled times, the infant mortality rate per thousand of births reached the absurd figure of 1063.3.[282] Burnett-Hurst was convinced that 'Bombay must have the inglorious distinction of possessing probably the highest infant death rate in the world.'[283]

Most of the infantile deaths, quite expectedly, occurred among the poor people. Right since the day the child was conceived, the problems started. The pregnant women did not have much to eat or drink. There were no facilities of life in the dirty rooms and the surrounding areas. On top of it, they had to go on doing tough physical labour till very late in pregnancy. All these put heavy strain on the mother and, therefore, on the child. The mother also did not get any skilled attendance during the delivery and had to return to her work very shortly after confinement. The infant did not get sufficient nourishment because the mother herself was often underfed and she did not have enough time to give to the child. When she went to her work in the mill, the child was left in the care of either the elder children or some neighbour. Even if the mother took the infant to the factory, the situation was not much better as there were no crèches provided by the mills[284] and the child had to stay with the mother in the polluted atmosphere of the mill. To keep the children from crying and disturbing they were given pills of opium which kept them quiet at home as well as in the mills.[285] The ill-ventilated, ill-lighted and damp rooms, covered with smoke morning and evening and with so many people living in them, were hardly the ideal homes for a new-born. And when they contracted some diseases, there were no proper medical facilities. Even the milk supplied to them was contaminated.[286] So, all that was left for them was to die.

The Health Officer to the Municipal Commissioner reached the heart of the matter when he wrote:

> The causes of these epidemics lie, I believe, in poverty of the people, and the misery in which they live. The poverty of the great masses of the people in this city is incredible. Obliged to support large families, and compelled directly or indirectly to lay portion of their incomes for marriage and other ceremonies, they live on what I may without exaggeration call a starvation diet. As the natural result of their poverty they crowd together, and in houses where there should be only one family, there are a dozen.

He further added: 'Looking to the great number of poor people in this city and considering their weakly and puny constitutions, I am convinced that we may expect to have every three, four or five years an outbreak of one or the other of the epidemic diseases; it may not be cholera, it may not be small pox, but some disease will arise and sweep off the most effete of the population.'[287]

THE DAILY LIFE OF A COTTON MILLWORKER[288]

A cotton millworker had to get up very early in the morning at about 4 or 4.30 a.m. After making his ablutions, he cooked his meals if he was alone. If he had a family or ate at the *khanavali,* he either took a quick meal or simply started for work and had his meals brought to the work-place later in the day. He could not afford to be late because fines would be imposed otherwise. In his worry not to be late, if he arrived at the factory a bit too soon he lay down on the pavement besides it and took a short rest till the factory gates opened. Then he had to insert his '*chappa*' or the 'ticket of presence into its proper slit in the box kept for the purpose'.[289] After this, he was allowed in.

By now the machinery had already started moving; the temperature and humidity inside the mill kept increasing partly because certain levels were required for the purpose of manufacture, and partly because so many people were crammed in an ill-ventilated space. If the worker was new to the city and the work, the sight of these 'vast, dim, cavernous places, with their bewildering vistas of rotating wheels and belts and shaftings',[290] must have filled him with awe. Even if he was an old hand, running to-and-fro among the ceaselessly moving intricate machinery demanded a kind of attention which would soon exhaust him. And he did get exhausted and wanted some respite from this alienating work which was to continue for so many more hours. So he asked permission to go out to answer the call of nature. Here there was a problem. The tickets allowed for going out were limited in number and, if a few others had already gone out, he had to wait and prolong his work till his turn came. He sometimes waited his turn, but at other times, he asserted himself and went out either with a verbal permission from the jobber or supervisor or even without it. Now he tried to spend as much time outside in the mill compound as possible. He feared the machinery which might any time cripple or kill him; he simply feared its size; he felt very belittled before the enormous mass of it; he sometimes or often disliked his work; and he dreaded the hot and stuffy atmosphere inside the building. So he wanted to remain out until the time he could evade penalty. Meanwhile his work was attended to by another adult worker or a substitute doffer boy. He would return this favour when his colleague went out. He resumed his work and waited for the time when the jobber could allow him to take his meal which either he had brought with himself or someone else had brought for him. So, three or four hours after starting work, at 9 or 10 a.m. he sat down to eat 'behind his machine'.[291] After eating he went out to wash his vessels and hands, and soon resumed his work. This work continued till midday interval. By this time he was so exhausted that 'As soon as the speed of machines slacken perceptibly, our workman pushes the strap on to the loose pulley, spreads his apron on the floor, and folding his hands and legs to suit the size of the cloth, lies down to sleep.'[292]

In case he had not brought his meal or it had not been brought, he had to immediately rush out either to his home or to the *khanavali* or to some other eating joint. He had to really hurry to finish his food and come back because before the Act of 1891 the actual period of the midday interval was not more than 15 minutes.

The time till the midday break was just about half the time he was supposed to spend in the mill. The other half was still before him and this was even more tiring because his interest in the work had slackened more perceptibly. His going out became more frequent and, if not allowed, he could even fight for this. As the closing hours drew close, he became more restless, sweating profusely, with 'flaccid and weary limbs, eyes dazed with unending roar' and with the 'ceaseless monotony' of his work.[293]

When the work was over he felt an immense relief. Now his real life started; but he was too tired to enjoy it. If he could afford it he went to the liquor shop; he sometimes borrowed for it or asked for credit at the shop itself. There he drank with his friends, chatted and relaxed. Then he went home or to a *khanavali* to eat. After eating, if he still felt like it, he might spend some time with his neighbours and friends singing *bhajans* or other songs. Otherwise he immediately went to sleep in the room he shared with many others if it was monsoon or winter season or on the street if it was summer. The area in which he lived was very crowded and noisy and he 'cannot go to bed before 11 p.m.'.[294]

Now he could get only about 5 or 6 hours of sleep, after this long day's work, before he embarked upon his next day's travails. He and many others like him started in the morning 'dragging themselves to work again before the sun is above horizon, their countenances set and hopeless, bodies only half-rested from the previous day's labour, a gait that denotes unutterable lassitude in every mechanical movement'.[295]

NOTES

1. J.C. Kydd, *A History of Factory Legislation in India* (Calcutta, 1920), p. 4.
2. Ibid., p. 6.
3. Report of the BMOA, 1875 & 1875-6, p. 6.
4. The details about the nationalist opposition to the commissions and the consequent Factory Acts is given in Chapter 5 of this volume.
5. J.C. Kydd, *A History of Factory Legislation in India*, p. 7.
6. Ibid., p. 5. One of the members, Munguldass Nathoobhoy, registered his minute of dissent which regarded legislation even in the mildest form as unnecessary because, in his opinion, 'it is calculated to check an important and new industry in its infancy'.
7. R.K. Das, *History of Indian Labour Legislation* (Calcutta, 1941), p. 52.
8. Report of BMOA, 1875, p. 30.
9. FC, 1875, pp. 91-2.
10. Ibid., p. 128.
11. Ibid., p. 121.
12. Ibid., p. 123.
13. Ibid., pp. 121, 122, 123 passim.
14. Ibid., p. 91.
15. Ibid., p. 93.
16. Ibid., p. 92.
17. Bipan Chandra, *Economic Nationalism*, pp. 328-9.
18. FC, 1885, evidences of Narayan Surkoji and N.M. Lokhanday.
19. FC, 1885, the evidence of Genoo Babaji.
20. Ibid., evidence of Narayan Surkoji, the Card-Room jobber at Anglo-Indian Mill.
21. Ibid., pp. 4-5.
22. Report of the BMOA, 1891, p. 43.
23. FC, 1875, p. 8.
24. IFLC, 1908, II, p. 64.
25. Ibid., p.75.
26. 'There are no standard hours of labour; each mill works as many hours as daylight allows them to; the number of hours varies with variation in lighting and processes in different mills; the new mills, long, high and narrow, with nearly half of their walls fitted with windows, make much better time than the old mills do.' Drewet, RCL, 1892, p. 132. Cited in Morris, *Industrial Labour Force*, p. 101.
27. IFC, 1890, p. 11.
28. FC, 1885. Evidences of Raghoo Bhicaji and Genoo Babaji.

29. Ibid., pp. 53, 56, 61 passim.
30. IFC, 1890, pp. 22, 23, 31.
31. FC, 1885, evidence of Jones, para 62.
32. *ITJ*, 1890-1, p. 59.
33. FC, 1885, p. 19.
34. IFC, 1890, p. 11.
35. Report of BMOA, 1875 and 1875-6, p. 75.
36. FC, 1875, p. 8.
37. FC, 1875, p. 121, evidence of J. Helm.
38. FC, 1885, evidence of Narayan Surkoji.
39. IFC, 1890, pp. 8-9 : 'there is one point on which Indian operatives are practically unanimous; it is in demanding that this concession (Sunday holiday) shall be granted to them.'
40. FC, 1885, evidence of Narayan Surkoji.
41. IFC, 1890, p. 23.
42. Ibid., p. 10.
43. Report of BMOA, 1891, p. 8.
44. Ibid., 1875, p. 30.
45. *Din Bandhu*, 7 July 1895. In *Report on the Native Newspapers for the Presidency of Bombay* (hereafter *RNP*), 13 July 1895.
46. Report of BMOA, 1893, p. 10.
47. *Annual Report on the Working of the Indian Factories Act in the Bombay Presidency* (hereafter *AFR*), 1895, p. 19.
48. Ibid., 1896, p. 7.
49. Report of BMOA, p. 17.
50. *AFR*, 1898, p. 7.
51. Report of BMOA, 1899, p. 11.
52. The *Times of India* (*TOI*), p. 7.
53. Speech in BMOA meeting, 11 August 1905. Cited in *TOI*, 13 September 1905, p. 7.
54. Speech in BMOA meeting, 11 August 1905. Cited in ibid. Part of the vehemence of his speech may be said to have derived from the fact that his mill had no electric lights and so he suffered in competition. But this did not seem to be the case because in his evidence before the IFLC he said that no legislative interference should be made to restrict the hours of work.
55. Report of BMOA, 1888-9, speech by D.M. Petit.
56. *TOI*, 13 September 1905, pp. 6-7.
57. *Indian Textile Journal* (hereafter *ITJ*), 1890-1, p. 15.
58. *ITJ*, September 1905, pp. 365-6.
59. *Praja Bandhu*, 24 September 1905, in *RNP*, 30 September 1905.

60. See Chapter 5.
61. *TOI*, 13 September 1905, p. 7.
62. *Oriental Review*, 27 September 1905, in *RNP*, 30 September 1905.
63. IFLC, II, p. 156.
64. IFLC, I, p. 7.
65. *TOI*, 25 September 1905, p. 4.
66. Report of BMOA, 1905, p. 8.
67. Ibid., 1906, pp. 17-18. The IFLC noted with concern that 'the Millowners' Association was powerless to enforce its resolution in favour of a 12-hour day, as against the individual members of the Association', IFLC, I, p. 7.
68. Ibid., p. 7.
69. Sir Bhalchandra Krishna, IFLC, II, p. 102.
70. Captain Houston, in ibid., p. 55.
71. Shavakshaw Dhunjeebhoy, in FC, 1875, p. 123.
72. Thomas Stevenson Weir, Health Officer to the Bombay Municipality, in ibid., p. 129.
73. Muncherjee Nowrojee Banajee, Secretary to the New Great Eastern Spinning and Weaving Co, in ibid., p. 131.
74. J.H. Bower, manager of the Fleming Spinning and Weaving Mill, in ibid., p. 132.
75. Ibid., p. 9. This was a paradox in most of the Bombay mills that despite having enough number of windows and other openings, proper ventilation could not be ensured. The enforcement also became difficult because when the Inspector arrived for checking, the windows were thrown open. IFLC, II, p. 56.
76. FC, 1885, pp. 198-201.
77. Ibid., p. 3.
78. Report of BMOA, 1895, p. 134.
79. Ibid., 1895, pp. 15 and 134-40.
80. *AFR*, 1895, p. 17.
81. Ibid., p. 18.
82. *AFR*, 1896, p. 19.
83. *AFR*, 1897, p. 6.
84. *AFR*, 1898, p. 13.
85. *AFR*, 1902, p. 1.
86. *ITJ*, March 1903, p. 165.
87. General Department, 1903, vol. 42, p. 253. MSA.
88. The workers' reluctance in opening the windows were stated in various forms according to the predilections of the witnesses. One mill secretary stated blatantly that the 'people do not suffer from heat, as they are used to it, and they moreover work almost naked'. FC, 1875, p. 123. Dr. Thomas Stevenson Weir, the Health Officer of Bombay Municipality, gave another interpretation

to it: 'if all the doors and windows were opened there would be such a draught created that the Mill hands, lightly clad as they are, most of them with nothing but a shred of cloth over their middle, could not endure it or work in it', ibid., p. 129. Thirty years later, many witnesses giving evidences before the IFLC, 1908, corroborated this view. Captain Houston, PA to the Surgeon General with the GOB, stated that the 'windows were kept closed for fear of the breeze snapping the threads. Even in the hottest weather the windows were closed, and . . . the operatives themselves preferred it so', IFLC, 1908, II, p. 58.

A.K. Leslie, of the Greaves Cotton and Company, expressed his firm opinion that the 'only person who objected to open the windows was the operative', ibid., p. 62.

89. *AFR*, 1902, p. 2.
90. Ibid.
91. *AFR*, 1906, p. 2.
92. Ibid.
93. *AFR*, 1907, p. 2.
94. *AFR*, 1908, p. 2.
95. K.A. Keluskar, Secretary of the Maratha Aikyechhoo Sabha, IFLC, II, p. 86.
96. S.M. Rutnagar, editor of *ITJ*, in ibid., p. 110.
97. N.N. Wadia, in ibid., p. 112.
98. J.H. Cooper, in ibid., p. 149.
99. Report of the BMOA, 1909, pp. 74-81.
100. *ITJ*, August, 1911, p. 375.
101. *AFR*, 1911, p. 2.
102. *AFR*, 1912, p. 4.
103. *AFR*, 1913, p. 4.
104. The data on accidents in the cotton mills are available only for four years between 1892 and 1911 for which the data are available for all the factories. However, as the accidents of all varieties in the cotton mills formed about 80-85 per cent of the total for all the factories in Bombay, the other figures may be taken as an approximation. See Appendix II.
105. FC, 1875, p. 7.
106. For example, S. Dhunjeebhoy said: 'The machinery is well protected in Alliance Mill. It is not . . . protected in all the mills', in ibid., p. 123.
107. FC, 1875, p. 7. N. Dadabhoy, the acting manager of the Morarjee Gokuldass Spinning and Weaving Mill, said that the accidents were 'due to the carelessness of the men themselves and not to any other causes. Such accidents could not be prevented by any care on the part of the owners', ibid., p. 124. Another witness, T. Dhunjeebhoy, the manager of the Alliance Spinning and Weaving Co, said that the accidents were 'caused through the negligence of the workpeople themselves, and not due to any want of protection of the machinery', in ibid., p. 126.

108. *AFR*, 1895, p. 21.
109. *AFR*, 1896, p. 21.
110. *AFR*, 1895, pp. 20-1.
111. Ibid., p. 21.
112. *AFR*, 1896, pp. 21-2.
113. FC, 1875, p. 127.
114. FC, 1875. J. Helm, the manager of the Bombay United Spinning and Weaving Mill, said that there were no 'special provision . . . made for a man . . . thus incapacitated for work', ibid., p. 121. His statement was corroborated by M. Bhagoobhoy of Mazagaon Spinning and Weaving Co and many others.

    One worker, Shaik Mahomed, stated before the Factory Commission of 1890 that 'I had my finger cut off for which I got nothing and lost one month's work and wages', FC, 1890, p. 24. Another worker, Syed Akram Ali, said: 'I was wounded in a mill, but got no pay during the time I was off work', ibid., p. 45.

    The fact that either nothing or very little compensation was given was repeated time and again and the workers were unanimous in demanding compensation.
115. Report of BMOA, 1875 and 1875-6, pp. 74-5.
116. Ibid., p. 56.
117. James Helm, in FC, 1875, p. 121.
118. Motiram Bhagoobhoy, in ibid., p. 123.
119. Nusserwanjee Dadabhoy, in ibid., p. 125.
120. FC, 1885, evidence of Raghoo Bhicajee.
121. Ibid., evidence of Genoo Babajee.
122. IFLC, II, pp. 62, 68, 93.
123. Report of BMOA, 1888-9, p. 1.
124. Ibid., 1891, p. 15.
125. Ibid., 1893, p .41.
126. Ibid., 1897; also, AFR, 1897, pp. 7-10.
127. *Report of Industrial Disputes Committee*, 1922, p. 2.
128. Morris, *Industrial Labour Force*, p. 155.
129. *Report of the Industrial Disputes Committee*, p. 2.
130. *ITJ*, October 1893, pp. 5-6.
131. IFLC, 1908, I, p. 21.
132. *Report of the Indian Industrial Commission*, 1916-18, I, p. 18.
133. S.M. Rutnagar, *Bombay Industries: The Cotton Mills* (Bombay, 1927), p. 322.
134. ITB, 1927, II, pp. 46, 331.
135. ITB, 1927, I, p. 113.
136. Morris has constructed an index on the money wages from 1882 to 1921

basing on the *Prices and Wages* series. The above percentage increase is derived from that. See, Morris, *Industrial Labour Force*, p. 223.

137. K. Mukerji, 'Trends in Real Wages in Cotton Textile Mills in Bombay City and Island, from 1900 to 1951', in *Artha Vijnana*, 1959, vol. 1, no. 1.
138. Ibid.
139. Cited in ITB, II, pp. 336-7.
140. Calculated from the index given in K. Mukerji, 'Trends in Real Wages'.
141. ITB, III, p. 443.
142. Ibid., p. 444.
143. Ibid., p. 470. Raj Chandavarkar also comes to the conclusion that 'Sizeable sections of the labour earned considerably less than the statistical averages which the Labour Office calculated for the occupational categories of their own making.' Chandavarkar, *Industrial Capitalism in India*, p. 309.
144. Most of the witnesses before the FC, 1875 and IFC, 1890 agreed that fines are imposed regularly on the workers.
145. ITB, 1927, II, pp. 352-3. The Girni Kamgar Mahamandal complained that even for 'insignificant mistakes' the workers were fined heavily and at times 'the fines are so big as to swallow the whole of a month's pay of a worker', ITB, III, p. 566.
146. Given in *LMI*, II, p. 64.
147. ITB, I, p.113.
148. A.L. Mirams, Consulting Surveyor to the GOB; in IIC, IV, p. 366.
149. *Wages and Hours*, 1921, p. 8.
150. *ITJ*, October 1893, pp. 5-6.
151. IFLC, II, p. 99.
152. FC, 1875, p. 24.
153. S.M. Edwardes, *The Bombay City Police: A Historical Sketch, 1672-1916* (London, 1923), pp. 64-5.
154. *Census of City and Island of Bombay, 1881*, p. 36.
155. IFLC, II, p. 128.
156. *ITJ*, September 1905, p. 366.
157. IFLC, II, p. 85.
158. Ibid., p. 126.
159. IFLC, I, p. 22.
160. Given in the Report of BMOA, 1908, p. vii.
161. IFLC, II, p. 114.
162. *Indu Prakash*, 27 September 1905, in RNP, 30 September 1905. Both Nare and Talcherkar, as upstart workers, had severe contempt for any deviations they perceived among the workers.
163. T.A. Kulkarni, General Secretary, Social Service League, in the *Report of the Excise Committee*, 1922-3, vol. II, p. 23.

164. Ibid., p. 23 and N.D. Kadam, Social Service League, in ibid., p. 45.
165. R.G. Pradhan, in ibid., pp. 131-2.
166. Ibid., p. 3, evidence of D. Dorabji Gilder, Secretary, Bombay Temperance Council.
167. Ibid., p. 483.
168. Ibid., p. 460.
169. Ibid., p. 78.
170. JD, vol. 99, File No. 5059, 1908, p. 136.
171. IFLC, II, p. 114.
172. Evidence of BMOA, *Report of the Excise Committee, II*, p. 458. Also, Saklatwala, in ibid., p. 460.
173. R.V. Vandekar, Joint Secretary, People's Union, Bombay, in ibid., p. 47.
174. IFLC, II, p. 88.
175. *ITJ*, February 1912, p. 171.
176. IIC, 1916-18, vol. IV, p. 366; RCL, 1929, vol. 1, part 2, p. 234. According to some other accounts, however, about 50 per cent workers were reported to be in debt. IFLC, 1908, II, p. 116. Burnett-Hurst, on the basis of his survey during the war years, concluded that '62 out of 121 households, i.e., 51 per cent were in debt', Burnett-Hurst, *Labour and Housing*, p. 69. On the other hand, the BMOA talked of the 'heartrending . . . (and) helpless condition of indebtedness in which almost all the labourers are steeped'. Report of BMOA, 1915, p. ix.
177. IIC, IV, p. 366, evidence of A.E. Mirams.
178. Burnett-Hurst, *Labour and Housing*, pp. 13-14 and 70.
179. Ibid., p. 70.
180. A.E. Mirams, in IIC, vol. IV, p. 365.
181. See TLIC, vol. II, pp. 66-7.
182. *Census of the City of Bombay*, 1864; Dr Leith's Report, quoted in *Census of the City of Bombay, 1872*, p. 1. The *Bombay Builder*, in September 1866, reported about the 'coolies and other workmen finding the greatest difficulty in housing themselves even in the most miserable and unwholesome lodging', quoted in S.M. Edwardes, *The Rise of Bombay, A Retrospect* (Bombay, 1902), p. 293.
183. *Census of the City of Bombay, 1872*, p. 9.
184. See Appendix V.
185. *Census of the City and Island of Bombay, 1881*, p. 71.
186. Quoted in *Census of India, 1901*, vol. X, part IV, History, p. 147.
187. See Appendix IV.
188. *ARMC*, 1886-7, p. 270, reported: 'These 5 Sections of Worlee, Mahim, Parell, Sewri and Sion (F and G Wards), covering the northern confines of the Island, having an area of 8,192 acres, a little more than one half of the Island, have only 8 persons to a square acre.'

189. *Census of India, 1901*, vol. XI, part I, Report, p. 17.
190. *Census of the City of Bombay, 1872*, p. 156. The corresponding BMOA's estimate is 8,816. It is possible that there are many shortcomings in the Census enumeration or the casual mill labourers might have registered themselves as 'General Labourers'. So, the Census figures are generally lower than the actual number of workers daily employed in the cotton mills. But the BMOA's figures give the total numbers and not the area-wise distribution. Therefore, for the purpose of comparison, all the Census figures are taken. Also see Appendix V.
191. R.K. Newman, *Workers and Unions*, p. 23.
192. *Bombay Builder*, September 1866, quoted in Edwardes, *The Rise of Bombay*, p. 293.
193. Quoted in ibid., p. 294.
194. *Census of the City and Island of Bombay, 1881*, p. 37.
195. *Census of India, 1901*, vol. X, part IV, History, p. 151. Also *ARMC*, 1886-7, p. 269: 'The density of population has not been relieved by the numerous buildings erected to the north through Byculla and Parel'.
196. Calculated from Censuses.
197. *Census of India, 1901*, vol. IX, part I, Report, p. 67.
198. Ibid., p. 67. The *Census of the Town and Island of Bombay, 1906* (p. 23) also reports: 'The sections containing the largest number of houses, whether occupied or unoccupied, are: Sion, Mahim and Worli but in all these sections . . . there is a large number of scattered huts.'
199. Burnett-Hurst, *Labour and Housing*, p. 20.
200. Ibid., pp. 19-20.
201. *The Gazetteer of Bombay City and Island, 1909*, vol. 1, p. 195.
202. *ITJ*, July 1897, p. 246.
203. Ibid., p. 248.
204. Report of BMOA, 1901, p. 60.
205. Ibid., p. 33.
206. Ibid., p. 60.
207. Ibid., p. 34.
208. Ibid., pp. 61-2.
209. Ibid., 1903, p. 99.
210. Ibid., 1907, p. V.
211. IFLC, I, p. 22.
212. Report of BMOA, 1908, p. VIII.
213. Ibid., 1909, pp. 42-3.
214. Ibid., 1913, p. VII.
215. Ibid., 1914, p. V.
216. Ibid., 1915, p. IX.
217. *ITJ*, June 1916, p. 263.

218. RCL, Memorandum from the Government of Bombay, 1929, p. 22.
219. TLIC, 1937-8, II, Final Report, p. 269. The BTLU, in 1926, claimed that there were only 17 out of 80 mills which provided accommodation for some of their workers. There were 52,000 people working in these mills, but the number of total rooms were only 4,600. Therefore, the 'percentage of housing provided to the total number of workers is thus not more than 8.61', in *Labour Movement in India: Documents* (*LMI*), II, p. 161.
220. IIC, I, Report, p. 156.
221. Ibid., p. 158.
222. IDC, 1922, p. 7, para 14.
223. ITB, III, p. 449. Written statement by the BTLU.
224. Ibid., p. 563.
225. Ibid., p. 512.
226. ITB, I, p. 141.
227. IIC, I, Report, p. 156.
228. IIC, IV, p. 301. Evidence of A.E. Mirams.
229. ITB, I, p. 140.
230. RCL, Report, p. 274.
231. TLIC, II, p. 272.
232. ITB, II, p. 139.
233. LMI, II, p. 162.
234. TLIC, II, p. 272.
235. LMI, II, p. 162.
236. *ARMC*, 1892-3, p. 384.
237. Ibid., 1875, p. 127.
238. Ibid., 1897-8, p. 653.
239. Ibid., 1898-9, p. 709.
240. Ibid., 1894-5, p. 525.
241. Ibid., 1879, p. 295.
242. Ibid., 1892-3, p. 386.
243. Ibid., 1888-9, p. 319.
244. Ibid., 1884-5, p. 224.
245. Ibid., 1875, p. 127. In 1909, the Municipal Commissioner complained that the 'number of cesspool carts for the conservancy of F and G Wards is now totally inadequate for the regular emptying of the contents of the cesspools', ibid., 1909-10, p. 36.
246. *The Gazetteer of Bombay City and Island, 1909*, pp. 210-11.
247. The Municipal Commissioner complained: 'The practice of throwing refuse is very common amongst the people and warnings prohibiting the objectionable practice given by the distribution of hand-bills and notices in the papers have no effect'. *ARMC*, p. 221.

248. IIC, I, Report, p. 155.
249. Many of the contemporary observers thought that it was due to high rents beyond the means of the lodgers that the overcrowding occurred. It was reported that 'one of the heaviest items of expenditure in the domestic budget of workers in Bombay is house rent. About 85 per cent of the population lives in tenements of one room and among these a large proportion are forced to share their quarters with others', *Report on an Investigation into the Causes of Malaria in Bombay, 1911*, p. 4.
250. The number of persons per acre was only 16 in Sion, and Byculla was the highest containing 161 per acre in 1921. Compared to the 699 per acre in 2nd Nagpada, 737 in Kumbharwada, 489 in Chakla, it was very low. See Appendix IV.
251. *Report on Malaria*, pp. 4-5.
252. Burnett-Hurst, *Labour and Housing*, p. 29.
253. Calculated from Censuses.
254. 2nd Nagpada had about 67 persons per house. Kumbharwada and Chakla were also equally crowded. *ARMC*, 1886-7, pp. 273-4.
255. Burnett-Hurst, *Labour and Housing*, p. 29.
256. IIC, I, p. 155.
257. *The Gazetteer*, 1909, p. 211. Also, *Report on Malaria*, p. 5.
258. Quoted in Burnett-Hurst, *Labour and Housing*, pp. 28-9.
259. *ITJ*, 1890-1, p. 37.
260. *TOI*, 1 May 1903, pp. 4-5.
261. *TOI*, 13 September 1905, p. 7.
262. *ARMC*, 1875, p. 128.
263. See Appendix VI.
264. IFLC, II, p. 58. Evidence of Captain Houston.
265. Calculated from the Appendix VI.
266. See Appendix VI.
267. See Appendices VI and VII.
268. *Report on Malaria*, p. 10.
269. See Appendices VI and VII.
270. Phthisis was the most important occupational disease in a cotton mill, *ITJ* (April 1902, p. 195), gave an account of the disease contracted through the inhaling of the cotton dust: 'The injurious effects of dust from cotton first gives the person a slight catarrh, noticeable by dryness and tickling in the larynx; next coughing and later on hoarseness appears, followed by hard breathing and in turn consumption. . . . A recent investigation amongst cotton mills has shown that in a well ventilated cotton mill out of 100 sicknesses, 75 cases referred to more or less acute cases of consumption. It must be remarked that this instance referred to a healthy location, the mill at the same time providing good tenements for their help, and the food taken being of the best kind.'

Many of the witnesses before the IFLC said that instances of phthisis were more common among millworkers than in others. Major Street, Presidency Surgeon, Bombay, said that 'tuberculosis glands of the neck are particularly common in young operatives'. IFLC, II, p. 52. Dr Turner, Executive Health Officer, Bombay, admitted that phthisis was more prevalent among millworkers, ibid., p. 41.

271. IFLC, II, p. 86. Evidence of K.A. Keluskar.
272. See FC, 1885.
273. For example, Dr Turner before IFLC, II, p. 41.
274. IFLC, II, p. 52.
275. IFLC, I, p. 24.
276. RCL, I, Report, p. 246: 'these millworkers have a noticeably low average weight compared with other classes of labour . . . the average weight being lowest in Bombay.'
277. Major McDonald, Acting Presidency Surgeon, 2nd District. IFLC, II, p. 53.
278. *ARMC*, 1887-8, pp. 329-30.
279. Dr Turner said that 'a possible explanation of the low mortality among millhands was that large numbers might on falling ill return to their country where they spent their remaining days', IFLC, II, p. 43.

Dr Chavan, who hailed from Ratnagiri and had a practice among the workers, said: 'the mortality returns would naturally be found to be less in Bombay for directly they become ill they proceed to their villages', ibid., p. 123.

Major Street opined that although it was possible to obtain some statistics from the J.J. Hospital, 'the word "labourer" would be used to describe all forms of labour and mill operatives were probably not specially described', ibid., p. 53.

Captain Gordon Tucker, I.M.S., stated that 'often a man did not come in until he had been ill for three months. That meant that he had been out of work for three months, and when asked about his occupation he would reply "none".' Ibid., p. 46.

280. See Appendices VI and VII.
281. *ARMC*, 1921. Quoted in Burnett-Hurst, *Labour and Housing*, p. 35.
282. As in 1900. See Appendix VI. Probably the registration of deaths was more than that of births.
283. Burnett-Hurst, *Labour and Housing*, p. 35.
284. Only three mills provided crèches by the early 1920s. Burnett-Hurst, *Labour and Housing*, p. 54.
285. The Report of the lady doctor, appointed by the GOB to investigate into conditions of women industrial workers, stated: 'Ninety-eight per cent of the infants born to women industrial workers have opium administered to them', quoted in ibid., p. 38.

286. *ARMC*, 1900-1, pp. 167-9.
287. Ibid., 1875, pp. 148-9.
288. The following account pertains only to the male workers. The problems of the female workers were different. They could go to the mills somewhat late and come back a little early. They could also afford to take more intervals to take care of their children. Moreover, the departments in which most of them worked were not mechanized and the work was less strenuous. At the same time, however, they were relatively underpaid and had much more responsibility at home. See Chapter 3.
289. *ITJ*, 1890-1, p. 37.
290. *TOI*, 13 September 1905, p. 7.
291. *ITJ*, 1890-1, p. 37.
292. Ibid., p. 59.
293. *TOI*, 13 September 1905, p. 7.
294. Keluskar, IFLC, II, p. 87.
295. *TOI*, 13 September 1905, p. 7.

CHAPTER 3

Women and Children

WOMEN AND CHILDREN were the two most vulnerable sections of Indian industrial workers. Considered easy to control and easy to dispense with, they were underpaid and tyrannized by the jobbers and supervisors. The axe of rationalization fell on them most severely and their ratios in the industry declined over the years. In Bombay, however, the women held to their position until the early 1930s after which the introduction of the shift system, combined with the prohibition of their night-work, resulted in the relative decrease in their numbers. The problem of the children was a little more complex. Despite the restriction on the age of the employable children, they were covertly employed. Moreover, as the age for their legal employment kept varying with each Factory Act, it was difficult to say who actually constituted the category of children and, therefore, most of the children could be legally defined as adults at various periods. The employers took advantage of the situation and kept employing, legally and illegally, at least till the 1910s, a sizeable number of those who were defined as children by the Act of 1922.

THE WOMAN WORKER

There has been some debate on the declining ratio of the women in the workforce, particularly during the inter-War period. It has been argued by some historians that this decline has been due to the attempts by the opinion- and decision-makers 'to reform the working class family'.[1] While in the pre-War period the 'ideological construction of skill and suitability' pushed the women workers into low-paid jobs while giving the men access to higher-paid ones,[2] in the inter-War period the assumption about the women workers as basically 'mothers and wives—ones who also work' created a situation in which they were further marginalized and pushed into the background.[3] All the surveys and enquiries undertaken during the inter-War period aimed at creating a rationalized and reformed working class family and 'At the centre of all these activities stood the concept of woman as mother—in particular, the working class woman as mother of the second generation proletarian.'[4] These assertions have been disputed by some other historians who have pointed out that the 'predominance of single male migration . . . has not been the result of managers' strategies'.[5]

In the pre-War years in Bombay there was not much change in the proportion of the women in the cotton textile labour force. Between 1884 and 1919 the proportion of women to the total workforce in the cotton mills remained at around 20 per cent. In fact, this trend continued till 1931 after which the percentage of women began declining. According to Morris, this decline 'can be attributed to the widespread adoption of night-shift working after that date', as the women could not, according to law, work at night.[6] The earlier laws which restricted the hours of work for women to 11 per day did not lead to a decline in the numbers of women workers in the Bombay mills as women were chiefly employed as reelers and winders. The reeling department, which was unmechanized, was mostly filled with women. Although there were some women in other departments also such as spinning, their number was negligible. The lower-caste women, employed as waste-pickers in the preparatory departments, could also adjust their time of work according to their needs to some extent. After the implementation of the Act of 1891 which restricted the number of working hours for women, it was reported that, contrary to the fears of many, it did not have any adverse effect on women's employment. In fact, some increase in their numbers was reported from 1892 onwards.[7]

When the commissions of enquiry were appointed and investgations conducted, there were fears expressed in several quarters that the working of the laws might prejudice the chances of women's employment in the mills. Those expressing such apprehensions included the millowners and the colonial officials. The IFC expressed apprehensions that any attempt to effect separate limitations in the working hours of women workers would result in their replacement 'by male adult operatives or half-time children'. It warned that 'The law, supposed to be passed for their benefit, will inflict serious permanent injury on these skilled mill-hands and deprive them of the chance of earning a living in these factories'. It further commented: 'To tell a thousand poor women that they cannot be allowed to work in this manner for 12, 13 or 14 hours, and that they must in consequence give up their work, will, we feel sure, not commend itself to the judgement of the public.'

It, therefore, recommended that if any law in this regard must necessarily be passed it should exempt the 'women who are now working with moving machinery' or it 'should authorize Local Governments . . . to exempt certain female operatives from the provisions of the section requiring a limit of 11 hours of work'.[8]

Only S.S. Bengali among the members raised an objection to this proposal 'to permit women to work in factories for more than 11 hours in a day'. But his reservation was never intended to push the women from mill work to the raising and rearing of a family. As an alternative, he proposed the shift-system whereby women's work could be automatically limited to about ten hours in a day.[9]

Actually, in Bombay, the women, particularly the reelers who formed the majority of the women workers, did not work more than 11 hours even earlier and observed a certain flexibility in their working. Although some witnesses before the Factory Commission of 1875 remarked that the hours of work of women were the same as those of men,[10] there were others who said that the women did different work from men and were: 'thus enabled to work an hour and a half less than the men. They are given a certain amount of work daily, after finishing which they are at liberty to go home. To get through their allotted work they need neither come early nor stay so late as the men. In this way they work generally an hour and a half less than the men.'[11]

Another employer stated that 'as soon as they finish their daily allotment of work, which they do about an hour and a half sooner than the other operatives, they are at liberty to leave'.[12]

Almost all the witnesses before the FC 1885 said that the women generally worked less hours than the men.[13] N.M. Lokhanday also stated that to women 'even at the present time some leniency is shown in the matter of attendance'.[14] The women workers testifying before the FC 1885 stated that their working hours were less than those of men.[15] On the basis of all this evidence the Commission concluded that in the Bombay cotton mills: 'although we found in some cases low-caste women working on machinery as long as men, the almost invariable rule is to treat women with leniency and consideration, and to give them light hand work such as reeling and winding, which admits of their coming later and leaving earlier than the men.'[16]

Most of the witnesses, including women, before the IFC, 1890, admitted that the women worked lesser hours than the men. The Commission, therefore, reached the conclusion that the women, particularly the reelers 'as a rule, work less than 11 hours'.[17] It further remarked that there was no 'desire on the part of the female operatives to have their present hours of work shortened. On the contrary, they have often expressed themselves against any interference which will subject them to the risk of being turned out and deprived of the means of earning their livelihood.'[18]

Therefore, the creation of separate enclaves of women's work tended to save them from the operation of factory laws. It did not, however, mean that the problems faced by the women workers were less than those by men. The reelers, who enjoyed certain relaxed hours, had to go to the mills even on holidays if the work was pressing. One female worker neatly summed up the situation: 'There is no great difficulty in getting leave if there is sufficient yarn in the factory ready. But if there is press of work, even if one died in her family, she cannot get leave, and, therefore, if absent without leave, is fined two days' pay.'[19]

Such fines pinched hard as the woman's earning was not just supplementary income to a working-class family. In most cases, it formed the mainstay of the family's economy. One survey put the proportion of widows among all the women at 38 per cent and that of women with unemployed husbands at 17 per cent.[20] Thus the ratio of women workers without earning husbands stood at 55 per cent of the total. And even in the remaining cases their wages were as important for the survival of the family as those of men. Yet the consideration of their earnings as supplementary tended to depreciate their wages. The women were almost universally less paid. In 1914 and 1921, the monthly earnings of the women workers were half of those of male workers. The men earned Rs. 18-6-8 per month in 1914 and Rs. 34-15-2 in 1921. The corresponding wages of women were Rs. 10-0-10 in 1914 and Rs. 17-6-6 in 1921.[21] In the time-rates for the same category of work, the women were paid less than men even while their piece-rate earnings were almost the same as those of men. Thus, the average daily earning of men in time category was Rs. 1-2-8, while these of women was only Rs. 0-12-6. But in piece category, while the men earned Rs. 0-12-8 per day, the women also earned 0-12-2 per day. Their equal earnings in piece-rates shows that they worked the same as the men.[22]

Reacting against this discrimination the BTLU stated that:

> the wages given to women were not even subsistence wages and must be increased considerably. It is wrong to suppose, as is mentioned in certain quarters, that the women's wages form only a supplementary income to the families and, therefore, the inadequacy of their wages does not become a factor worthy of

serious consideration. The Union does not accept this statement. There is . . . no data which shows that most of the textile workers are grouped in families the male and female members of which are engaged in the mills. On the contrary. . . a vast bulk of the operatives are such as have separate financial interests.[23]

The life of a woman worker with a family, with or without husband, was a hard one. She had to get up at 3 o'clock in the morning to fetch water and cook the meal for the family, including herself. The infants had to be fed and clothes were also to be washed. After that she went to the work. In the recess at midday, she often returned home to look after her small children. If she carried her infants to the mill, she had to feed them at regular intervals, besides keeping a watch over them. In the afternoon, she again had to go to the mill to finish the day's work. And, after a hard day's work, she 'returns to her room in the evening only to face more household duties—to fetch water, cook the food and clean the utensils'.[24] In the night, while the men could sleep outdoors in the warm weather, she had to sleep, with other women and many children, inside the hot, unventilated room which had been rendered hotter due to the cooking done there.

The burden on a pregnant female worker was even harder. Besides carrying out all the household duties, she had to go on working in the mill with the child in the womb till the last day. The fear of losing her job as well as the temptation of earning money till the last kept her going and there were cases in which the children were delivered inside the mills. Even after the child-birth, the mother would not get more than a week's rest and had to join work immediately. There were no medical help available for her throughout the pregnancy and thereafter. Thus child-bearing also became quite a painful experience for the female worker.[25]

THE CHILD WORKER

The question of the employment of children in Bombay mills in this period is a little problematic. Not only did the legal definition of who constituted children kept changing, but there were also reports about the evasion of law regarding their employment. According to one source, the proportion of children in the workforce in the late 1870s was about 10 per cent, while the census estimated that the children below the age of 15 years constituted about 23.76 per cent of all the workers.[26] Morris expresses doubts on these figures and states that 'Children, legally defined, never exceeded 5.6 per cent.'[27]

But the situation seemed to be more complex. Before the Factories Act of 1881 the children remained an undefined category. Their minimum age was often stated in the records but the upper age limit fluctuated depending upon the perceptions of the individuals. Even the lower limit of the employed children was more a matter of guess than their actual age. The Factory Commission of 1875 faced this problem when it reported: 'Much uncertainty seems to exist among the witnesses as to the precise age of the children. Some of the witnesses, judging probably from the appearance of the children, state the youngest to be not older than 5 or 6 years, while others state the minimum age to be 7, 8, or 10 years.'[28]

As for their absolute or proportionate numbers there is not much information in this report. One employer, however, said that in his mill there were 155 children, including 11 girls, 89 women and 781 men.[29] This puts the proportionate share of children in the workforce at about 15 per cent.

They were employed under the same conditions as the adults and worked for about 12 hours in the standing position. Most of the employers conceded that their hours of work were too long and should be limited.[30]

The Act of 1881 defined children as those between the age of 7 and 12 years and limited their hours of work to 9 in a day with one hour of rest. These restrictions did not quite suit the owners because the timing of 9 hours did not fit in the pattern of mill work and it seems that the legal employment of the children somewhat declined. There were complaints from the workers' side also that such legal enactments would throw the children out in the streets and deprive them of their means of livelihood. One worker's representative complained before the Commission of 1885 that the 'smaller children have all been turned out of our mill in consequence of the Act'. He appealed to the government to devise some method to facilitate the employment of children even below the legally-allowed age of 7 years. Speaking about the decisions taken at workers' meetings conducted to formulate their grievances to present before the Commission, he said: 'We thought that the Government ought to make some arrangement by which the smaller (children) could be employed in some way or the other. The smaller children should be employed 8 or 9 hours. It should be regarded as a hardship if the smaller children were not allowed to work, because they would not be able to afford the same amount of support to their parents.'[31]

N.M. Lokhanday also complained that the Act of 1881 'has not answered the purpose for which it was passed chiefly because the children for whose benefit it was passed have become its victims, having all been turned out of their employment'.[32] And his solution was that the children 'should be employed, well fed and better clothed than be idle and badly fed'.[33]

Since it was impracticable to employ those who cannot work the entire time that the machinery was in motion, it was reported that 'All children under 12 have been dispensed with.'[34] But what is important to note here is that although those working 9 hours (and, therefore, by definition, children) were now very rarely employed in the mills, it does not mean that children were not employed. The parents, with active support of the jobbers and willing connivance of the managers, still sent their children to work as full-timers. This fact was clearly brought to the notice of the Indian Factory Commission which found in the course of its visits to various mills in Bombay and interviews with the workers of all ages and sexes that there was hardly anybody working only 9 hours in the mills. In most of the cases either the age of the children was overstated or, simply, the law was evaded. Similar practices prevailed in other parts of India. The commission, therefore, concluded:

> We have satisfied ourselves that 12, the present maximum age for children, is too low, it being impossible to guess with accuracy the age of any child who may be over 10 and under 13. The result of the present law has been that hundreds of children between the ages of 9 and 12 are now daily employed in India as full-timers, doing 12, 13, and 14 hours of work, to the great detriment of their health.[35]

It was because of this practice of employing the children as full-timers that the legally-defined children became invisible in the Bombay mills. On the recommendations of these commissions of enquiry, the Act of 1891 now defined children as those between the ages of 9 and 14 and restricted their hours of work to 7 a day with half-an-hour rest. Despite the adjustments in the timing whereby two sets of children could be employed, there were again complaints about the decrease in the number of children.[36] The Factory Inspector concluded on the basis of the figures that 'child labour is steadily losing in popularity among employers'.[37]

If, however, we take the stipulation of the Factories Act of 1922 with regard to the age of children, it applied to those between the ages of 12 and 15. During the course of their evidence before the IFLC, many employers pointed out that persons of the 14 to 17 years age group constituted from 35 to 50 per cent of the entire workforce in various mills. 'There are about 35 per cent of young persons between the age of 14 and 17 working in the various departments', said a mill manager. He further added that 'it would be impossible to work any cotton spinning mill without the help of young persons, who are employed as doffers boys and piecers in the various preparing and spinning processes'.[38] Another manager pointed out that any attempt to create a class of young persons was 'sure to determine the working hours of the mill. A major proportion of the hands employed in the spinning department and a good number of work-people in the mill come from the proposed class of young persons'.[39] Bhiwa Ramji Nare, a then retired weaving master, asserted that up to '60 per cent of mill-workers are between the ages of 14 and 20 and about 40 per cent are between 14 and 16 years', and if the hours of work of these people were restricted then 'the mills would have to close after these hours'.[40] It was said that the mills with ring spinning were to be most severely affected as half of the ring spinners belonged to this category and any legal restriction on their working hours would 'have the effect of partially closing the factories'.[41]

It seems that the introduction of ring spinning led to the employment of children from this age group of 14 to 16 years in considerable numbers and, as no restrictions applied to their working hours, they could be worked for long hours with less expenditure. In 1905, a reporter of the *Times of India* noted:

> There are a large number of boys working in the mills who are little more than 14 years of age. They are certified adults, and they are compelled to work these intolerable hours under these debilitating conditions. They are still, to all intents and purposes, mere children, not labouring of their own free will, but because they are made to. One has only to examine them as they leave the mills, to note their exhausted condition, the symptoms of intense fatigue, the hollows under their eyes, to realise that they are slaving under conditions which will make them prematurely old and decrepit.[42]

P.B. Haigh, the Chief Inspector of Factories in Bombay, confirmed this: 'At present a considerable number of so called "adult" workers are mere children.'[43]

Almost all the employers, therefore, stoutly resisted the Commission's proposal of creating a separate class of 'young persons' whose hours of work could be regulated by law.[44] The crucial significance of this group of child-workers could be gauged from the fact that the employers would rather have the general restriction placed on the working hours than any attempt to fiddle with this group. The BMOA gave vent to this feeling when it passed a resolution in a special meeting held on 20 August 1908 on this issue: 'In the opinion of this Association, if it is intended to restrict the hours of adult factory labour, it should be done by direct legislation by restricting it to 12 hours, and that the recommended creation of a young persons' class be dropped.'[45]

Again, as we see, the decline in the number of child-workers was more a matter of definition than fact. The invisibility of the children in the mills applied mainly to the legally-defined group and not to the actual children in terms of age, physique or mental capacity. And it was not only a problem of employing the children who were not legally defined so. The evasion of law, with the willing consent of the parents or guardians, was also quite frequent. Right from the beginning of the legislation on this issue, the practice of evading the law as well as its poor enforcement was quite openly noticeable. The Factory Commission of 1885 pointed out that children between the ages of 7 and 12 years were 'most inefficiently' protected.[46] The IFC made a more clear statement saying that 'children under 12 are, to their great injury, employed as full-timers, working 12 hours or more'.[47] Some of the worker witnesses also testified to this fact. Matha Bux, a worker in the Howard in Bullough Mills, said that all the children in his mill worked full time.[48] A girl named Anoo Shiva, of 10 or 11 years of age and working in the same mill, said that she had been working for one year always as a full-timer.[49] There were many such cases. Although in some instances the children worked willingly, there were cases in which the children were forced to work by their parents. For example, a boy named Tanoo Dewkiya said that he did not want to work, but his 'parents send him'.[50] Similarly, the girl Anoo Shiva complained that 'Her father has sent her to work. She has not come of her own will.'[51] Another woman worker, then aged 25, said that she had been working since the age of 10 and that 'her parents beat her and compelled her to the mill' when she was a child.[52] A boy, named Atma and aged 9 or 10 years stated that 'His father made him come. He would not come otherwise.'[53]

The *Times of India*, in the course of its investigations about the conditions of work in the Bombay mills which were working the largest number of hours till date, reported that 'many of the mills appear to violate both the prescriptions of the law and the dictates of humanity by employing considerable numbers of helpless children for an excessive number of hours'.[54]

Marking the children as half-timers and limiting their hours of work seemed to have facilitated their employment for the whole day under different names. During the periods when immediate labour was required, the schools opened in the mill compounds supposedly for providing education to the children served as the reserve pool of cheap labour. The IFLC noted that 'the so-called school has been used solely for the purpose of retaining the children at the mill during the whole working day, in order that this additional supply of labour might be utilized either as a regular measure, or temporarily when the occasion demanded.'[55]

In 1913, a Committee appointed by the Government of Bombay to enquire into the education of factory children reported: 'The economic conditions of their (the children's) parents are such that they (the children) will work for the remaining six hours at other mills under other names and it is next to impossible for the present to stop this practice which is notorious.'[56] And the Factory Inspector reported in 1914 that 'child labour is exploited to a regrettable extent, much to the disadvantage of the child'.[57]

How much this 'regrettable extent' amounted to was not quantified, but it remains certain that there was a substantial amount of surreptitious and illegal use of children as a reserve pool of cheap, disposable and pliant labour as a means to tide over the daily fluctuating demands of the industry.

NOTES

1. Radha Kumar, 'Family and Factory: Women in the Bombay Cotton Textile Industry, 1919-39', *IESHR*, 20, 1 (March 1983), p. 81.
2. Samita Sen, *Women and Labour in Late Colonial India: The Bengal Jute Industry* (Cambridge, 1999), p. 90.
3. Ibid., p. 143.
4. Radha Kumar, 'Family and Factory', p. 81.
5. Arjan de Haan, 'The *Badli* System in Industrial Labour Recruitment: Managers' and Workers' Strategies in Calcutta's Jute Industry', in Parry, et al., eds., *Contributions to Indian Sociology*, special issue, vol. 33, nos. 1 and 2 (January-August 1999), p. 276.
6. Morris, *Industrial Labour Force*, pp. 65-7.
7. *AFR*, 1893, p. 11, para. 14. See also the *AFR* for the year 1895 (p. 19, para. 20) which reported that between 1892 and 1895 the increase in the number of women workers had been 2,436.

8. IFC, 1890, p. 3.
9. Ibid., p. 15; note by S.S. Bengali.
10. FC, 1875, pp. 121, 123.
11. Ibid., p. 125, evidence of N. Dadabhoy, acting manager of Morarjee Goculdass Spinning and Weaving Mill.
12. Ibid., p. 131, evidence of M.N. Banajee, secretary to the New Great Eastern Spinning and Weaving Company.
13. See FC, 1885, answers to questions 60 and 61.
14. Ibid., evidence of Lokhanday, para. 48.
15. Ibid., evidences of Sakoo and Akoo.
16. Ibid., p. 5.
17. IFC, 1890, p. 2.
18. Ibid., p. 4. After the passage of the Factories Act of 1991, the *Din Bandhu* (2 March 1890) sarcastically remarked: 'God save us from our friends, and the female mill-operatives have sufficient reason to invoke divine help to save them from their legislators. The Supreme Legislative Council has enacted that women should work only for 11 hours, while, as a matter of fact, the women in the Bombay mills work on the whole for 9 hours at the most, inclusive of recess hours', In *RNP,* 8 March 1890.
19. IFC, 1890, p. 22, evidence of Awdi. Another woman, Dhoorpathee, said, 'She cannot get any Sunday holidays. She does not even get the native holidays, because the reelers have to go, when the engine is not working, to work up the cops', ibid., p. 26.
20. Kanji Dwarkadas, *Forty-Five Years with Labour* (Bombay, 1962), pp. 98-9.
21. *Wages and Hours,* 1921, p. 8.
22. Ibid., pp. 15-16.
23. ITB, III, p. 453.
24. Burnett-Hurst, *Labour and Housing,* p. 54. Also, Kelman, *Labour in India,* pp. 145-6.
25. Kelman, *Labour in India,* pp. 181-91; FC, 1875, pp. 121, 123, 128; *ARMC,* 1902-3, p. 168.
26. Morris, *Industrial Labour Force,* p. 70.
27. Ibid., p. 65.
28. FC, 1875, p. 7.
29. Ibid., p. 130, evidence of M.N. Banajee.
30. Ibid., pp. 121, 122, 123 passim.
31. FC, 1885, evidence of Narayan Surkoji.
32. Ibid., evidence of N.M. Lokhanday, para. 4.
33. Ibid., para. 84.
34. IFC, 1890, p. 3.
35. Ibid., p. 5.

36. *AFR*, 1893, p. 11; ibid., 1895, pp. 19-20.
37. Ibid., 1895, pp. 19-20.
38. IFLC, II, p. 70, evidence of S. Meyers, representing the David Mills nos. 1 and 2 and the Standard Mill.
39. Ibid., p. 80, evidence of H.B. Warden, manager of the Victoria Mill.
40. Ibid., p. 115.
41. Ibid., p. 96, evidence of C. Dorabji Panday, manager of Emperor Edward Mill.
42. *TOI*, 13 September 1905, p. 7.
43. IFLC, II, p. 49.
44. Ibid. Various witnesses.
45. Report of BMOA, 1908, p. 11.
46. FC, 1885, p. 5.
47. IFC, 1890, p. 3.
48. Ibid., p. 42.
49. Ibid., p. 43.
50. Ibid., p. 43.
51. Ibid., p. 43.
52. Ibid., p. 44.
53. Ibid., p. 44.
54. *TOI*, 13 September 1905, p. 7.
55. IFLC, I, p. 15.
56. Quoted in IIC, IV, p. 365, evidence of A.E. Mirams, Consulting Surveyor to the Government of Bombay.
57. *AFR*/BP, 1914, p. 6.

PART II

IDENTITY AND MOBILIZATION

CHAPTER 4

Communalism and Working Class: The Riots of 1893

THE HINDU-MUSLIM riots which ravaged Bombay city in mid-August 1893 witnessed, albeit negatively, the first collective mobilization of workers on a grand scale. Its tremours were felt throughout the city and in all the circles which counted. The press, both Indian and Anglo-Indian, duly noted this development and the pacification of the workers became a major duty for both the official and self-appointed peace-makers. The situation was further complicated by the fact that none of the peace-makers seemed to have any influence over the workers.[1] Until the workers went back to their work the apprehension remained and the situation was not declared as 'completely normal'. Unlike the riots in 1929, these riots had not originated in the workers' quarters, but once they engulfed them, their magnitude became truly enormous. The government of Bombay noted apprehensively 'this capacity for cooperation which the Bombay mill-hands are beginning to display' and urged the necessity 'for strengthening the police for a new development of this kind'.[2]

Reporting about the riots, the Commissioner of Police, R.H. Vincent, did not have the slightest hesitation in attributing 'the origin of the ill-feeling between the two races to the anti-cow-killing agitation of the Hindus. . . .'[3] As Vincent's remarks soon got public through the medium of the Anglo-Indian press, the debate about the origins of the riots was joined in the columns of the newspapers by the leaders, editors, correspondents and the general public.[4]

The *Mahratta* considered this view prejudiced against the Hindus.[5] Even before that, Tilak had written in the *Kesari* on 15 August 1893 criticizing the Muslims for their 'boorish and arrogant attitude' and blamed the government for the 'encouragement' it supposedly gave to the Muslims. He warned the administration that if the 'policy of strict neutrality is not observed by the Government, then the Hindus have to fight in self-defence as they did in Bombay'.[6] He convened a meeting on 10 September 1893 possibly 'with the intention of publicly condemning the action of Government and the Muhammadans and expressing sympathy with the Hindus'. But, finally, succumbing to the pressure from the moderate leaders and some of his own supporters, he decided not to press the issue.[7]

Later on, Dinshaw Maneckji Petit, the president of one of the cow-protection societies, reacted to Vincent's accusations by stating that the Go-Rakshak Mandali was 'a constitutional body composed of some of the most eminent and respectable citizens of Bombay which aims principally at the improvement of the agricultural resources of the country'. He felt 'deeply grieved to read the reflections cast upon it by Mr Vincent' and asserted that 'nowhere else in the Presidency it has ever been suggested that the cow-protection movement has had anything to do with the riots in the moffusil'.[8]

However, Vincent reiterated his charge in his letter of reply to the Under Secretary, Judicial Department, GOB, on 26 June 1894. He conceded that the other communal riots during this period, particularly the one at Prabhas Pattan, provided 'the spark which exploded the mine' and speculated that 'but for this . . . it is not impossible that there would have been no outbreak at all'. But he stuck to his point that the vigorous campaigns by the cow-protection societies prepared the ground for the Bombay riots.[9]

The written debate on the responsibility for the riot continued between the officials of the GOB and the leaders of the cow-protection societies. But it had by then become mostly an academic debate because much before this the GOB had decided that it was injudicious to lay the blame for the riots on any particular group for several reasons. As many prominent citizens were involved in the cow-protection societies, they could not be held responsible for the riots. It also wanted 'to avoid gratuitously wounding the feelings of Hindus' and, therefore, 'the Governor in Council hesitates to adopt the opinion that the cow-protection movement was the principal cause of these riots.' On the other hand, the Government could not hold the Junagarh state, 'a most friendly . . . first class state in subordinate alliance with Her Majesty', responsible for the earlier riot in Prabhas Pattan which was considered by many as a precursor to the Bombay riot.[10]

Finally, when the GOI prepared its 'Report on the Causes of Recent Riots between Muhammadans and Hindus in Various Parts of India', the nature of the arguments changed. They now had a general framework for placing the riots occurring in British India as well as those which had supposedly taken place during the earlier times or in the Natives States. The report asserted that 'Religious disturbances in India are no novelty' and that it was 'a mistake to suppose that under the native regimes such occurrences were or are unknown'. In this view, therefore, there was no difference between the 'religious disturbances' of the British period from those of the earlier periods. But the report did acknowledge that these disturbances had become more numerous during the British times. It was, the report stated, because in a Native State 'one or the other religion is dominant in the administration' and the subordinate religious group had 'to submit to the loss of the privileges which it would enjoy if it were in the ascendant or free to carry out its rites'.

The British administration in India, on the other hand, was characterized, according to the report, by 'the impartiality in reference to all forms of religious creeds' and it 'does not permit one party to impose its will upon another'. But the British officials were said to face enormous difficulties in 'the impartial administration of justice and the equal treatment of all creeds' because of the offending nature of the rites of the 'religious opponents' among whom there was now 'a general tendency towards assertion of religious privileges'.

As such, this 'impartiality' and 'equal treatment' were assumed to be sufficient reason 'to increase the frequency of dissensions'; but the writers of the report had in mind some other causes as well. The first of these was 'the greater frequency of communication and the interchange of news by post and telegraph between different parts of the country'. Another was 'the greater forwardness of the Hindus in the race of life' which had embittered the minds of the Muslims 'against the Hindus and reflections on their past state of supremacy contribute to keep this feeling active'. This 'religious discord' was bound to happen in a country 'where religion lies at the basis of all relations of life'. The third cause was the 'Hindu revival' which, as the report analyzed, was basically 'a reaction against the spread of religious indifference, which was the first effect of Western education'.[11]

It was a typical colonial document, a part of the colonialist discourse. The great majority of the Indian peoples were divided into 'the two great religions' which were described to be in perpetual antagonistic relationship. Whenever and wherever the state power was in the hands of the kings or administrators of one faith, they suppressed the rites and rituals of the other religious group. In such a situation religious antagonism was bound to occur and the 'zealots of either creed', on many occasions, engineered 'bloody outbursts of fanaticism'.[12]

The onset of the British rule in India delivered the subject peoples from religious and political oppression and established the rule of impartial and even-handed justice which 'does not permit one party to impose its will upon other, or to prevent the observance of religious rites which, though repugnant to its own feeling, are sanctioned by the sentiments of its opponents'.[13] But this impartiality of the state was not taken in its right spirit by these religious groups who had become more prone to the 'assertion of religious privileges'. In fact, the beneficent measures introduced by the British rulers in India such as the post and telegraph, railways, printing press, Western education and impartial and non-religious administration had all been perversely used by these fanatics to spread religious discord. In this official view, the entire blame for the sectarian strifes lay squarely on the shoulders of the Indians themselves and the colonial administration had nothing to do with them.[14]

However, the one most important thing missing from these accounts is the role of the British administrators, ethnographers and historians in constructing the image of antagonistic religious communities out of the diverse array of castes, sects, classes, and linguistic groups. This 'historical reconstruction was characterized also by an emptying out of all history—in terms of specific variations of time, place, class, issue—from the political experience of the people, and the identification of religion, or the religious community, as the moving force of all Indian politics.'[15]

This construction by the colonial rulers helped in transforming the localized sectarian strifes into supra-local communal riots and the vast, diverse mass of Indian people into (basically two) warring religious communities. The roots of progression from the caste and sect identities to the community identity in the late nineteenth century and finally to full-grown communalism of the twentieth century lay in the colonial intervention.[16] The neutral instance maintained by the colonial state did not preclude the possibility of intense intrusion. The state attempted to influence all facets of 'corporate religious life—from the shape, height and use of a building to the format of a religious procession'.[17] Such interventions by the state upset the balance between various groups—not only the religious groups, but between sects, castes, linguistic groups as well—which had evolved and were accepted by most people over the centuries.

The role of the colonialists was not limited only to the ideological construction of the entire Indian history as a narrative of feuding religious communities; it was also reflected in the policies and practices initiated by the colonial regime. The one potent example was the role played by the colonial censuses which acted 'not merely as a passive recorder of data but as a catalyst for change'.[18] The flawed perception of the Indian society by the British officials had a major role to play in the consequent response of the Indian groups. While the British censuses exercised remarkable restraint in matters of religious enumeration, the Indian censuses accepted religious demarcation as their foundation. 'Religion in the minds of the census officials was not merely a basic category but a factor which cut across nearly all human existence.'[19]

There were expected responses from their subjects. Many of the enumerated people had also begun thinking and projecting themselves in terms defined by the censuses. The Census of 1901 duly noted the process of crystallization of religious communities, particularly in the wake of census operations. Various socio-religious groups which had hitherto been engaged in heterodox practices had started moving towards orthodoxy. It was reported that the Lingayats who had earlier refused to recognize caste distinctions and the authority of the Brahmans had, in 1891, submitted 'numerous representations' to the census authorities 'claiming the right to be described as Virshaiv Brahmans'. Some of them had also submitted 'a complete scheme' showing the fourfold *varna* divisions among the Lingayat community.[20] By 1901, these attempts by the Lingayats 'to revert to Brahministic Hinduism' had become even more pronounced.[21] Similarly, it was reported that the Sikhs had been registering themselves in the censuses as 'Nanakshahi Hindus' for two decades.[22] Therefore, while their actual number in 1901 in Bombay was 150,000, in the census figures the number of Sikhs had been put down at 1,502, the rest being counted as Hindus. Along the same lines, the Animists whom the census of 1891 in Bombay had enumerated at 292,000 had declined to 95,000 in 1901, and one of the main reasons for this decline was said to the 'the tendency of such tribes to become converts to Hinduism with a view to raising themselves in the social scale'. In the view of R.E. Enthoven, the Chief Census Officer for Bombay, this trend could be attributed to the fact that the 'improved communications are tending, in some instance, to introduce uniformity where, at an early stage in the history of the country there was only diversity, and the evidence certainly seemed to indicate the extraordinary attraction exercised on rival religions by the doctrines and social orders of orthodox Brahminism.'[25]

Some of the truly heterodox sects like the Kabirpanthis who believed neither in the Vedas nor in the Koran and respected neither the Brahmans nor the *Ulema*, faced a vertical division and dissolved themselves into Hinduism and Islam. Thus, the Census of 1901 in Bombay returned from among the erstwhile Kabirpanthis 8,000 Hindus and 1,300 Muslims.[26]

It appears, therefore, that most of the heterodox sects such as the Lingayats, Satnamis, Margis, Swami Narayanis, etc., were being increasingly subsumed under the overarching fold of Hinduism. The census had set in motion the process whereby most of the population had started defining themselves in terms of a few great religious traditions.

There was yet another level at which the intervention by the colonial officials tended to consolidate community identities. At the time of the Census of 1881 in the Bombay city, there were apprehensions that the entire exercise was viewed 'with much suspicion by the masses'. It was reported that there was general fear of 'social disasters' and 'material losses' and stories were circulating about 'conscription of labour, to extend even to women, to recruit the forces beyond the Indian frontier'.[27] To overcome these obstacles and to ensure the 'sympathy and good will' of the people, the officials decided to rely upon so-called community leaders whom they called 'the elements of popular influence'.[28] For this purpose the supposed leaders of various religious communities were invited to the municipal office and meetings were held. For the Muslims, 'A meeting of "ulama" and prominent Muslimin was assembled'. Mohammad Ali Roghay and Badruddin Tyabji were some of those present. It was resolved that the leaders from each community should call meetings with people of their own religion, that the Anjuman-i-Islam and Majlis-Akhwan-i-Sufa should play prominent roles in holding meetings with all classes of Muslims and familiarize them with the 'objects of the Census', advise them to 'co-operate with the Census officers', and help in distributing posters and pamphlets brought out by the municipal authorities, that the names of the community leaders be included in the posters and pamphlets, and last, but equally important, Muslim enumerators should be employed for the enumeration of the Muslim population.

Meetings with Hindu leaders were held along the same lines and it was resolved that 'a general Committee of influential Hindoos should be formed to explain publicly the objects of the Census, and to disarm suspicion'. Following this, a meeting of the 'Hindoo inhabitants' was held at Madhav Bag and speeches were delivered by Varjivandas Madhavdas,

Gopalrao Hari Deshmukh, Javerilal Yajnik, Raghunath Narayan Khote and others. Likewise, a meeting with the Parsi leaders was held in which Nowrozjee Furdoonjee suggested that the Parsi 'priests should be employed to explain to the lower classes the objects of the Census'.[29]

Thus, even prior to the census operations the people of Bombay were neatly divided into religious communities and some men were assumed as community leaders with influence on all classes of people, supposedly following a particular religious faith. These communities were further assumed to be impervious to the influences from any other except the leaders from their own communities. All these assumptions derived warm and positive responses from these supposed community leaders who were equally anxious to assume and defend their leadership roles.

Once the construction of the communities was done around these assumptions, the British found it convenient to make diplomatic use of the one community against the other when it suited them.[30]

However, the responsibility for generating communal discord cannot be laid entirely at the door of the colonial rulers. There were intense community-oriented social and cultural activities in Bombay in the later half of the nineteenth century. Certain reform movements, like that of the Arya Samaj, tended, sometimes unintentionally, to encourage the closing of the community boundaries in basically two ways. First, the reforming attempts were centred at religious or caste groups and tried to redefine, reform and purify the religious and caste practices often resulting in weaning away the people from the shared traditions. Second, these reform activities antagonized, revived and energized the conservative and reactionary sections within the community or caste and prompted them to close ranks and display aggressive behaviour not only towards the reformers but also towards the government and other religious groups.

The reform activities sometimes combined the religious and cultural with social and economic. The improvement of a community's position in education and jobs was at times an important objective of the community/caste associations. Thus, B.M. Malabari, one of the most ardent and famous nineteenth-century reformers, feared the decline of the Parsi position in economic, social and educational spheres. 'We are afraid,' he wrote in 1883, that 'the future of the Parsi community in Bombay is a very unpromising one. With the loss of money they are losing their social prestige. In fact, they are being pressed out by the Hindus and the Mahomedans, till there is scarcely room for them in Bombay.'[31]

Various castes among the Hindus such as Prabhus, Sonars, Sutars and the Marathas were organizing their caste associations for improvement of their social and economic position. In 1885 a group of Konkani Marathas numbering about 25,000 and consisting of 'millhands, office peons and private messengers' founded organizations called Kshatra Dharma Pratipadak and Dharma Fundolejaka Sabhas. There were organizational activities among the Telugu-speaking Kamathis aiming towards consolidation of the community and for self-improvement. The Jains and Jews had formed similar bodies to consolidate their communities' position and highlight their problems.[32]

The caste activities among what is termed as the 'Maratha-*kunbi* caste cluster' was particularly noticeable. There was a rapid emergence of Maratha identity during the 1860s and 1870s and several endogamous Maharashtrian peasant castes began to claim the Maratha identity, along with Kshatriya status. There was a constant movement among the Kunbi peasantry in the whole of Maharashtra to register themselves as Marathas in the censuses. Many of them had also started wearing the sacred threads (*janeyu*) associated with the twice-born among the Hindus. In Bombay city, this movement for upward social mobility was particularly noticeable with all the Kunbi migrants registering themselves as Marathas while nobody registered himself/herself as Kunbi in the Census of 1901.[33] This social consolidation was also reflected in political assertion and as this group formed about half of the city's total population and more than half of the textile workforce, no big mobilization was possible without taking them into account. Numerous caste-based associations mushroomed in the mill areas. Thus, we find Maratha Aikyechhoo Sabha, Maratha Temperance Association, Maratha Educational Conference, Maratha Advisory Board and a host of other bodies based on this particular identity.

Among the Muslims also both the caste- and community-based associations were the order of the day, particularly among the elite. Both the traditional and modern elite were active in organizing and participating in associations which would boost their social position and competitive abilities in trade and jobs. The Khojas, Bohras, Memons and Konkanis were becoming increasingly self-conscious not only in terms of caste but also the sect identities like Sunnis and Shias. Even the unifying bodies like the Anjuman-i-Islam were more successful when they took up communal issues like mourning the death of the Turkish Sultan in 1876, collecting funds for the Turkish armies in 1877 or working for the promotion of Urdu as the language for all the Muslims than while trying to improve the educational standards of the Muslims or introducing secular reforms. Many of these groups also tried to eliminate the earlier shared customs and practices and impose a puritanical version of Islam on their members.[34] These identities and activities seemed to have led to the Muslim-Parsi riots in 1851 and 1874.

Although all these activities tended to generate an atmosphere of communal antagonism, the cow-protection movement proved to be the most potent factor in mobilizing the Hindu masses and antagonizing the Muslims. The cow, as an essential symbol of Hinduism, could provide the platform where the broad community identity could be forged, where the high and low, the orthodox and heterodox, the *Shetias* and Western-educated, the Kunbis and Brahmans, the south Indian Kamathis and north Indian Hindus, the Gujarati and Marathi speakers, all could unite.

These activities were simultaneously going on in various parts of the country organized and propagated by activists mainly associated with the Arya Samaj.[35] In Bombay also, Swami Dayanand held many meetings in June 1882. In one of them he urged the necessity of protecting cows and stopping their slaughter as their milk was an important source of protein for the vegetarians. His plea was enthusiastically taken up by some groups, particularly the Bhatias, who memorialized the Bombay government 'requesting the prohibition of cow-slaughter'.[36]

In Bombay, the society for the preservation of cows and buffaloes, named Gaurakshak Sabha, was first established on 28 July 1887. Its president was the very prominent Parsi mill owner, Dinshaw Maneckji Petit, who was awarded the knighthood previously. Of the two secretaries 'one (was) Hindu and one Parsi'.[37] We get a slightly different structure of the organization in the words of its president:

> This Society, of which I have the honour to be President, Mr Damodar Gokaldas Manji, Hon. Secretary, and Mr Manmohan Dayaldas, Hon. Assistant Secretary, Mr Tribhovandas Varjivandas Madhavdas, Vice-president, consists of 1,500 members. Its Committee of Management consists of 75 members out of whom 35 are Justices of Peace and one a distinguished member of Bombay Legislative Council. The Society has 110 Life-member(s) of whom 11 are Parsees, 1 a Jew, 1 a Chinese and the rest, Hindus.[38]

This was stated in a letter written by Dishaw Maneckji Petit to refute the allegations earlier levelled by Vincent and others that the cow-protection societies were responsible for the Bombay riots. He claimed that some Muslims were also the members of the society and a few had contributed to its funds.[39] He also indirectly accused the British of being insensitive to the religious feelings of the Hindus by suggesting that some of the Muslim kings had 'respected the religious sentiments' of their 'Hindu subjects by discouraging the slaughter of kine' and stated that 'wise and enlightened Mahomedans have always been careful to treat the feelings of their Hindu neighbours'.[40] The basic aim of the society was, he claimed:

> to adopt measures for the preservation of Horned Cattle, such as kine, oxen, he-buffaloes and she-buffaloes which are very useful for cultivation and other purposes in an essentially agricultural country like India, and to acquaint people by means of lectures, essays, pamphlets, and newspapers with the difficulties attendant on the diminution of cattle, and to encourage the establishment of Go-shalas or Dairy-farms for the improvement of Horned Cattle so far as the finances of the Society might permit.[41]

Vincent, in his response to this letter, asserted that the Muslim members of the Society were the Khojas and Memons who, prompted by their 'intimate business connections with the Bhatias and Banias', allowed 'their names to be entered in the list of the members'. He further alleged that the Parsis and other non-Hindus were basically the 'sleeping partners in the concern'. Speaking in the heat of the argument and prompted by his colonialist training, Vincent completely denied any collaborative ventures between members of different faiths. It might, however, be true that the most active members were the Bhatias and Banias, who were generally vegetarians as well as keen to establish their leadership role in a changing religious environment.

The original intent and purpose of this society, other than protection of horned cattle, are not known.[42] Most probably they did not have any other motives. The presence of the members of different religious groups and of those who were very 'honourable' in government records, seemed to prove it. Meanwhile, the cow-protection societies were active in holding meetings in different parts of the Presidency, like Ahmedabad, Poona, etc., apart from Bombay, where speeches were made to mobilize support for stopping the killing of cattle.

Some of the activists who identified themselves with the Congress were also active in the cow-protection movement. Whether they found it as an already existing base to mobilize support for the nationalist cause or whether they considered the cow-protection itself as a nationalist cause is not known. But anti-British sentiments did appear. Shriman

Swami, who had some links with the Congress and was a prominent cow-protectionist in the North-West Provinces, went about lecturing in Poona, Sholapur and Bombay. It was reported that on 14 July 1889 in Sholapur he said that 'from want of unity between Hindus and Muhammadans the whole wealth of the country is carried to England'. He, however, ended his speech by appealing to the people to stop the cow-killing.[43] In Bombay also he spoke in a meeting on 3 November 1889 on this issue.[44] He was reported to have again lectured about cow-protection in Bombay on 18 and 28 December 1889.[45]

One police report goes to the extent of stating that the entire cow-protection movement was the handiwork of the young generation of Hindus who visited Europe and imbibed 'their hatred for the British from the foreigners' and 'their vanity is equal to their political cheek and they look upon the British as aliens who feed upon and keep them from their birth-right'. It asserted that the 'cow-protection movement was only a means to an end'.[46]

The police assessment might have been hyperbolic, but it is true that there were attempts to use the platform of the Congress to promote the movement. Already in 1887 there were efforts to pass a resolution at the Congress meeting 'calling for cow killing to be made a penal offense'.[47] In a meeting of the representatives of the Congress held at Jalgaon on 28 July 1889, Chintamanrao Vakil of Bhusaval gave a lecture on the issue.[48] In yet another instance, during the convention of the Congress in Bombay in December 1889, the Nagpur Cow-protection Association distributed thousands of pamphlets entitled *Prarthana* exhorting the people to agitate against cow-killing.[49] Sometimes the cow-protection and anti-British propaganda got so mixed up that there were some who blamed the Congress for the riots.[50] However, the Congress as an organization was never involved in this venture and, as McLane points out, such activities by persons associated with Congress 'embarrassed the Congress leaders who insisted they represented the interests of all Indians'.[51]

There were wider links of these cow-protection bodies all over India. Shriman Swami toured the Bombay Presidency several times. The Bombay Gaurakshak Sabha sent one Jairam to lecture in Ahmedabad on 27 January 1892.[52] Such instances were very common during this period. Activities were going on in the entire Bombay Presidency around the cow-protection movement. Associations similar to that of Bombay had sprung up in various places like Sholapur, Nagpur, Kolhapur, Satara,

Khandesh, etc., either on their own initiative or fostered by emissaries from other places. Although these activities had not 'gained much hold' in the Bombay Presidency as compared to north India, the official circles were worried about the 'feeling of unrest and religious antagonism' which this agitation was causing and had started talking about 'watchfulness' and 'precautionary measures'.[53]

The meetings and propaganda of the Bombay Gaurakshak Sabha went on as before. It had, since its inception, six honorary preachers and two or three paid preachers. They held meetings and delivered lectures to people at places 'where Christian Missionaries are wont to do and also at Chinchpoogli and Grant Road'.[54] On 25 April 1890, a big meeting of the Sabha was held at the Mulji Jetha Market. It was announced that the subscriptions collected from 2 August 1887 to 30 June 1888 was Rs. 11,932. The firm of Morarji Gokuldas presented 83,000 sq. yards of land in Chembur for construction of cattle sheds. Again in September 1890, a public meeting was organized in which Swami Achyutanand gave lecture on the protection of cows.

Though not much evidence is available, it is perhaps about this time that the cow-protection agitation in Bombay was undergoing a change. Its meetings became more frequent. Cooperation from societies in other parts of the Presidency was sought and given. More and more money was collected from wealthy people. A change in the method also came about. Earlier this society had satisfied itself with holding the meetings and distributing the pamphlets and handbills. But now it started more active mass contact programme by collecting signatures and selling and distributing pictures which made more appeal to the illiterate masses. In January 1891, pictures and illustrations of the cow 'supplicating for protection were on sale at a pice a piece in Bombay'.[55] R.H. Vincent, the Commissioner of Police, reported that 'pictures and pamphlets illustrating the sanctity of cow and the sin of slaughtering it were also sold and distributed in thousands all over the Presidency, but chiefly in Bombay'.[56] Another picture was that of a 'cow looking quite "gharib" . . . being milched by a handsome matron (in the dress . . . of a Dakshini Brahmini). A plump healthy child . . . playing near. In the background a Brahmin in a reverent posture, worshipping the cow, with on the other side a Mahomedan "Mlechcha" of a butcher, with a hangdog, villainous face, brandishing a long knife and looking sinisterly at the cow'.[57]

Such pictures and posters would obviously hurt the feelings of the Muslims. In August 1891, one Abdul Rahman of Bombay distributed an Urdu pamphlet in Ahmedabad 'strongly attacking the Gaurakshak

Sabha and stating that the agitation was only meant to excite the Muhammadans and to cause ill-will throughout the country'.[58]

The cow-protection propaganda, however, went on apace. In November 1891, 3,000 signatures were collected to be presented to the Hindu members of the Legislative Council. On 7 November 1891, the Secretary of the Gaurakshak Sabha asked the Police Commissioner of permission to parade cows on the roads in Bombay after the general meeting to be held on 8 November 1891. The Commissioner declined to grant permission for the procession. The meeting, however, was held before an audience of about 4,000 people and some cows were brought to the meeting.[59] In March 1892, six men from Sholapur arrived in Bombay to collect funds 'for the purchase of cows which had fallen into the hands of butchers' due to famine there. By the end of September 1892, the Nagpur Gorakshak Mandali sent four delegates to Bombay to collect Rs. 60,000 for the Nagpur Fund. Pandit Keshav Narain Vaidya from Kolhapur published 25,000 copies of four pamphlets on cow-protection and distributed most of them in Bombay. A meeting of the Bombay Sabha, held on 29 October, circulated a printed appeal which exhorted people to contribute to the Nagpur Fund.[60] In April 1893, the Sabha again wanted to take out a procession with 'thousands of cows', but permission was not granted.[61] The anniversary meetings of the Sabha, however, were held on 15 and 16 April 1893. Delegates from all parts of India attended the meetings and there was a huge gathering.[62] It was reported:

> On the former date [i.e. 15 April 1893] there was an immense procession (of) about 12,000 people, of Hindus, chiefly Kachis, with a sprinkling of Parsis, in the quarter of the town inhabited by them. Houses were covered by flags & c., some 200 milch cows gaily decorated were collected in Madhav Bagh, and a great many speeches were made in favour of the movement. On 16th, a sort of regular meeting was held in the Madhav Bagh, which was attended by some 20 delegates and about some 15,000 persons. Addresses were delivered and prizes bestowed on the owners of the best-fed cows. Medals were also given to the lecturers who had worked zealously in the cause. Many Hindu shops were closed in the honour of the event, and a theatrical performance took place in the New Alfred Theatre in the aid of the Gorakshak Mandali.[63]

One of the songs sung at the meeting ran as follows:

> You males wearing moustaches, wearing turbans and fastening weapons do (you) effect cow-protection. You valiant Aryan brothers, do sacrifice (your) courage and (your) wrath, rush among the waves of the battle-field, do rout (or

bury!) the stupid Mlechas (Musalman unbelievers). They take the lives of lakhs of cows, kill the best of animals, while you Aryan brothers are sitting—run, rush to die. What, are you wearing bodices . . . ? You have the strength in your arms of the Aryans; for once, rise, rise, oh, why do you fear?[64]

The preachers of the Sabha had now begun holding meetings in the localities with substantial or majority Muslim population. This created more tension and it was feared that they might be assaulted. On the eve of Bakr-Id which fell on 25 June 1893, some of the members of the Sabha tried to collect information from the Hindu police constables about the areas where cattle might be sacrificed. The secretary of the Sabha also approached the Police Commissioner asking him to put a ban on the cattle-slaughter. In his letter to the Police Commissioner he had also warned ominously that a failure to prevent slaughter 'might lead to disturbance of peace by the Hindus'. The authorities feared that riots would take place because 'feelings were running very high indeed'. Then came the news about terrible riots at Azamgarh, Rangoon and some other places and both sides were reported to be very highly charged and the police had to maintain constant vigil to avoid any disturbance.

In July 1893, another cow-protection society was formed in Bombay. It was named as Gaupalan Updeshak Mandali. Its president was the Bhatia mill owner, Lakhmidas Khimji, who was once a very enthusiastic reformer and had been involved in intense conflict with the conservative Bhatias who were said to be the main driving force behind the Gaurakshak Sabha. The new society took an even more extreme position and its 'leader and members displayed still greater virulence in the dissemination of their views'.[65] Its foundation meeting was followed by a big demonstration in which the president 'was carried about in procession with band and banners' and 'violent speeches and warlike songs were read and sung'.[66]

Now both the societies started competing with each other in taking more active steps to stop the killing of cows. So while the members of the Gaurakshak Sabha had taken turns to prevent the sacrifice of the cows in various localities on the occasion of Bakr-Id, the Gaupalan Mandali 'obtained a large plot of land at Lonavala, where they intended to keep all cattle intercepted and purchased by their agents *en route* to Bombay'.[67] While one Society brought out a magazine called *Kamdhenu* advocating cow-protection, the other one started publishing another entitled *Gau Upadeshak* preaching the same.[68] The societies also tried to make inroads in the police and administration and sometimes succeeded. In such atmosphere, even minor incidents had potential for a major disturbance. So, when a restive cow, which was being escorted to the cattlehouse by a Muslim constable, fell into a ditch and died, there was possibility of a riot. People gathered and accused the constable of intentionally murdering the cow and they did not allow the carcass to be removed for 16 hours.[69]

Such activities and incidents were bound to have their impact sooner or later. In the minds of the Muslim middle-class and Shetias, some sort of sectarian sentiments were already injected during the 1870s and 1880s by various religious and other associations which espoused the cause of the Muslims ranging from education and reservations in government jobs to pan-Islamic issues such as the defence of Turkey and the Khalifa. But these sentiments were mainly limited to the upper and middle strata. The cow-protection propaganda, however, reached down to the lower levels and created fear in the minds of the poor Muslims that they would be deprived of their cheap article of food. Some zealots of the Sabha also went into the Muslim-dominated areas and preached their creed, despite warnings from several quarters. All this was slowly preparing the ground for a conflagration by emphasizing separate community identities and alienating both communities from each other and creating tension between them. In such a surcharged atmosphere came the news of the riots at Prabhas Pattan.

It is true that the news of riots from other places had already been reaching the city and people's feelings were getting divided over them. But the physical proximity of Prabhas Pattan made it possible for both sides to carry on intense propaganda which aroused sectarian feelings. The riots at Prabhas Pattan (in the princely state of Junagarh whose head was a Muslim) had occurred in the end of July 1893, on Muharram Day, in which many Hindus were killed.

The agitation fever in Bombay rose a few notches higher. On 30 July 1893, a meeting of the Gaurakshak Sabha was held on this issue. In his speech Javerilal Yajnik demanded 'condign punishment for the offenders' and talked of 'avenging justice'. He further said that 'not only one of the most sacred temples dear to the Hindus had been defiled, but the holy *Bithal* of the god Shree Krishna wantonly polluted, innocent monks and religious ascetics . . . were, in violation of inter-communal laws, ruthlessly massacred'.[70] Other speakers also adopted the same tone.

The other society, the Gaupalan Mandali, also held a much-publicized meeting on 3 August. Then on 6 August 1893 a joint meeting of both the societies was held. The last big meeting on the issue held by the cow-protection societies was on 10 August. Many smaller meetings were regularly being held in different localities and subscriptions collected for legal action against the offenders. Dr Deshmukh of Gaurakshak Sabha organized a meeting of Maratha Hindus at Thakurdwar. Many others went around making inflammatory speeches. Shivram Sudhale and Narayan Trimbak Vaidya went around on one Sunday 'from house to house to urge people to sympathise with Prabhas Pattan sufferers'.[71]

There were many such instances. Thousands of rupees were collected, speeches were made denouncing the Muslims and appeals were issued to support the afflicted Hindus in Prabhas Pattan. In one meeting by Gaupalan Mandali, Lohanas, Banias and Bhatias 'outbid each other in their subscriptions'.[72] There were attempts made to hold meetings among the mill workers also. We have evidence of one such attempt by the Gaupalan Mandali which, however, later denied it.[73] But, judging by the pitch of propaganda, it was not unlikely that such meetings were held. In any case, the mill workers were as much a part of the Bombay population as others and the possibilities of their participation in the movement were always there.

The Muslims were not far behind. Aga Khan, in a meeting, talked about the killing of his co-religionists, desecration and destruction of their mosques by the Hindus in Prabhas Pattan. There were many such meetings. Many Muslims from the affected area in Junagarh arrived in Bombay 'complaining to their co-religionists and afterwards to (the Police Commissioner) that they had not received fair treatment at the hands of the local (Hindu) authorities'. Subscriptions were also collected for the defence of the accused in the Prabhas Pattan.[74] There were rumours that the Muslims were discussing this issue in various mosques in the city.[75] On 10 August 1893, there were definite reports of a large meeting convened 'to arrange for the legal defence of the accused, and Rs. 12,000 were subscribed on the spot'.[76] In the morning of 11 August, there were reports of a 'large meeting of Mahomedans especially (lower classes) . . . at the house of Haji Kasam Haji Ismail in the Abdul Rehman Street. About 1000 persons who could not be accommodated were standing from 7 to 8 in the streets'.[77]

The riots started in the afternoon of 11 August.

It was city's third inter-religious riot in the nineteenth century. The first one was in 1851, when a Parsi journalist named Byramjee Ghandi had printed a portrait of Prophet Muhammad in his journal.[78] The Muslim crowds attacked the Parsis, injuring them and destroying and looting their property. The second one took place in 1874, again between the Muslims and the Parsis, when a Parsi named Rustomjee Jalbhoy made an indiscreet reference to the Prophet Muhammad in his translation of some works of Washington Irving.[79] But in none of these two the magnitude and intensity of the riots were anywhere near those of 1893. It was because the Parsis were few in number and limited to a few areas while the Hindus and the Muslims were spread all over the city.

When the riots started the police was not exactly caught unawares. Since weeks past rumours were afloat about the possibility of riots. The administration did not take much precautionary measures and 'as Bakr-Id, Muharram and several Fridays passed without any disturbances', it was lulled into a false sense of security and order.[80] Although there were strong rumours that the riots might start on 11 August,[81] not much arrangements were made to meet such a contingency. There were some policemen posted outside Juma Masjid, but their number was grossly inadequate given the enormity of the problem.

When the worshippers went into the Masjid for prayer, they were not carrying any sticks or weapons. The only thing observed was that 'the attendance of worshippers exceeded the usual number by about a thousand souls'.[82] But when the worshippers came out of the Masjid after prayer, many of them were carrying sticks and other weapons which lends credence to the opinion that the riots were pre-arranged.

Coming out of the mosque at around 1.45 p.m., the Muslim crowd started shouting *'Deen, Deen'* and rushed towards the Hindu temple situated in the nearby Hanuman Lane. The policemen posted there tried to restrict them, and a fight ensued in which stones and other missiles were freely used by the crowd. Some of the policemen got injured. But, with the arrival of the reinforcements, the rioters were repulsed with many injuries and some arrests were also made.

As soon as they were driven from this area, they spread out in other areas and, joined by others, started rioting there. Thus rioting crowds could be seen in Bhendy Bazaar, all along Erskine Road, Null Bazaar, Falkland Road, Duncan Road, Jagjivan Keeka Street and Cowasjee Patel Tank Road. They attacked the passing Hindus and sometimes the others. Passing vehicles and the tramcars were pelted with stones. The Commissioner of Police reported, 'Infuriated mobs of Musalmans surged from street to street, carrying havoc and destruction in all directions. To trace the course of the tumult is beyond my powers, for the rioters seemed to be in every place at once.'[83]

The military was called to handle the situation. Many companies of Marine Battalion, 5th Bombay Infantry, Bombay Light Horse, etc., were ordered. But even this did not prove much effective because when the rioters were:

> driven back and dispersed by the Police and Military from one locality, it was only to unite again in another and wreak their wanton rage on the hated Hindus and any who sought to hinder them. Wherever they went their tactics were the same. Sticks and bludgeons were the weapons generally employed, and only too frequently with fatal results. Volleys of stones, broken tiles and other missiles were flung both from the streets and from the windows and tops of houses.[84]

Many Hindus temples in Nissanpada, Kumbharwada and other localities were desecrated, their idols broken and thrown on the streets. To the killing and desecration of the religious places, another motive was soon added, that of loot. One pay clerk of GIP Railway Company was assaulted and robbed of many thousands of rupees. Many shops in Bhendy Bazaar were looted and their property destroyed.

It was only to be expected that the Hindus, among whom communal propaganda had been going on for some time and who were so preponderant in number, would soon retaliate. In some areas, the Hindus were also prepared for this as they had been forewarned and supplied with necessary equipment. Within an hour of the outbreak, Muslims in some areas were attacked. In Falkland Road, Jagjivan Keeka Street and Duncan Road, there were pitched battles between the Hindu and Muslim *talimwalas*. In Arthur Road and Grant Road, several groups of Hindus assaulted the Muslims and committed other acts of violence. At Kamathipura, a large body of Hindus attacked the mosque in that area and intense fighting ensued. In Umarkhadi and neighbouring areas many groups of Hindus attacked solitary Muslims and at Chinch Bunder, both parties fought pitched battle. The intensity and the range of rioting was such that even on the very first day it was described as 'the most furious and bloodthirsty encounter known to the city since the inauguration of British rule'.[85]

The mill workers also joined the fray right on the first day. In Chinchpoogly, the Hindu mill workers attacked the Muslim weavers only to be dispersed by the military, and 'towards midnight of the 11th, 300 Hindu mill-hands came out, bent on revenge, at the Arthur Road; but were kept back in their chawls with great difficulty'.[86]

While people from both communities attacked each other, desecrated temples and mosques, looted property, both of them 'turned upon

European and native Police and Military'. Little regard was shown for the authority and the military and the police fired in several instances, when attacked, killing and injuring many. The Military report says:

> No sooner was one district reduced to comparative quiet by the presence of troops, than fresh riots broke out beyond the spheres of existing patrols; and as darkness came on, the difficulty of watching long lines of streets with innumerable intersecting gullies increased enormously. It was felt, therefore, that the force employed was insufficient, and urgent orders were despatched to Colaba for four field guns and the Loyal North Lancashire Regiment to parade at once and proceed to Paydhuni.[87]

This was on the first day. The second day brought the mill workers fully into the vortex of the riots. Though they might have been influenced by the cow-protection propaganda and the Prabhas Pattan riots, the immediate cause of their participation seemed to be the riots in Bombay itself. It was a Saturday, a normal working day for the mills. But many of the mills were closed because they were working short-time. The workers of these mills went around mobilizing the workers of other mills, occasionally by throwing stones at their mills. This way, after some time, all the mills were closed and about one lakh workers were on the streets. The majority of the workers being Maratha Hindus, they started attacking and killing the Muslims and destroying and looting their property. They dispersed in most of the northern parts of the city. Many of them were 'carrying pieces of firewood, and attacked the Musalmans at Chinchpokli, Arthur and Parel Roads, Siwri, Mazagaon and the vicinity, killing and wounding many'.[88] Some three hundred of them went to Mama Hajani, a mosque very sacred to the Muslims, situated in Worli on the rocks surrounded by water. They attacked the people inside the mosque with stones and sticks and 'brought down a portion of it by means of thick long bamboo sticks'.[89] On this day, most of the northern areas were ruled by the workers. The *TOI* reported:

> Early in the morning at about 8 o'clock, they (the mill workers) took possession of the whole of the Girgaum Road, the Girgaum Block Road, and their adjacent localities, and ran like mad fanatics, raving and crying out 'Mahadev Ki Jeh', and belabouring, and in some cases murdering stray Mahomedans who happened to meet them in the streets. They attacked every shop owned by Mahomedans in these localities, and robbed and plundered right and left. . . . A strong party of mill-hands then attacked the mosque of the Borees in a by-lane called Mangalwady on the main Girgaum Road, and having brought out the doors and windows and furnitures, including even the cooking pots, of the mosque

into the street, set fire to them, causing a great panic to the inhabitants of the locality.[90]

When confronted by the police or the military, the workers sometimes resisted and at other times laid down their sticks only to pick them up after the withdrawal of the forces. These rioters roamed around the railway lines attacking the Muslim employees at the stations, on the road leading to Dadar and at other places in the northern parts of the city all at once. They conducted these operations with much cleverness. The authorities found it hard to check them, because

> the rioters having learnt where the Military and Police guards were stationed, took advantage of this to select isolated spots for their operations and proceeded to murder and plunder such victims as they could find. The Police and troops were frequently unable to reach such places for some time; and the marauders were thus able to carry out their nefarious intentions with comparative impunity.[91]

Although on Saturday the field was held by the Hindus, chiefly the mill labourers, the Muslims were also active in many areas. Early morning, a large group of Julahas came out from Madanpura 'with old knives, razors and other weapons tied on the end of sticks, crossed the flats beyond the Byculla Club, and severely injured a number of Hindus'. They also created trouble at Duncan Road, Khoja Street, Paydhuni Road and other places by throwing stones at the passers-by and the passing vehicles.[92] In Khetwadi and Girgaum, some of the Hindu temples were wrecked; in Arthur Crawford Market, Hindu shopkeepers were attacked; two Hindu temples at Durga Devi and Falkland Road were destroyed. They also attacked and fought with the police and military whenever checked. In one instance, a Muslim burial party, consisting of three to four thousand men, turned violent and was fired upon by the military 'killing half a dozen and wounding about forty or fifty'.[93] In another instance, when the police were transferring about seventy prisoners from a police station, desperate attempt was made by a large group of about 1,500 Muslims armed with sticks, clubs, and stones to rescue them. They would have succeeded, but for the arrival of an infantry group. The crowd was fired upon and many were injured and killed. At another place, a group of Julahas were reported to be violent. When the policemen posted there tried to restrain them, they were attacked and some of them received injuries. Again they were saved by the arrival of a military party which fired on the rioters, killing one and wounding many. In yet another instance, the policemen were surrounded and attacked with sticks and stones and they had to seek shelter in a nearby house. At the Jackeria Masjid, the policemen were attacked and one policeman got killed. [94]

At several places, many groups of the Hindus and Muslims fought each other bitterly. In Chinchpoogly, 'a free fight had taken place between the two rival factions . . . and there were eight men killed and about a hundred seriously injured'.[95] In Kamathipura and Northbrook Gardens, the Julahas and the Kamathis were involved in violent clashes. In Islampura, a fight occurred between the Muslim Chili Chors and the Hindu residents of the area in which many of the former were seriously injured.

The mill workers were very active in these riots. They attacked the Muslims in their areas as well as in other areas, not sparing their Muslim fellow workers. In one instance, a chawl on Parel Road, whose upper storeys were occupied by Muslim workers 'had been forced into a state of siege by Hindoos all over the way, who, armed with lathis, had come down in hundreds, driven the occupants into their quarters, and hurling volleys of stones at them to close every shutter, and hopelessly stand a siege'.[96] In another instance, many Muslim workers wanted to leave the mill areas and go to Nagpada which was dominated by the Muslims and they had to be escorted by the police through besieging Hindu workers. In another incident, one Muslim was killed while carrying food for his relative at Kaiser-e-Hind Mill. Such incidents were quite common. All the other identities seemed to have dissolved into communal identities. Thus not only were the Hindu mill workers attacking and killing the Muslim workers, but the Julahas from the North-West Provinces were injuring and murdering their countrymen who were Hindus and vice versa.

Loot was also one motive induced into the riots. Property was plundered from religious places, shops and private houses. Passers-by were also robbed and sometimes the loot became the principal motive. It was reported that in some instances, so 'little regard was felt by the *Budmash* element for their religious principles . . . that the shops of both Musalman and Hindu were robbed by members of their own race and creed'.[97]

On 13 August, some Hindu mill workers learnt that some Muslims had been given protection by a Parsi at Girgaum Road. They went to him and demanded some money 'threatening that if it was not given they would force their way into the place and murder'. The Parsi paid them Rs. 10. After some time, another batch of workers came demanding the same. On being refused, they broke open the gate and entered the house but, finding nobody there, returned.[98]

On Sunday, the mills remained closed and the assault, loot and desecration were taking place in most of the mill areas. In Worli, Matunga, Parel, Mazagaon, Lalwady and other places hordes of workers could be seen going around and involving themselves in many riotous activities. At Curry Road, four Muslims were killed by them.

Although some such incidents were still taking place, by the evening of Sunday, 13 August, the worst was over. On the 14th, there were some disturbances in Kamathipura. In Chinchpoogly, two Muslims were murdered and in Worli, two *dargahs* were desecrated and demolished.

The mills remained closed on Monday, 14 August, because the workers refused to attend on the ground that in their absence their families would be attacked. They also caused some trouble in Parel, Elphinstone Road and Fergusson Road. But when the military came, they put down their sticks and went away. Even after a week since the beginning of the riots, the mill workers were refusing to join their work. It was only on Saturday, 19 August, that most of them went to their mills. But even then they did not feel quiet and calm as false alarms kept sounding time and again. In one instance, 'The Hindu mill hands working in the mills at Kala Chowkey Road stopped work about midday on Saturday and turned out into the roads on hearing a report that the Mahomedans were coming to attack them. Having awaited outside the mills for about ten minutes, and being assured that it was a false alarm, they resumed work.'[99]

Events took a more serious turn on Sunday, 20 August, when a similar false alarm was sounded at Pydhowni. This time the Hindus who had gathered did not go back even after learning that the alarm was false. They started attacking stray Muslims and it was only after the arrival of the military that they dispersed. Other alarms were raised at Bhuleshwar, Chokshi Bazaar, and Bhoiwada. The situation was such that even after four weeks since the riots had broken out, the Police Commissioner did not feel confident enough to conclude that everything was over and the peace had been fully restored.

The main rioting had taken place only on three days but its intensity was such that, according to the official estimates, 81 persons were killed, 700 injured and 1,550 arrested; property worth lakhs of rupees was looted and destroyed. The riots caused disruption of many civic services, the most important being the sanitary works carried out by the municipality. The Hindu *halalkhors* and the Muslim cart-drivers both were threatened and attacked. In a city where about 850 tons of night-soil was removed by hand every day, it was a great difficulty. The Municipal

Commissioner thought the situation to be very serious: 'On Sunday 13th there was an impurity in the air which was distinctly perceptible almost everywhere, and had the Health Department been unable for a day or two longer to resume its labour the health of the city would almost certainly have been affected.'[100]

There was also individual and mass migration of the people during and even after the riots. Right since the beginning of the riots, people has started moving to the areas where their co-religionists dominated. During the course of the riots, the police and military had to escort these migrating groups and such escort parties were attacked in some instances. Tens of thousands of people left Bombay for their native places. It was reported that 'there were not enough railway carriages to carry all the passengers who presented themselves at the stations during the day'.[101]

There have been many interpretations to explain the links between the working classes and communalism. The relationship between the cow-protection movements, along with related riots, and the differential involvement of various groups has also received a lot of scholarly attention. John R. McLane, in a detailed study of the movement and the riots, attributes these developments to a variety of factors and motives ranging from economic ('to improve agriculture and the health of Indians')[102] and social beliefs (regarding 'Muslims as alien offenders of Hindu custom')[103] to political factors (like struggle for ascendancy within Hinduism and the role of some local Congress leaders).[104] Sandria Freitag argues that in the movement during the 1880s and early 1890s there were broad-based initial attempts to define the 'community identity' which, however, did not quite succeed and the identities remained localized.[105] Peter Robb puts more emphasis on the British search for 'definitions and certainty' which 'encouraged assertiveness and polarization among Indians'.[106] He also stresses the role of the 'petty zamindars and more substantial tenants' whose attempts to preserve their social and economic position in the rural society led to their widespread participation.[107] Gyan Pandey, on the other hand, emphasizes the 'very substantial' and 'autonomous' role played by some 'non-zamindari castes' such as Ahirs, Kurmis and Koeris in the movement and riots in Bihar.[108]

With respect to the urban workers, this debate has been particularly intense in the context of the jute millworkers in Calcutta. Dipesh Chakrabarty finds a significant growth of sectarian tendencies which he describes as 'community consciousness', 'communal culture', and 'communal divisions' among the workers in the 1890s.[109] This he further defines as 'a consciousness to which religion was of crucial importance'.[110] Even though this consciousness developed in the 1890s, he charts it as something inherited, 'as an ensemble of relationship one is born into, as opposed to "class" which is based on an associational principle'.[111] Thus the notions of community or/and communal consciousness, as emerges from his arguments, were phenomena not related to particular historical and contextual developments. He reconfirms this position when he says that 'The jute workers . . . acted out of an understanding that was prebourgeois in its elements.'[112]

Many historians have criticized the inadequacy and ahistoricity of this analysis and emphasized the colonial context as crucial to the development of such identity. They have stressed the centrality of economic and political factors as decisive in shaping the consciousness and actions of the workers. [113]

What was the nature of the riots in Bombay in 1893? It is true that the workers were imbued with religious consciousness which was reinforced in the alienating atmosphere of the city. It did not, however, mean that it automatically led to communalism. The ideology of communalism must have a conception of the 'other' and this emerged and was shaped by the colonial ideology, policies and practices and was reinforced and strengthened by the political mobilization which took place in response to the colonial reality. The communal atmosphere and the consequent riots have to be placed in the particular historical context. The growth of communal ideology in India was as recent a phenomenon as the development of the factory industry. British policies and historiography turned the sectarian strifes into communal riots and constructed distinct communities with disconnected culture and customs out of the varieties of castes and sects with shared traditions. What were until then feuds between different groups were transformed into persistent battles between all-India communities defined by their religion. But the responsibility for this was not entirely that of the colonial rulers. Several times the actors from within the Indian social and political milieu mobilized opinions and people and their actions did not always conform to the rulers' ideology and interests. They also stood against the state. Therefore, the notion of communities based on religions was not inherited but was acquired during the late nineteenth century.

But the growth of communal identity could not be explained in purely political-economic terms. Although the political mobilization in the form of caste and community associations was taking place and the cow-protection movement pushed it forward on a much larger scale, the process of identity-formation was social and cultural also. Why would a person or a group assume a certain identity and not another was also decided by their socio-cultural backgrounds and had its roots in the inherited consciousness of the people. In such situations, the socio-cultural inheritance interacts with political movements to shape a particular identity for a person or group.

The people who participated in the riots had a variety of motives. Although the cow-protection propaganda and the Prabhas Pattan riots and the agitations connected with them might have started them in Bombay, once the riots were on, they had a logic of their own. The feeling of communal revenge, of personal defence, of group rivalry and desire to loot kept them going. Communal violence was, of course, one of the strongest motivating factors. In some cases, the rioters on both sides were paid by their co-religionist patrons. According to a police report, 'the ten or fifteen Pardeshis who were near the Bhuleshwar temple on Saturday, the second day of the riot, and Sunday have been paid by the shetias on Saturday morning'. The report further added: 'I saw about 70 Maratha Ghatis loitering about in Kandewadi, they were very much agitated and all had sticks. I asked them whether they were paid, promised payments, but they bitterly complained about the *Shetias*, and on Sunday some of Malvanis threatened Mr Vizbookandass.'[114]

Similarly we find that 'cartloads of sweetmeats were supplied by wealthy Hindus to be distributed among their poor co-religionists . . . the Mahomedans also have been distributing *nans* and plantains to the poor of their community'.[115]

However, payments were not very common. Only in a few instances the rioters were paid, but in most others they participated on their own. Loot, mostly, though not invariably, on communal lines was a stronger motive. But even loot did not form the primary motive on the whole. The desecration and destruction of small temples and *dargahs* were not motivated by the desire for loot.

The cow-protection propaganda and the agitations related to the Prabhas Pattan riots were initiated and carried on basically by the trading and millowning bourgeoisie (the *Shetias*) and the middle classes. But the people who participated in the riots were almost exclusively from the lower classes. And just by the fact of being from the lower strata they, in the official and some of the non-official vocabulary, were rendered 'disrespectable' and 'badmashes', basically interested in plunder. It became a matter of self-congratulation in several quarters that the so-called 'respectable' people were not seen participating in the riots. The *Bombay Gazette* felt: 'One gratifying circumstance in this outbreak of lawlessness is that amongst the hundreds that have been arrested, there is scarcely a respectable Hindu or Mahomedan, and it was manifest that the main cause of the misbehaviour was a desire for plunder and loot, and not the defence or vindication of religious principles.'[116]

The Police Commissioner, reporting on the very first day of the riots, stated that 'Only the lower and lowest classes of the Musalmans took part in the riots.' This 'low and disreputable portion of the population commonly known as *badmashes*' were said to be basically interested in 'robbing wayfarers and plundering shops'.[117] Even in a meeting of the 'representative members of the Hindoo and Mahomedan communities' convened by the Municipal Commissioner on 15 August 1893, this view was expressed by many that 'it was the lower classes of the communities which had given and giving them a lot of trouble'. [118]

So who were the people involved in the riots? Were they the 'migratory Sidis and Pathans' displaying their 'spirit of greater freedom and lawlessness in which they are bred'?[119] Or the 'Mussulman rabble who had apparently broken loose from the influence of their elders?[120] Or the turbulent mill workers? Or the 'ruffianly' Chili Chors? Or the 'fanatical Julahas'? Or the troublesome Ghatis? The official and some non-official accounts constructed a variety of stereotypes around the participants.

Among these lower classes the mill workers were also prominently involved in the happenings. Their involvement was viewed with much concern and was termed as a 'most serious aspect' and 'absolutely unprecedented'. The intensity and the spread of the riots was in large parts attributed to the 'capacity for cooperation which the Bombay mill-hands are beginning to display'.[121]

The so-called community leaders, who seemed to have no influence at all with the people, had washed their hands off these happenings. They had joined the ranks of the 'respectable people'. Persons like Varjivandas Madhavdas, Haji Cassum, Vizvookandas Atmaram, Lakhmidas Khimji, Damodar Tapidas, Amiroodin Tyabji, etc., who had been quite active earlier in communal propaganda had started participating in peace meetings and issuing appeals to the people to restore peace. Anjuman-i-Islam, which was one of the organizations active in raising the communal temperature in the pre-riot period, held a meeting soon after the riots on 16 August and declared that 'there were no differences between the leading Hindus and Mahomedans'.[122] Amiroodin Tyabji, a leader of the Mussalman Patan Ryots Defence Commitee, which was another such organization, claimed that the main purpose of the meetings conducted by his organization was 'to cooperate' with the Hindu organizations.[123] The leaders of the cow-protection societies also loudly disclaimed any responsibility whatsoever of any involvement in the riots. Lakhmidas Khimji, leader of the more active society and accused by the police of being a precipitating factor behind the riots, termed these criticisms as 'ill-informed and unfounded'. He ridiculed his critics for 'crediting him with an amount of power and influence of the possession of which I was hitherto ignorant'. He, however, defended his role with regard to the cow-protection movement and denied any links between this and the riots.[124]

Another person, writing under the pseudonym of 'justice' defended the agitation undertaken by the Muslims for protection of their co-religionists in Prabhas Pattan, severely condemned the 'mob rule' and bemoaned that 'henceforth no movement, however legitimate or necessary, can be undertaken lest the ruffians and budmashes of the town threaten to rise and commit excesses'.[125]

During the meeting of the 'Hindoo and Mahomedan leaders' held on 15 August, this problem again came to light that although there were some recognizable leaders who claimed to exercise some influence on certain sections of the Muslims and promised to restrain them, there was nobody who could exercise a similar restraint on the Hindus, particularly the mill workers.[126] This put a question mark on the supposed leadership of these 'leaders'. A letter in the *Bombay Gazette*, written under the name of 'M.B.K.', put the problem in perspective with a touch of sarcasm:

> May I be allowed to suggest to the authorities concerned that the Maratha, the Pardeshi, and the Camattee Hindoo communities do not acknowledge those who can glibly quote from John Bright, Burke, or Buckle, and stand on a platform and make fine speeches. They certainly have no influence at all over the masses, who can only be reached through their recognized leaders, generally quiet and unassuming men. The mill-hands . . . look up to their mukadums; the Purdesees, the Ghatees, the Kamatees, and other follow the dictates of their headmen who are not budmashes but quite as much respectable and peace-loving as fine speakers on the platforms above referred to. The Mahomedans have their mullas and kazis; the Sidhis their kings and queens.
>
> If the authorities could only secure the good offices of these heads, the

present disturbances would not only terminate, but soon be forgotten; peace and good-will would reign among us and business flourish.[127]

These official and unofficial assessments about the role of the masses pointed towards relatively autonomous actions by people who, in most cases, did not belong to the criminal underworld and whose motivations varied widely.

Another thing which was clear during the course of the riots was that although the lines were drawn across the Hindu and Muslim divide, the people who participated were mobilized and could be recognized as Julahas, Pathans, Ghatis, Kamathis, Kolis, Pardeshis (the Hindu migrants from north India), Chili Chors (the Muslim migrants from Kathiawar) and mill workers. In very few cases—at least that is the picture we get from contemporary accounts—do we find the action organized along larger communal lines. That's why the leadership was localized and located into the caste groups or in smaller migratory communities based on linguistic or regional identities even though these smaller identities identified with the larger identity of religious communities.

This identification of the localized groups with the larger community was the factor which propelled the Telugu Chamars and Mahars, reported to be 'not only cow-eating but cow-carrion-eating',[128] to side with the Hindus and which allowed the cow-protection propaganda carried on mostly by a Gujarati leadership to acquire such influence among the Hindu lower classes of Bombay and which prompted the north Indian Julahas to attack people from their own region and linguistic groups. The speed with which the warring groups appeared on the streets and in the alleys pointed towards a process that had been going on for quite some time and that had helped to crystallize associational and conflicting identities making such massive mobilization possible in the course of these riots. So, although a variety of motives went into the making of the riots, the lines between 'we' and 'they' were drawn along communal identities. All other motives and identities tended to be dissolved into communal identity at that point of time. Caste, class, region and occupation were subordinated to the communal identity.

However, this was only for the time being. There were no congealed communal identities, at least for quite some time to come. The relative population of the Hindus in the Muslim-dominated areas or the Muslims in the Hindu-dominated areas did not show a major decline over the years, despite a few migrations. The Hindus, despite endeavours from various quarters to dissuade them, kept participating in the Muharram processions.[129] There were no communal riots again till 1929 and soon other loyalties were manifested in different kinds of sectarian strifes. The Sunnis attacked the Bohras in 1904 and the Julahas in 1908 at the time of Muharram. In 1911, on the Muharram day, Muslims and Hindus fought together against the police and in the police firing many Hindus were killed and injured along with many Muslims.[130]

NOTES

1. See *Bombay Gazette*, This volume of the paper from 11 August 1893 to the end of the month was reprinted and kept in the Judicial Department files, vol. 194, *MSA*. It consists of events and opinions expressed in the paper relating to the riots and their aftermath. Hereafter it will be referred to as BG for all subsequent references to it in this chapter. pp. 32-4.
2. Judicial Department (henceforth JD), vol. 281/94, 1894, p. 19. *MSA*.
3. Ibid., p. 2. Letter from the Commissioner of Police to the Secretary, JD, GOB, dated 12 August 1893.
4. See, for example, the *Bombay Gazette* and *Times of India* for the months of August 1893. (This volume of the *Times of India* consisting of reports and opinions relating to the riots is also kept in the JD, vol. 194 in a booklet form. Hereafter it will be referred to as *TOI* for all subsequent references to it in this chapter.)
5. *Mahratta*, 20 August 1893, in Cashman, *The Myth of the Lokamanya: Tilak and Mass Politics in Maharashtra* (Berkeley and Los Angeles, 1975), pp. 68-9.
6. Quoted in D.V. Tahmankar, *Lokamanya Tilak: Father of Indian Unrest and Maker of Modern India* (London, 1956), pp. 55-6.
7. Government of Bombay, *Source Material for a History of Freedom Movement in India*, vol. II, 1885-1920 (henceforward *SMHFM*, II), pp. 201-2. Also, Cashman, *The Myth of the Lokamanya*, p. 70.
8. Home Department (Public), August, 1894, Proceedings nos. 214-20, pp. 11-14. Letter from Dinshaw Maneckji Petit to the Secretary to the Judicial Department, GOB, dated 26 May 1894. NAI.
9. Ibid. Letter from R.H. Vincent to Under Secretary, JD, Bombay.
10. Home Department (Public), Proceedings nos. 169-89, 26 October 1893, letter from G.C. Whitworth, Acting Secretary, JD, GOB to the Secretary to the GOI, pp. 72-4. NAI. Also, JD, vol. 281/94; letter from the Secretary of State for India, dated 17 November 1893, pp. 16-22. MSA.
11. Home Department (Public), part A, December 1893, Proceedings nos. 210-13, pp. 5-9. NAI. Letter dated 27 December 1893 from Lansdowne, A.E. Miller,

H. Brackenbury, C.B. Pritchard, J. Westland, and A.P. MacDonnell to Earl of Kimberley, Secretary of State for India.

12. Ibid., p. 5.
13. Ibid., p. 6.
14. For the colonialist representation of the Indians as the 'primitive Other' who were irrational, fanatic and ignorant, see Gyan Pandey, 'The Prose of Otherness', in David Arnold and David Hardiman, eds., *Subaltern Studies, VIII* (Delhi, 1994), pp. 195-7.
15. Gyan Pandey, *The Construction of Communalism in Colonial North India* (Delhi, 1992), p. 24.
16. See Sandria B. Freitag, *Collective Action and Community : Public Arenas and the Emergence of Communalism in North India* (Delhi, 1990).
17. Ibid., p. 54.
18. Kenneth W. Jones, 'Religious Identity and the Indian Census', in N.G. Barrier, ed., *The Census in British India: New Perspectives* (Delhi, 1981), pp. 73-4.
19. Ibid., pp. 80-1.
20. *Census of India, 1901*, vol. IX, part I, Report, p. 183.
21. Ibid., p. 58.
22. Ibid., p. 61.
23. Ibid., p. 57.
24. Ibid., p. 65.
25. Ibid., p. 183.
26. Ibid., p. 61.
27. *Census of the City and Island of Bombay, 1881*, report by T.S. Weir, p. 4.
28. Ibid., p. 4
29. Ibid., pp. 4-6.
30. For a discussion of the British policies in fostering the growth of communalism, see Bipan Chandra, *Communalism in Modern India* (Delhi, 1984), pp. 237-89.
31. *Indian Spectator*, 26 August 1883; quoted in Christine Dobbin, *Urban Leadership in Western India: Politics and Communities in Bombay City, 1840-1885* (London, 1972), p. 218.
32. Ibid., pp. 224-8.
33. For a detailed discussion on this emerging Maratha identity, see Rosalind O'Hanlon, *Caste, Conflict and Ideology*, pp. 41-9.
34. Ibid., pp. 229-46.
35. For a detailed discussion of the cow-protection movements in various parts of India, see John R. Mclane, *Indian Nationalism and the Early Congress*, pp. 271-331; Gyan Pandey, 'Rallying round the Cow: Sectarian Strife in the Bhojpuri Region c. 1888-1917', in Ranajit Guha, *Subaltern Studies, II*, pp. 60-129; Sandria B. Freitag, *Collective Action and Community*, pp. 148-74; Peter Robb, 'The Challenge of Gau Mata: British Policy and Religious Change

in India, 1880-1916', *Modern Asian Studies*, 20, 2 (1986), pp. 285-319.

36. Christine Dobbin, *Urban Leadership in Western India*, pp. 257-8.
37. JD, 1893, vol. 194, p. 156.
38. Home Department (Public), August 1994, Proceedings. nos. 214-20, p. 11, letter from Dinshaw Maneckji Petit to the Secretary to the JD, GOB, dated 26 May 1894.
39. Ibid., p. 14.
40. Ibid., p. 12.
41. Ibid., p. 11.
42. Peter Robb says that 'whatever the undoubted influence of different social and economic forces, the identification was inevitably anti-Muslim', 'The Challenge of Gau Mata', p. 292. It might be so in north India, but it seems that in its earlier phase in Bombay the movement was sustained by a variety of intentions. The involvement of respectable Parsis and other non-Hindus meant that it was not primarily disposed towards a militant communal tone in the beginning.
43. Home Department (Special), 1893, F. no. 1002, p. 373. *MSA*.
44. Ibid., p. 374.
45. Ibid., p. 375.
46. JD, 1893, vol. 194, pp. 157-8.
47. McLane, *Indian Nationalism and the Early Congress*, p. 304.
48. Home Department (Special), 1893, F. no. 1002, p. 374.
49. Ibid., p. 375.
50. Letter by Ameer Mahomed Khan to BG, p. 42.
51. McLane, *Indian Nationalism and the Early Congress*, p. 304.
52. Home Department (Special), 1893, p. 378.
53. Ibid., p. 171.
54. Home Department (Public), August 1894, Proceedings nos. 214-20, p. 13.
55. Home Department (Special), 1893, p. 376.
56. JD, 1894, vol. 281/94, p. 3.
57. JD, 1893, vol. 194, p. 158.
58. Home Department (Special), 1893, p. 377.
59. Ibid., pp. 377-8.
60. Ibid., p. 378.
61. JD, 1894, vol. 281/94, p. 3.
62. Ibid., p. 3.
63. Home Department (Special), 1893, p. 380.
64. Home Department (Public), August 1894, Proceedings nos. 214-20; letter from R.H. Vincent to the Under Secretary, JD, GOB.
65. JD, 1894, vol. 281/94, p. 3.

66. Home Department (Public), August 1894, Proceedings nos. 214-20; letter from R.H. Vincent to the Under Secretary, JD, GOB.
67. JD, 1894, vol. 281/94, p. 3.
68. Home Department (Public), August 1894, Proceedings nos. 214-20; letter from R.H.Vincent to the Under Secretary, JD, GOB.
69. Home Department (Special), 1893, pp. 380-1.
70. Quoted in the Pioneer; given in *BG*, p. 48.
71. JD, 1893, vol. 194, p. 155.
72. JD, 1894, vol. 281/94, p. 3.
73. *BG*, p. ii.
74. JD, 1894, vol. 281/94, p. 3.
75. Home Department (Special), 1893, p. 383.
76. *BG*, p. 11.
77. JD, 1893, vol. 194, p. 156.
78. *TOI*, 12 August 1893. According to S.M. Edwardes, however, this riot was a result of 'a very indiscreet article on the Muhammadan religion which was published in . . . a Parsi newspaper'. S.M. Edwardes, *The Bombay City Police: A Historical Sketch, 1672-1916* (London, 1923), pp. 36-7.
79. *TOI*, 12 August, 1893. Edwardes again gives a slightly different version: 'the Parsi-Muhammadan riots of February, 1874 . . . ensued upon an ill-timed and improper attack upon the Prophet Muhammad, written and published by a Parsi in a daily newspaper', in Edwardes, ibid., p. 68.
80. JD, 1894, vol. 281/94, p. 1.
81. Ibid., p. 1. On 10 August, in a meeting of the Gaupalan Mandali in Madhav Bagh, many speakers asked the Hindus to be prepared as the Muslims would create disturbances on 11 August.
82. Ibid., p. 4. The following account of the riots is based on the this document as well as the BG and the *TOI*.
83. Ibid., p. 5.
84. Ibid., p. 5.
85. *TOI*, August.
86. JD, 1894, vol. 281/94, p. 6.
87. Given in ibid., p. 13.
88. Ibid., p. 7.
89. *TOI*, 14 August.
90. Ibid.
91. JD, 1894, vol. 281/94, p. 7.
92. Ibid., p. 7.
93. Ibid., p. 8. Also, BG, p. 6. The burial parties were sometimes a popular way of duping the authorities. It was reported that in the course of the Muslim-Parsi riots of 1874, 'hundreds of Mahomedans accompanied the well-covered biers

of some Mahomedans to the Sonapore burying ground, where it was discovered that, while only one of the biers contained a corpse, the others were filled with clubs and weapons of formidable character, which the mourners, on their way homeward, used against the Parsees residing in the street near the Dady Sett fire-temple'.

94. *BG*, pp. 6-7.
95. JD, 1894, vol. 281/94, p. 7.
96. *TOI*, 14 August.
97. JD, 1894, vol. 281/94, p. 8.
98. *BG*, p. 9.
99. Ibid., p. 20.
100. JD, 1894, vol. 281/94, p.10.
101. *BG*, pp. 9, 13 and 28.
102. McLane, *Indian Nationalism*, p. 308.
103. Ibid., p. 274.
104. Ibid., p. 273, 296, 308.
105. Freitag, *Collective Action and Community*, pp. 148-74.
106. Robb, 'The Challenge of Gau Mata', p. 292.
107. Ibid., p. 291.
108. Gyan Pandey, 'Rallying round the Cow', p. 63.
109. Dipesh Chakrabarty, 'Communal Riots and Labour: Bengal Jute Mill Hands in the 1890s', Occasional Paper no. 11, October 1976, Centre for Studies in Social Sciences, Calcutta.
110. Dipesh Chakrabarty and Ranajit Das Gupta, 'Some Aspects of Labour History of Bengal in the Nineteenth Century : Two Views', Occasional Paper no. 40, October 1981, CSSS, Calcutta, p. 7.
111. Ibid., p. 22.
112. Chakrabarty, *Rethinking Working-Class History*, p. 212.
113. Das Gupta, 'Material Conditions and Behavioural Aspects of Calcutta Working Class, 1875-1899', Occasional Paper no. 22, January 1979, CSSS, Calcutta; Das Gupta, 'Some Aspects of Labour History'; A.K. Bagchi, 'Working Class Consciousness', *EPW*, vol. XXV, no. 30 (28 July 1990), PE54-PE60; Parimal Ghosh, 'Communalism and Colonial Labour: Experience of Calcutta Jute Mill Workers, 1880-1930', *EPW*, vol. XXV, no. 30 (28 July 1990), PE61-PE72.
114. JD, 1893, vol. 194, p. 157.
115. *TOI*, 15 August 1893.
116. *BG*, 13 August 1893.
117. JD, 1894, vol. 281/94, pp. 2 and 5.
118. *BG*, p. 31.
119. *Deccan Budget*; given in *BG*, p. 45.

120. *Indian Spectator, BG*, p. 45.
121. Home Department (Public), Proceedings nos. 169-89, 1893, p. 72.
122. *BG*, p. 35.
123. Ibid., p. 39.
124. Letter by Lakhmidas Khimji, in *BG*, p. 40.
125. *BG*, p. 40.
126. Ibid., pp. 31-5.
127. Ibid., p. 39.
128. JD, 1893, vol. 194, p. 158.
129. Jim Masselos, 'Change and Custom in the Format of the Bombay Mohurrum during the Nineteenth and Twentieth Centuries', *South Asia*, n.s., 5, no. 2 (1982), p. 57.
130. Jim Masselos, 'Power in the Bombay "Mohollas" 1904-15: An Initial Exploration into the World of the Indian Urban Muslim', in *South Asia*, 6 (December 1976), pp. 83-7.

CHAPTER 5

The Nationalist Links: The Protests Against Tilak's Conviction in 1908

THE COTTON MILL workers were the crucial component of the crowds which participated in violent protests following Tilak's imprisonment and conviction in June-July 1908. This agitation was an important landmark not only in the history of the workers' movement but also in the history of the relationship between the nationalist leadership and the working classes. These events attracted wide attention and Lenin thought that 'the proletariat (in India) has already developed to conscious political mass struggle'.[1] This observation of Lenin set the trend for the historians of the Left in general and from the former Soviet Union in particular. Thus D.C. Home described these events as a 'class conscious action of the working class'.[2] L.A. Gordon, writing about the 1908 strikes and protests, suggests that prior to this, there were 'vigorous activities' by 'the radical democratic wing of the Indian national movement among the Bombay proletariat'.[3] He further asserts that 'the Bombay strike was no longer a spontaneous outburst of the workers. It was a more or less conscious anti-imperialist and democratic movement.'[4] Similarly, A.I. Chicherov states that the 'political strike of the Bombay proletariat in 1908 vividly revealed that the Indian working class was already taking an active part in the national movement'.[5]

On the other hand, V.B. Karnik thinks that it was just 'a spontaneous and elemental outburst'. According to him, it was only 'a momentary affair. It blazed for a few days and then died without leaving a trace. There was no repetition of that revolutionary action for many years. It left no memories; it left no landmark. Workers were soon back at work as if nothing happened.'[6] Richard Cashman also agrees with him.[7]

The contemporary colonial authorities themselves were puzzled by the enormous response given by the workers and others on this issue. One official stated: 'I am compelled to say that the ignorance of the Bombay police as to the agency and methods used for engineering the strike is nothing short of appalling.' He concluded that these events were 'a spontaneous exhibition on the part of the mill hands'.[8]

On the other hand, the Commissioner of Police, Bombay, commented: 'I do not think (that) the movement was spontaneous.'[9] This view was supported by the Governor of Bombay who wrote that 'the conspiracy in this part of India (is) better organised than I thought'.[10] S.M. Edwardes, writing later, asserted that 'the trouble was not a sudden and spontaneous outburst of popular feeling and that the rebellious mill-hands were the victims of an unscrupulous agitation, based on malevolent falsehood'.[11]

Between these two extreme views one has to tread cautiously in order to find the level at which organization and spontaneity constantly intermingled; one has also to delineate the complex nature of workers' consciousness where elements of anti-imperialist and democratic consciousness interpenetrated with religious consciousness which perceived Tilak as a magico-religious figure and harbinger of better days.

In the early period, there was a near unanimity in the Indian press of all opinions that legislative interference in labour issues was unnecessary and uncalled-for. Initially, most of the nationalists were not interested in labour matters. They were almost completely silent on the extreme hardships endured by the workers in the industrial situation. There is no mention about the 'misery of the labouring classes' in Ranade's *Essays on Indian Economics*, or in vigorous speeches and writings of Dadabhai Naoroji, or in R.C. Dutt's massive *Economic History of India*. There was no reference to the problems of the workers in the early resolutions of the Indian National Congress.

Right since the first Factory Commission was appointed in 1875 to investigate the working conditions of the Bombay factory workers, nationalist opinion was critical of any sort of legislative enactment on this issue.[12] When the Bill was introduced in the Legislative Council in 1879 and after the Factory Act was passed in 1881, the nationalists bitterly opposed even these half-hearted measures to ameliorate the conditions of the mill workers. The *Amrit Bazar Patrika* set the tone for this strident reaction by declaring that 'A larger death rate amongst our operatives is far more preferable to the collapse of this rising industry.'[13] Later on it rubbed the point, a little heartlessly: 'If great zulum (tyranny) is practised upon them (workers), why do they not seek employment elsewhere?'[14]

Among the nationalists of the Bombay Presidency the uproar was even more marked as the Act was basically concerned about the factories in Bombay. In the words of the *Quarterly Journal of the Poona Sarvajanik Sabha* there was not 'the least justification for a legislative enactment to regulate factory labour'.[15] Many arguments were advanced to show that the lot of the factory workers was better than many others in India. Even the children, for all their long hours in the mills, were said to 'enjoy better health than those who attend school'.[16]

The reason behind this extreme reaction by the nationalist press was the involvement of the Lancashire's cotton mill owners who visualized the Indian cotton mills as competitors, particularly in the Indian market, and sought to deny them any advantage. Thus *Mahratra* (13 March 1881), in its reaction to the government's first labour legislation, bewailed: 'our factories are ruined . . . the infant industry is doomed'.[17] The *Bombay Samachar* thought that 'since no hardships are actually so inflicted (on the workers), the Act cannot achieve any good purpose'. It further added that the colonial government was doing so only in the interests of the 'Manchester cotton manufacturers'.[18] The *Gujarat Mitra* (20 March 1881) was certain that the law was enacted only to serve the 'selfish' motives of the British cotton industry and 'the measure is certain to make the condition of the mill-labourers worse than it is'.[19] The editor of the *Indian Spectator* was sarcastic and more aggressive: 'It seems the lachrymose wails and philanthropic denunciations of a few short-sighted enthusiasts, worked up by the saints of Manchester, have been too much for a hysteric Government to resist.'[20]

There was almost a repeat performance by the nationalist press during the later process of the appointment of the Factory Commissions of 1885 and 1890 and the passing of the Factory Act of 1891. Here again the nationalists were suspicious about the Manchester's professed interest in the welfare of Indian labour, critical about government's interference, protective about the indigenous industry and dismissive about the alleged poverty and misery of the workers.[21]

The issue was joined again in 1905 when the *Times of India*, on 13 September, in an article entitled 'The Bombay Slaves', depicted the miserable conditions of the Bombay mill workers and demanded its mitigation through state interference. The moderate opinion expressed through papers like *Rast Goftar*, *Oriental Review*, *Jam-e-Jamshed* supported it and condemned the 'inhuman practice of exacting work from the mill operatives for 15 hours at a stretch'.[22] And the *Indian Social Reformer* later congratulated the *TOI* 'on the success of its endeavours to mitigate the evil of long hours in the local mills'.[23] There were workers' meetings supported and organized by the Maratha Aikyechhoo Sabha to memorialize the government to ameliorate the conditions of the workers. But the nationalist opinion was generally hostile. The *Praja Bandhu* (24 September 1905), while conceding 'certain well-known defects in the present-day management of the cotton mills', was critical of the 'hysterical' manner in which these views were ventilated. It queried whether it was 'meant to be a counterblast to the Swadeshi movement' and declared that the 'agitation must have been inspired by the vested interests in Lancashire and their agents in Bombay'.[24] The *Bombay Samachar* wrote that 'the meeting was a hollow demonstration got up by wire-pulling from behind'.[25] The *Indu Prakash* published articles by V.A. Talcherkar (who later became the president of the Kamgar Hitwardhak Sabha) and S. Tavde attacking the stand taken by the *TOI* and claiming that the conditions of the workers were not so bad.[26] The *Mahratra* dismissed the report by the *TOI* as 'a hollow ebullition based more on imagination than on facts'. It further remarked: 'Is it not significant that the eyes of the Anglo-Indian editor should be attracted by the so-called slavery of mill-hands, when slavery of a more real and crushing kind is to be met with in so many other walks of Indian life mainly as a result of foreign rule in the land?'[27]

When, faced with agitating workers, critical public opinion and the threat of the government intervention, the BMOA passed a resolution asking the millowners to restrict their hours of work to 12 in a day, the extremist nationalist opinion was censorious of the move to pressurize the Association. The *Kal* thought that there was an organized conspiracy to force the millowners 'by means of riots'.[28] The *Vihari* bitterly criticized the BMOA for such proposal to reduce the working hours, almost suggesting an exclusion of the concerned workers from the 'people of India': 'It is a great shame that the mill-owners should have acted upon the suggestion of the *TOI* to shorten the hours of labour in the mills. The lot of the people of India is a thousand times worse than that of the so-called Bombay slaves, and the *TOI* advocates a perpetuation of their lot of servitude.'[29]

The *Mahratra* condemned the 'riots' by the millworkers against the long hours of work and contended that the 'so-called "slaves of Bombay" have ... come forward in good time to help the *TOI*' in its 'irresponsible' agitation and was sure that it all was 'being carefully manufactured by a kind of wire-pulling'.[30] In a similar vein, the *Kalpataru* wrote: 'The Swadeshi movement will possibly cause some new mills to be started in

Calcutta. To nip them in the bud, the Bombay *TOI* had shed crocodile tears for the mill-hands under the pretext of humanity.' Although it admitted that the workers should not be worked for such long hours, the reason behind the agitation, it asserted, was the 'sordid animosity of Europeans against the Indians' and then warned that 'these Europeans will receive what they pay us . . . at quadruple interest'. It finally summed up the stated and unstated arguments of the nationalists: 'There was a custom among the Hindus to offer a living human being to propitiate the goddess or god concerned at the time of building a castle or a palace. We have to build a nation and it matters not if all the mill hands are placed at the altar of martyrdom.'[31]

In this unanimity of opinions, the *Kal*, edited by a Tilakite, Paranjape, introduced a discordant note not by supporting the workers on this issue but by seeing in them a potential ground for nationalist mobilization. It asserted that 'If any patriot were to make an industrious effort, he could easily get up a mass meeting of 25,000 mill operatives.' It praised the workers for their use of 'native-made articles' and added that the: mill operatives are deeply imbued with patriotism and earnest zeal to further the cause of the Swadeshi movement. These people deserve to be congratulated upon the fact that the seed of patriotism, which inspires man to put forth every possible effort for the progress of their country, has taken firm roots in their minds. We want such men for furthering the cause of our country.[32]

The nationalist reaction was prompted by the twin concern for the promotion of the indigenous industry and opposition to the colonial government. They were not so much opposed to the betterment in the conditions of the workers as such unless it supposedly clashed with the interests of the Indian industries. And, as in social matters or even more so because here even some moderates had joined in, the government interference in labour issues was perceived as undesirable and industrial reforms were considered as an internal matter. Thus, in 1890, the *Mahratra* advised the millowners to allow one day of weekly rest to the workers,[33] and was pleased to note that the BMOA had proposed that the workers should be given one full holiday in a week and the mills should close two hours earlier on the previous day for cleaning.[34]

When the workers' interests clashed with those of the colonial state, the nationalists, particularly the extremist variety, supported the workers fully. This was illustrated by the support extended by the nationalists to the strike by the signallers of the GIP Railway in 1899. The support did not remain confined to words and the nationalist press issued appeals to the public for raising funds for the strikers.[35] Similarly, regarding the conditions of the mint workers the *Madhukar* wrote, 'The *Times of India* was profuse in its sympathy with these "Bombay slaves", but what has our contemporary to say about the slaves at the mint? As the mint is a Government concern, the *Times* is perfectly silent over the hardships of the Mint employees. But why is the Mint worked for such long hours?'[36]

In the event of a postal strike, the nationalists supported the striking employees. The *Indu Prakash* (18 August 1906) requested the public not to blame the strikers for their inconvenience because 'In a quarrel between the rich and the poor, it is so easy to take the side of the rich.' It held the postal authorities responsible 'who by their own attitudes brought the men to their frame of mind'.[37] The *Mahratra* also supported the strike and criticized the authorities for their 'half-hearted response' to the demands submitted by the employees who had 'real grievances'.[38] The *Kesari* went further and professed the need for trade unions in India:

> In civilised countries there are trade-unions to safeguard the interests of the labour against the tyranny of capital. . . . There is an outcry against the long hours of work prevailing in Indian mills, but Government seems to be heedless of the conditions of labour in some of their own concerns like the Post Office. If strikes are regarded as a legitimate weapon of agitation in Europe, why should they be considered illegal in India, which is crushed under the domination of foreign traders and highly-paid bureaucrats?[39]

In the course of the celebrations of the Ganapati festival in Poona, Tilak 'urged the necessity for having unions and organizations throughout the country similar to those in England, America and Russia to represent the grievances of the public', and said that the recent strike of postal peons in Bombay failed 'for want of a union'.[40]

But this sympathy for labour and the need for their organization evaporated when the Textile Factories Labour Committee and the Indian Factory Labour Commission were appointed in 1906 and 1907 respectively. The nationalist press opposed any recommendations regarding 'reduction in the hours of labour or the prohibition of the labour of women and children.'[41] Any 'state interference' was considered 'highly injurious to the best interests of the mill-industry'[42] and the government was advised to direct its attention to the rural 'millions who suffer from fevers, cholera, plague and disastrous famines',[43] as if the workers were not part of this multitude, and the 'Lancashire men' were sarcastically told to hold their 'milk of human kindness' for the 'bond-slave of the hosiery or any other trade in England' instead of transmitting it 'six thousand miles away in order to gladden the life of the poor Indian operative'.[44] Some of the papers also protested against the non-inclusion of Indian members on the Committee[45] and some expressed their surprise over the fact that the 'Mill-owners' Association has not yet entered its protest against the one-sided constitution of the Committee.'[46]

The criticism against the appointment of TFLC continued in the Indian-owned press till the Committee gave its reports in May 1907. Its recommendations were thought to be innocuous.[47] And yet misgivings were expressed on the need of state interference in the matters of labour in the Indian-owned concerns. The *Kesari* (4 June 1907) neatly expressed the arguments: 'The Factories Committee has issued its report. We would not object to its recommendations regarding better hygienic conditions in the mills, but we do not think that the textile industry in India has made such progress as to necessitate the regulation of working hours by special legislations. We think the matter may be left to be decided by mutual agreement between millowners and their employees.'[48] Even stronger sentiments were expressed on the appointment of and recommendations of the IFLC.[49]

The tables seemed to have turned and the opposing camps changed their positions with the events of June and July 1908 as the mill workers prominently took part in the demonstrations and protests against the imprisonment and conviction of Tilak. While the Anglo-Indian papers like the *TOI*, followed by some of the Indian papers, condemned the incidents and put the blame on the 'wire-pullers', the nationalist, particularly the extremist nationalist press defended the actions of the workers on the grounds that the public believed that Tilak 'had been dealt with unjustly'.[50] The *Kesari* praised the workers as 'the descendants of those Maratha warriors whose fame for bravery and daring had once spread throughout the whole of India'.[51] The *Kal* denounced the government for inflicting 'barbarous sentences on popular leaders' and for 'spilling the blood of poor mill-hands in the streets of Bombay'. It asked the public to contribute to the funds 'in aid of the mill-hands', and declared: 'It is our duty to help the mill-hands in every way. The masses are our divinity. Had we worshipped them instead of government, the result would have been more encouraging.'[52]

As was clear, however, the nationalist motive was to praise and enlist the support of the workers for the nationalist cause and not to work systematically towards the mitigation of their conditions of work and living. Tilak's own speeches and activities also confirmed this.

Before 1905, Tilak did not show much interest in Bombay city. In 1905, to promote the message of Swadeshi, he launched the Swadeshi Vastu Pracharini Sabha which held several meetings there during 1905-6.[53] On 15 October 1905, he spoke in a Swadeshi meeting in Bombay where it was resolved 'to encourage . . . the use of country-made goods', to urge the millowners 'to stop increasing the price of locally manufactured clothes' and to completely stop using the foreign-made, specially English, goods.[54] Again on 22 and 25 October, speaking in 'largely attended' meetings, he urged people to promote the cause of Swadeshi and the necessity to boycott English goods.[55] On 9 September, 7 October and 21 October 1906, in the meetings in different parts of the city, he exhorted the people to 'further the cause of *Swadeshism*', to learn from the 'awakening of Persia, China and Afghanistan', and raise the export from India and reduce imports.[56] During this period he tried to mobilize the support of the middle classes, traders and the mill owners. While he managed to enlist the support of the traders and some sections of the middle classes, the mill owners rebuffed him.[57] However, no approach to the workers had been made so far.

In 1907, for the first time, Tilak showed some practical interest in the mill workers. During 1907-8, he addressed a few meetings of the workers in the city. In one of the meetings held at Chinchpoogly on 15 December 1907, he exhorted the workers to unite to promote Swadeshi which he described as the 'only remedy for our utter destitution'. He further urged the workers to abandon the consumption of liquor. He said that the colonial government wants them to drink alcohol to increase its revenue. He promised that if they acted according to his advice, their 'condition will improve', and they 'will command respect like the working class in England.'[58] In March 1908, in a workers' meeting he was reported to have said: 'Bombay belongs to you. It does not belong to the rich. If someone asks me to whom Bombay belongs, I will say it belongs to the labourers. If you do not work, the Bombay mills will have to be closed.'[59]

In another meeting held on 6 June 1908, on the occasion of a Satyanarayan Puja held by the mill workers at Victoria Road, he again spoke about the bad effects of liquor and criticized the government for encouraging drunkenness. He also 'advised the mill hands, especially the Jobbers and Head Jobbers, to form committees of mill hands in their respective mills for the purpose of discouraging liquor drinking among the mill hands'.[60]

He spoke to the mill workers on a few other occasions as well and although his speeches were basically concerned with nationalist issues and were not on specific labour problems, he seemed to have become quite popular among the workers. On his initiative, an organization called The Bombay Millhands Defence Association was also formed.[61] But it did not seem to have lasted long.

After his release from prison in 1914, Tilak did not remain much in contact with the Bombay mill workers. But, in the later years of his life, he seems to have been influenced by the Fabian Socialist, Joseph Baptista, who was his close associate from 1914 till the end.[62] Under this influence he occasionally expressed some pro-labour views. Therefore, in 1920, he was reported to have said that it was 'the duty of the Government to make the mill owners give better wages and to introduce legislation for the purpose, if necessary, and to introduce a profiteering law or real control of prices'.[63] How far this reflected Tilak's actual opinion is difficult to say because during most of his active life he battled against any legislative interference by the colonial government in Indian affairs. His pro-labour stand, however, cannot be denied as it was stated again in the Manifesto of the Congress Democratic Party drafted by Tilak in 1920. There he declared his support for 'a fair share of the fruits of labour, a fair minimum wage, reasonable hours of work, decent house accommodation' for the workers.[64] But such occasions were too few to be taken as his unstinted support for the cause of labour. This was evident in his speech on 29 November 1919 in a meeting behind the Elphinstone Mills in Bombay where he said that 'Everyone in this country could be described as a majur or labourer' and that there should be no distinction 'between men as labourers and masters.'[65]

Some of the Home Rulers like Joseph Baptista, Kanji Dwarkadas and B.G. Horniman were active among the workers in the post-war period. But they 'remained "outsiders" without control and sustained organized contact with the workmen'.[66] Their ineffective links with the workers were evident during three incidents between 1918 and 1920. In 1918, the influenza epidemic ravaged Bombay killing hundreds of people. The Home Rulers wanted to launch their own relief service but were unable to do so because of lack of organization. They were ultimately forced to join hands with N.M. Joshi's Social Service League.[67]

In the second instance, the Home Rulers tried to mobilize the workers to oppose the meeting called for presenting a memorial to the retiring governor, Lord Willingdon. Although they managed to mobilize a fair number of people, their support mainly came from the 'cloth markets and the personal followings of the Home Rule leaders'.[68]

The weak influence of the Home Rulers on the workers was again evident during the general strike in the cotton mills in 1919 and the strike of the postal workers in 1920. In both cases the Home Rulers, although involved in the strikes, did not have the capacity to influence the actions of the workers either way.[69]

This period also witnessed the emergence of Gandhi as an important nationalist leader. In the course of the Rowlatt Satyagraha, Gandhi visited Bombay and, on 4 April 1919, addressed a meeting of the mill workers near the Elphinstone Mill. Taking an ambiguous stand on involving the workers in the movement, Gandhi told them 'not to come out on Sunday unless they could obtain leave from their masters'. During the course of the Satyagraha, particularly on 10 and 11 April when the news of Gandhi's arrest had reached Bombay, the city witnessed quite a bit of turbulent activities by the crowds and cavalry charge and firing by the police. But the mill workers were only marginally involved in the events. In a meeting with Gandhi on 11 April the police authorities extracted a promise from him that 'he would not . . . do anything to induce the mill hands to join and . . . he would see that his Agents did not make any attempt to stir up unrest in that quarter'. Gandhi was reported to have told the authorities that 'he had no intention of bringing the mill-hands into the movement "probably for many a long day"'.[70] In view of Gandhi's dislike for the modern industry, it was not surprising that he was not very comfortable with the idea of involving the Bombay mill workers in his movement particularly because of the linguistic barrier and the indulgence of the crowd in occasional violence, another bugbear of his. Thus, with the ascendancy of Gandhi in the Congress and in nationalist politics, even the tenuous links between the Bombay workers and the nationalists seem to have further weakened.

Against this background of ambiguous and indifferent relationship between the nationalists and the mill workers in Bombay the events of 1908 stood as a towering instance of protest by the workers for the nationalist cause.

Tilak was arrested on 24 June 1908 in consequence of the articles he wrote in defence of the revolutionary terrorist tactics of Khudiram Bose and others. The first hearing of his case in the court was on 29 June. The authorities thought that Tilak's influence was limited to the students and 'a section of Brahmins'.[71] But even on 29 June, the assessment of the authorities was called into question as a 'large crowd collected outside the court house' and started shouting slogans and behaving in what the police thought a 'disorderly' manner. On being dispersed by the police they congregated in a nearby field and were addressed by 'one Kanchan Kumar, a swadeshi preacher'. The gathering was dispersed again. But now the crowd began pelting the police and the passing Whites with stones. The police arrested eight men. But even after that groups of people roamed the streets stoning the court building and 'isolated Europeans'.[72]

The hearing had been adjourned till 13 July. The events of 29 June seemed to have caught the police 'unawares'.[73] Therefore, now more preparations were made to face any such situation. Notices were issued 'prohibiting assemblies throughout the city between certain dates', many jobbers and others in the mill areas were contacted and warned 'of danger they ran in fomenting trouble', almost all mill owners were asked to enforce order among their workers 'as it was generally rumoured that in the event of Tilak being convicted the operatives intended to strike and make a demonstration on a large scale'.[74] The police in the city was kept on alert, the assistance of the military was sought and on 12 July, 'the Bombay garrison was reinforced by four infantry companies of the Northamptonshire Regiment and two squadrons of light cavalry'.[75]

In this way, the authorities took all precautions to meet any situation arising out of the strike of mill workers or any other section of the Bombay population. The police and the cavalry were posted outside the court building. Despite that, on 13 July (when Tilak's trial began again and continued till 22 July), many 'mill hands and others made their way to the Fort and attempted to assemble in the vicinity of the High Court'. But they were not allowed to assemble by the police and the cavalry and were 'dispersed in the evening'.[76]

On 14 and 15 July, the workers remained calm, but again on 16 July, the workers of the Queen and Lakhmidas Mills struck work and went to see the trial. They were joined by 320 workers of four other mills. On 17 July, the workers of 28 mills had struck work. In the Greaves Cotton Mill, where there had been resistance by the mill authorities, the workers had also broken furniture to effect the strike. They were dispersed by the arrival of the police and the military. On Currey Road, they attacked three Whites who then took refuge in a Parsi-owned shop. The shop was wrecked by the workers but the lives of the Europeans were saved by the arrival of the police and cavalry. When the police moved towards the chawls to rescue another European, they were 'greeted with a volley of stones from inside the courtyard of a *chal'*. The police fired but, according to the Police Commissioner, no one was injured.[77]

The events of 17 July showed the main pattern the later events were to follow. The first was the total defiance of authority inside the mill. The workers not only did not pay any heed to the warnings of the mill managers, etc., for not striking work but became violent on being denied the leave. The second was their hatred against the Whites which manifested itself in such a marked way that the authorities concluded that 'there is no doubt that the feeling against Europeans was most hostile'.[78] The third was their defiance of the authority of the police and military whom they stoned whenever confronted, particularly choosing the Whites among them. There were seven major confrontations between the workers and other protesters, on the one hand, and the police and military, on the other, as reported by the police authorities, during the entire course of events, and firing took place in each case.[79]

Anti-authority and anti-White sentiments were running very high among the workers but it was not organized at a broader level and manifested itself in sporadic events occasionally taking the form of a generalized strike. So, while on 17 July, 28 mills had struck work, the next day, the workers of only one, the Crescent Mill, had walked out. On 19 July, being Sunday, a holiday, all mills were closed, 'but everything was quiet'. But again on 20 July, the workers of Jacob Sassoon Mill, struck work and stoned the Morarji Goculdas Mill, bringing its workers out. When the police reached there, both together attacked the police, 'a European officer being especially picked out'. The workers fought a pitched battle with the police which fired on the crowd.[80] On 21 July, the workers of four mills struck work and posters in Marathi were found in the Petit mills stating: 'Why are you asleep! Awake, be ready, and assist your Parel comrades. Defile the mothers of the European police.'[81]

It was also reported that the Ghati labourers working in Mandvi, Masjid Bunder, Khand Bazaar, Argyle Road, the Docks and the adjacent localities became restive and it was only the intervention of the police that seemed to prevent the 'trouble'.[82]

On 22 July, while all mills were working normally, a six-year deportation sentence was passed on Tilak. The employees of the Mulji Jetha market decided to boycott work for six days, one day each for one year of Tilak's sentence. Even when the news reached the mill area on 23 July, only nine mills stopped working, though it was reported that a large number of mill workers 'were induced to take oaths not to work on certain days'.[83] It is clear, however, that the oaths were not very effective in themselves and the time-honoured method of stoning the mills was resorted to time and again to effect strikes on each day.

On 24 July, all the mills in the mill area and some others as well stopped working. The events on that day were typical and closely resembled those of 17 July but with much greater ferocity. The Police Commissioner reported:

> This morning 70 mills stopped work. At an early hour some mill hands belonging to the Western India Mill situated at Kala Chowki Road stoned the Bombay Cotton Mill which had commenced work, with the result that the employees came out and joined them. The crowd then proceeded along Chinchpoogly Road when they stoned the Rachel Sassoon Mill and the E.D. Sassoon Mill, causing the employees to come out. At this juncture Superintendent Mayers and Sub-Inspector Finan arrived on the scene and they kept the crowd moving along Chinchpoogly Road till it reached its junction with Albert Road. Here other Police Officers came up and the mob divided into two parties. One went into Albert Road and brought the hands of the City of Bombay Mill out by stoning the mill, who joined with them, and were dispersed by a party of cavalry under Lieutenant Summers, while the other drove the Police down the Chinchpoogly Road stoning them to such an extent that they had to fire their revolvers on them, killing three and wounding others.[84]

Such events continued throughout the day in various parts of the city, particularly the mill areas,[85] each episode invariably ending with police firing. It seemed as if some ritual was performed again and again. On that day alone, according to police reports, eleven people were killed and several injured.[86]

On 25 July also, most of the mills were closed and a few, like the Textile Mill which had started to work in the morning, were forced to close by the stone-throwing workers who 'attempted to wreck the mill, and attacked the European employees'. The police and military were called and firing was resorted to. Two of the protesters died and yet the mood of the crowd remained defiant.[87]

On 26 July, when the Governor came to Bombay from Poona to help in restoring peace, the protests intensified. The workers, the employees of the trading shops, the students and others blocked the road through which the Governor was to pass. It was reported:

> Black flags were hung across the street with Tilak's photographs and the words 'Tilak Maharaj-ki-jai' on them. The street became blocked from end to end with

dense crowd of people, all hostile and demonstrative. A party of European and Native Police came on the scene to clear the street and restore order, and as the crowd refused to disperse they charged them repeatedly. The crowd retaliated by stoning the police. A party of Cavalry with the Deputy Commissioner passed through later on and stones were thrown at them also. At about 5-20 p.m. a detachment of the Northamptonshire Regiment came up and they also were pelted with stones. . . . Four rounds were fired and four persons were picked up wounded.[88]

Events of a similar nature, in which the people defied the police and the military to register their protests, continued till 28 July, the sixth day after 23 July, the day on which oaths were supposedly taken not to work for six days. But even on 29 July, all was not quiet. At Sewri, a few mills were stoned and most of the workers had still not gone to work.[89] The mill areas were constantly in turmoil throughout the week. S.M. Edwardes, on the basis of his personal experience, observed:

Within the mill-district the rioting was fairly continuous and occasionally serious, and isolated Europeans whose duties obliged them to reside in the area north of Jacob's Circle found it wise to vacate their houses for the time being and seek shelter in Mazagaon, the Fort and other parts. Much damage was done to mill property, and in several encounters with the mob the European police were forced to use their revolvers and the troops had to fire in self-defence. The Indian cavalry were stoned from the *chals* on more than one occasion, and small parties of unarmed police fared badly at the hands of the rioters, who had accumulated considerable stores of brick-bats and road-metals at convenient vantage-points.[90]

The official figures of the total number of deaths in police and military firing was put at 16, the number of injured at 43, and those of arrested at 60.[91] But, according to unofficial estimates, the numbers of dead and injured in police action were 30 and 100 respectively.[92]

What propelled the workers to resort to such unprecedented levels of defiance to register their protests against official action against Tilak? The most favourite contemporary official explanation, supported by a large section of the press, was an organized conspiracy by Tilak and his followers. Following the lead given by the *Times of India*, the editor of the *Rast Goftar* was sure that 'Some secret organization is at work which has been responsible for the painful incidents which have convulsed Bombay for a week.'[93] These papers severely condemned the forces which instigated 'the mob to riot and disorder',[94] which 'either covertly or openly' incited 'the mill hands to violence',[95] and which converted the

'Peace-loving Bombay . . . into another Moscow.'[96] Later they regretted the fact that the government was not able to find out and arrest the 'miscreants, the ring-leaders and the wire-pullers'.[97] Edwardes, commenting on the events, asserted that the agitation was the handiwork of 'Tilak's agents and followers', some of whom were said to have 'declared during the trial that there would be a day's bloodshed for every year to which he might be sentenced by the Court'. His explanation of the *modus operandi* employed by 'Tilak's revolutionaries' was simple: 'Most of the "jobbers" who control the supply of labour were easily won over, and Tilak's Brahman emissaries from Poona found many co-adjutors among their own caste-men in Bombay, and among the Bhandaris and Konkani Marathas. . . .'[98]

The pro-Tilak section of the press, however, completely discounted this interpretation of the 'disturbances' by stating that 'all this talk of secret emissaries is unmitigated moonshine'.[99] Some mocked the government for failing to discover the supposed roots of the conspiracy: 'How is it that the smart Investigation Department of Bombay is not able to lay hands at these emissaries?'[100]

The Bombay police authorities were quite confused about the agency behind the 'disorder'. In a revealing sentence the Commissioner of Police wrote that the mill workers had 'no organisation, no leader, no common object and no weapons other than stones'.[101] The 'extremist' nationalist press also queried: 'why ill-fed, ill-clad and half-starved people should by one common impulse strike work and . . . do deeds, which expose them to the fire of trained military men?'[102] Their explanation was that the workers and others were agitated because of the injustice done to Tilak by the government.[103]

But Tilak was not the only one of the nationalist leaders to be on the receiving end of the prosecution by the Bombay Government. Many others were tried and convicted before him. Even when Tilak was convicted in 1897, there were no protests by the workers then. So what had changed by 1908?

As has been seen, the nationalists had not much practical interests in the workers. And whenever they took a stand it was not in favour of the mill workers even on a very crucial issue like the long hours of work. The workers were left to the non-Brahman activists and philanthropists like Bengali, Lokhanday, Bole and Keluskar who did some welfare and rudimentary organizational work among them. These people were not sympathetic to the Tilak's way of thinking. It is true that they did not have much influence on the activities of the workers but they were the only ones in touch with them.

A more immediate and potent form of influence on the workers was exercised by the jobbers. There are some evidences that Tilak and his followers had approached the jobbers in order to reach the workers. One jobber named Deoji Gunoo was said 'to possess great influence among mill hands generally'. He was one of those who 'had taken a prominent part in the movement started by Tilak'.[104] But these people, along with some others, were warned by the authorities not to create any problems. In any case, it would have been too much for any recognizable person to antagonize the authorities as well as the mill owners by inciting strikes and riots. Similarly, the 'Brahmin clerks' in the mills, whom the authorities, trying to find scapegoats, belatedly blamed for 'engineering' the riots,[105] had much to lose by any such activity. In fact, what rendered the task of law-enforcing agencies even more difficult was the absence of any recognizable bodies or persons whom they could approach or command to control the workers.

It is true that Tilak and his followers became somewhat active among the mill workers during 1907-8, but their involvement was too brief and impermanent; their activities and organization among the workers were never strong enough to mobilize support at this level when people would go for total defiance of authorities both at the workplace and outside it and dare to challenge the might of the state. The fearless resistance offered by the workers and others to the police and troops revealed the very strong motivation behind their protests. This motivation and zeal derived from a source different from what the organization and activities by a few half-interested individuals could manage.

Scholars have shown in other contexts the perception of Gandhi as a magico-religious figure by the masses who were ready to sacrifice their lives on his supposed appeals.[106] These were done even when Gandhi's connection with the involved people was much more remote. Tilak had been more closely involved with Bombay politics and the workers had seen or heard him or about him since long. Right since the 1890s, Tilak had become involved in Bombay's political events. He was very much upset by the riots of 1893 in Bombay and other parts of India. He believed that they were the result of the policy of 'divide and rule initiated by Lord Dufferin'.[107] According to him, the responsibility for the riots in Bombay lay at the doors of the Muslims and the Bombay police who, despite having full knowledge of 'the possibility of a disturbance' had done nothing to stop it. The 'unjustifiable and impolitic' support extended to the Muslims against the Hindus by some Anglo-Indian officials like Vincent was, in his opinion, at the root of the problem. He also praised the mill workers for taking retaliatory action during the riots.[108]

In order to dissuade the Hindus from participating in the Muharram and to send a message to the British officials, he initiated the public celebration of the Ganapati festivals by introducing several changes in the format of this traditionally popular festival.[109] These innovations, though initially introduced in Poona, soon became popular throughout Maharashtra. Government officials feared that the festivals were a vehicle for spreading seditious messages and 'the possibility of overthrowing the British Government was not an uncommon subject among the Tilak faction in Poona'.[110] But it seems to be an overexcited reaction of an apprehensive officialdom and the festivals in the early years were mostly used as channels to unite the Hindus and berate the Muslims, if the songs sung during the celebrations were any indication. For example, one of the songs exhorted the Hindus to remember that:

> The Arya religion is superior, other religions will not help you
> The Ghodepir [Muslim *tabut*] is not worthy of your salutations.[111]

Another song went along the same lines:

> Oh! Why have you abandoned today the Hindu religion? . . .
> Do not at all venerate the *tabuts*,
> The cow is our mother, do not forget her.[112]

There were a profusion of similar songs and sentiments in the early phase of the movement. But Tilak also had other aims in mind. He wanted this and other festivals to become channels for the politicization of the masses. Once he commented in the *Kesari* (on 6 September 1896): 'Why shouldn't we convert the large religious festivals into mass political rallies? Will it not be possible for political activities to enter the humblest cottages of the villages through such means?'[113]

In Bombay city also these festivals were celebrated with much enthusiasm in various quarters. The approximate number of festivals celebrated in Bombay city were 35 in 1895, 68 in 1896, 40-4 in 1900, 45 in 1906 and 46 in 1908.[114] The Bombay workers had also established many of their own Ganapati festivals modelled on the new lines.

The nature and character of these festivals began to change after 1900. They now acquired an anti-government tone. Songs exhorting people to abandon liquor, to adopt Swadeshi, to oppose the policies of the government, to regenerate Indian industries began to be sung in many of the Ganapati *melas.* Although the negative references to the Muslim rulers still remained and the fights of the Marathas against them were highlighted, it was through these channels that Tilak and others endeavoured to take an anti-imperialist stance. Thus, in 1901, in the course of the Shivaji festival in Poona, he declared that 'Shivaji was greater than all European heroes' because he did not believe in appropriation of other's property but in the 'redemption of his religion and co-religionists and the deliverance of Brahmins and cattle from molestation at the hands of the Muhammedans'.[115] Again, in 1902, he praised the Boers in South Africa who fought against the British by adopting a 'system of warfare . . . which Shivaji had adopted against the Muhammadans'.[116] The Bombay Police Commissioner, therefore, noted in 1910:

> The movement which began as an opposition show to the local Musalman festival began to assume the character of an annual anti-Government eruption. Exhortations to use home-made clothes, the purity of Hinduism, social reform, the plague, Government measures generally and Lord Curzon in particular, the Congress, the Moderates, Lal, Bal, Pal and other persons of the official Demonology—these subjects under the tuition of the Extremist agents gradually formed the themes of the songs sung in the festival.[117]

Therefore, part of the political education of the workers in the nationalist ideology took place through the medium of these religious festivals and through religious, even communal, vocabulary. Beyond doubt, the workers had their own economic grievances and they were struggling to get these resolved. They also had anti-imperialist feelings through their experiences in the course of the famines and the plague. When Tilak came to attend their Puja and spoke to them on other occasions on temperance and Swadeshi exhorting them to remember their ancestry, they must have felt elated and gratified. Even before that, through Ganapati and Shivaji festivals, a process of deifying Tilak had started by putting his photographs beside those of Ganesh and Shivaji. The workers, who also initiated and participated in such festivals, must have known Tilak long before he came to speak to them. Thus, in the minds of the workers and the poor in general as well as the lower middle classes, the image of Tilak was that of a demi-God who was fighting against the British and suffering at the latter's hands for their benefit. So, when asked what Tilak had done for them, the workers 'unhesitatingly declared that he was fighting their battle with the Government and that he was prosecuted because he attempted to rescue the people from the demon of drink'.[118]

And when they were told that it was not due to this that he was convicted, 'they flew into a rage'.[119] For many workers he was 'an incarnation of Vishnu'.[120] More often than not religious channels were used to disseminate the views of Tilak. It was reported that Tilak's 'doings and sayings were further spread by the many religious Hindu preachers, who are daily in the habit of reading *Puranas* to the millhands in their *chals*'.[121] Some posters put in the mills and other places to mobilize people stated that 'the man who would continue to work would be thought guilty of killing kine'.[122]

The process of myth-making reached such an extent that superhuman stories had started to circulate. One, for example, was that 'the ship on which Tilak was being taken away had been turned back by Divine Providence.'[123] In this situation it was no wonder that the 'multitude of people believed that Tilak was an incarnation of God and that a diabolical Government had put him behind bars'.[124] This sentiment was reflected even in the slogans shouted by the workers like '*Tilak Maharaj ki Jai*' and in their demand put before S.M. Edwardes, when he went to the mill areas to pacify the workers: 'Let us have a look at Tilak Maharaj'.[125]

These were the sentiments which propelled the workers towards valiant and desperate acts to articulate their feelings of resentment. At the same time, however, this religious appeal alienated those sections of workers who came from different religious backgrounds. The Muslim workers, who formed a sizeable section of the total workforce, not only kept away from the movement but also resented it. The police authorities congratulated themselves for the fact that . . . throughout the trouble the Mahomedans kept aloof, though strenuous attempts were made by the Hindus to induce them to join forces. . . . It is believed that had the disturbances continued much longer this feeling might have eventually brought the Mahomedan operatives into actual collision with their Hindu co-workers'.[126]

Therefore, despite the lukewarm response of the nationalists, including Tilak, towards workers' grievances and the equivocal relationship between them, Tilak's personal appeal among all shades of Bombay workers remained quite high till the end. On 29 November 1919, a meeting attended by about 10,000 workers decided to present him 'an address'.[127] And, after his death in 1920, a general *hartal* was declared to pay obeisance to him. The workers also struck work in many mills and joined the demonstrators in large numbers. On 9 August 1920, the tenth day of his death, a general strike in the mills and other concerns was observed and it was reported that:

> No previous hartal had evoked so much interest among the mill-hands, the dock-labourers, and the railway workmen of Bombay. The mills were all shut, and though the docks and the railway workshops remained for the most part in action the men absented themselves therefrom in large numbers. Crowds streamed down to Chowpatty throughout the day for the purpose both of bathing in the sea and of visiting the spot where Tilak was cremated.[128]

The sentiments of the workers towards Tilak, therefore, operated in the arena where the religious and the political intermingled. The workers' protests against Tilak's imprisonment and their continued attachment to him cannot be explained by the fact of what he had done for them (which was pretty little) or even in terms of workers' nationalist feelings. Their strong motivation seemed to derive from a domain beyond these. At the same time, however, their actions cannot be taken out of the historical context which turned Tilak from a provincial (Maharashtrian) and city (Poona)-based politician into the most prominent Indian nationalist ranged against the might of the British government in support of the Indian, particularly Hindu, customs and practices and for the liberation of the Indian people from foreign domination. Therefore, what did not happen in 1897, at the time of his previous incarceration, became possible in 1908, particularly with the working classes of Bombay.

NOTES

1. V.I. Lenin, *The National Liberation Movement in the East* (Moscow, 1957), p. 15, quoted in A.I. Chicherov, 'Tilak's Trial and the Bombay Political Strike of 1908', in N.M. Goldberg and I.M. Reisner, eds., *Tilak and Struggle for Indian Freedom*, p. 546.
2. Quoted in ibid., p. 546.
3. L.A. Gordon, 'Social and Economic Conditions of Bombay Workers on the Eve of the 1908 Strike', in Goldberg and Reisner, eds., *Tilak and Struggle for Indian Freedom*, p. 471.
4. Ibid., p. 530.
5. A.I. Chicherov, 'Tilak's Trial and the Bombay Political Strike of 1908', in Goldberg and Reisner, ed., *Tilak and Struggle for Indian Freedom*, p. 545.
6. V.B. Karnik, *Strikes in India*, pp. 52-3, quoted in Cashman, *The Myth of the Lokamanya*, p. 184.
7. Cashman, *The Myth of the Lokamanya*, p. 184.

8. Home Political-A, December 1908, File nos. 149-69 ; telegram from Officiating Director, Criminal Intelligence to Officiating Secretary to the GOI, Home Department, dated 5 August 1908.
9. J.D., vol. 99, file. no. 5059, 1908, p. 141.
10. Clarke to Morley, 31 July 1908. Quoted in Cashman, *The Myth of the Lokamanya*, p. 181.
11. Edwardes, *The Bombay City Police*, p. 143.
12. For discussion of various Factory Commissions and their recommendations and the consequent Factory Acts, see Chapter 2, the section on 'Hours of Work'.
13. *Amrit Bazar Patrika*, 2 September 1875, quoted in Bipan Chandra, *Economic Nationalism*, p. 336.
14. 12 November 1880, quoted in ibid., p. 333.
15. July 1881, vol. IV, no. 1, p. 39, quoted in ibid., p. 332.
16. *Journal of Poona Sarvajanik Sabha*, 4 January 1879, quoted in ibid., p. 335.
17. Quoted in ibid., p. 336.
18. 14 March 1881, in the *Report on Native Newspapers* (Bombay Presidency) (henceforward *RNP*), 19 March 1881.
19. *RNP*, 26 March 1881.
20. 20 March 1881, in *RNP*, 26 March 1881.
21. For details, see Bipan Chandra, *Economic Nationalism*, pp. 339-52.
22. Rast Goftar, 17 September 1905, in *RNP*, 23 September 1905.
23. *RNP*, 14 October 1905.
24. *RNP*, 30 September 1905.
25. 26 September 1905, in *RNP*, 30 September 1905.
26. On 27 September and 2 and 3 October respectively.
27. 1 October 1905, in *RNP*, 7 October 1905.
28. 13 October 1905, in *RNP*, 14 October 1905.
29. 16 October 1905, in *RNP*, 21 October 1905.
30. 15 October 1905, in *RNP*, 21 October 1905.
31. 24 September 1905, in *RNP*, 30 September 1905.
32. 6 October 1905, in *RNP*, 7 October 1905.
33. 16 March 1890, in *RNP*, 22 March 1890.
34. 22 June 1890, in *RNP*, 28 June, 1890.
35. For details, see Bipan Chandra, *Economic Nationalism*, pp. 379-85.
36. 2 December 1905, in *RNP*, 9 December 1905
37. *RNP*, 18 August 1906.
38. 19 August 1906, in *RNP*, 25 August 1906.
39. 21 August 1906, in *RNP*, 25 August 1906.
40. *SMHFM*, II, p. 218.

41. *Sind Gazette*, 6 November 1906, in *RNP*, 10 November 1906. Also see *Rast Goftar*, *Gujarati* and *Kaiser-i-Hind*, 11 November 1906, *Praja Bandhu*, *Jam-e-Jamshed*, 12 November 1906.
42. *Rast Goftar*, 11 November 1906, in *RNP*, 10 November 1906.
43. *Gujarati*, 11 November, 1906, in *RNP*, 10 November 1906.
44. *Kaiser-i-Hind*, 11 November, 1906, in *RNP*, 10 November 1906. Similar sentiments were voiced in *Gujarati Punch*, 18 November 1906, *Phoenix*, 17 November 1906, in *RNP*, 24 November 1906; in the *Hindi Punch*, 2 December 1906, in *RNP*, 1 December 1906; and *Praja Bandhu* 23 December 1906, in RNP, 29 December 1906.
45. For example, *Jam-e-Jamshed*, in its issues of 12 November 1906, in *RNP*, 17 November, 1906 and 24 December 1906, in *RNP*, 29 December 1906.
46. *Sanj Vartman*, 8 January 1907, in *RNP*, 12 January 1907.
47. For example, the *Indian Spectator* (8 June 1907) characterized it as 'an impartial document', and *Rast Goftar* (9 June 1907) described it as 'not a very terrible document', in *RNP*, 8 June 1907.
48. *RNP*, 8 June, 1907.
49. See, for example, *Gujarati Punch*, 17 November, 1907, *Bombay Samachar*, 3 December 1907, *Rast Goftar*, 1 December 1907, *Kal*, 6 December 1907, *Kaiser-i-Hind*, 28 December 1907. *Kal* questioned the very motive for the appointment of the Commission by saying that 'the secret aim of the Factory Commission (is) to deal a blow at the mill industries in India under the pretence of showing sympathy to the mill hands'.
50. *Gujarati*, 2 August 1908, in *RNP*, 8 August 1908.
51. 4 August 1908, in *RNP*, 8 August 1908.
52. 31 July 1908, in *RNP*, 1 August 1908.
53. Cashman, *The Myth of the Lokamanya*, p. 175, fn. 20.
54. *SMHFM*, II, p. 213.
55. Ibid., pp. 213-14.
56. Ibid., pp. 214-15.
57. Cashman, *The Myth of the Lokamanya*, pp. 174-5. Dinshaw Wacha, speaking for the Bombay millowning community, described the nationalists supporting Swadeshi as the 'economic Cheap Jacks who are now vociferously hawking the Swadeshi Shibboleth'.
58. *SMHFM*, II, p. 253-4.
59. Quoted in D.P. Karmarkar, *Bal Gangadhar Tilak* (Bombay, 1956), p. 166.
60. JD, File no. 5059, para 9.
61. JD, File no. 5061, p. 6.
62. Cashman, *The Myth of the Lokamanya*, p. 186.
63. *SMHFM*, II, p. 321.
64. *Mahratta*, 18 August 1920; quoted in Cashman, *The Myth of the Loakmanya*, p. 185.

65. *SMHFM*, II, p. 317.
66. S. Bhattacharya, 'Swaraj and the Kamgar: The Indian National Congress and the Bombay Working Class, 1919-1931', in Richard Sisson and Stanley Wolpert, eds., *Congress and Indian Nationalism: The Pre-Independence Phase* (Delhi, 1988), pp. 229-30.
67. Newman, *Workers and Unions*, p. 94.
68. Ibid., p. 95.
69. S. Bhattacharya, 'Swaraj and the Kamgar', p. 229.
70. *SMHFM*, II, pp. 742-50.
71. Clarke to Morley, 10 July 1908; given in Cashman, *The Myth of the Lokamanya*, p. 179.
72. JD, 1908, vol. 99, p. 135.
73. Home Political-A, 1908, File nos. 149-69, telegram dated 2 July 1908.
74. JD, File no. 5061; from Secretary to the Government, Bombay to the Secretary to the GOI, Home Department, dated 26 September 1908, p. 2.
75. *The Times*, 19 August 1908; given in Chicherov, 'Tilak's Trial', in Goldberg and Reisner, eds., *Tilak and Struggle for Indian Freedom*, pp. 596-7.
76. JD, File no. 5061, p. 2.
77. JD, 1908, vol. 99, p. 137.
78. JD, File no. 5061, pp. 5-6.
79. Home Political-A, December 1908, File nos. 149-69, p. 4.
80. JD, File no. 5061, p. 3; and JD, 1908, vol. 99, p. 138.
81. JD, File no. 5061, p. 3.
82. *TOI*, 22 July 1908.
83. JD, 1908, vol. 99, p. 136.
84. Ibid., p. 138.
85. *TOI*, 25 July 1908.
86. JD, File no. 5061, pp. 3-4.
87. Ibid., p. 4.
88. Ibid., pp. 4-5.
89. *TOI*, 30 July 1908.
90. Edwardes, *Bombay City Police*, p. 143.
91. JD, 1908, vol. 99, p. 144.
92. Ram Gopal, *Lokmanya Tilak: A Biography*, p. 325.
93. 26 July 1908, in *RNP*, 25 July 1908.
94. Ibid.
95. *Akhbar-e-Islam*, 20 July 1908, in *RNP*, 25 July 1908.
96. *Indu Prakash*, 29 July 1908, in *RNP*, 1 August 1908.
97. *Rast Goftar*, 2 August 1908, in *RNP*, 1 August 1908. Also *Jam-e-Jamshed*, 15 August 1908, in *RNP*, 15 August 1908.

98. Edwardes, *Bombay City Police*, p. 141.
99. *Rashtramat*, 1 August 1908, in *RNP*, 1 August 1908.
100. *Sanj Vartman*, 5 August 1908, in *RNP*, 8 August 1908.
101. JD, 1908, vol. 99, p141.
102. *Rashtramat*, 29 July 1908, in *RNP*, 1 August 1908.
103. Ibid. Also, *Bombay Samachar*, 31 July; *Indian Spectator*, 1 August; *Mahratta*, 2 August; *Rashtramat*, 1 August; *Kal*, 31 July, in *RNP*, 1 August 1908. *Sanj Vartman*, 5 August; *Gujarati*, 2 August; *Bombay Samachar*, 4 August; *Kesari*, 4 August; *Chikitsak*, 5 August, in *RNP*, 8 August 1908.
104. JD, File no. 5059, point 14.
105. Ibid., points 71 and 72: 'It is not unlikely therefore that the agitation, in whosoever's mind it may have originated, was engineered through the Brahmin clerks in mills.'
106. Shahid Amin, 'Gandhi as Mahatma: Gorakhpur District, Eastern UP, 1921-2', in Ranajit Guha, ed., *Subaltern Studies, III* (Delhi, 1984); Sumit Sarkar, 'The Conditions and Nature of Subaltern Militancy: Bengal from Swadeshi to Non-Co-operation, c. 1905-22', in ibid.
107. *SMHFM*, II, p. 203.
108. *Mahratta*, 20 August 1893, 'in Cashman, *The Myth of the Lokamanya*, pp. 68-9.
109. For a detailed discussion of Tilak's use of the Ganapati festival, see ibid pp. 75-97.
110. *SMHFM*, II, pp. 204-6.
111. JD, 1894, vol. 287, pp. 252-3, quoted in Cashman, *The Myth of the Lokamanya*, p. 66, fn. 81.
112. JD, 1894, vol. 287, pp. 263-4, in ibid., p. 78.
113. Ibid., p. 79.
114. Ibid., p. 226.
115. *SMHFM*, II, p. 210.
116. Ibid., p. 211.
117. JD, 1910, vol. 139, p. 167, quoted in Cashman, *The Myth of the Lokamanya*, p. 88.
118. *Oriental Review*, 29 July 1908, in *RNP*, 1 August 1908. Cashman (ibid., p. 177) argues against this by saying that most of the workers were drinkers. But to drink is one thing and to legitimize it and feel comfortable is another. The workers, despite their drinking habits, did not justify it and their guilt-conscience made them all the more vulnerable to someone who they thought was trying to liberate them from their present conditions.
119. *Oriental Review*, 29 July 1908.
120. Clarke to Morley, 24 July 1908, in Cashman, *The Myth of the Lokamanya*, p. 180.

121. JD, File no. 5059, para. 69.
122. *The Times*, 19 August 1908, quoted in Chicherov, 'Tilak's Trial', p. 593.
123. Ibid. In fact, Tilak was transferred from Bombay in a train.
124. Ibid.
125. *Indian Spectator*, 1 August 1908, in *RNP*, 1 August 1908.
126. JD, File no. 5061, p. 6.
127. *SMHFM*, II, p. 317.
128. Ibid., pp. 323-4.

CHAPTER 6

Towards Class Identity: Resistance, Protests, Strikes

THE WORKERS' REACTIONS to industrial life were expressed in a variety of ways. They had come to the city in search of work and those who found it felt gratified. But it was a different kind of work from the situation of work or worklessness they had experienced in their villages. They were expected to work in the mills daily, for long hours in an enclosed atmosphere, supposedly with few breaks in between, under the supervision of the jobbers or some other official.

There has been much debate on the differences in the nature of work in the pre-industrial and industrial environment and the imposition of time-discipline on the workers by the employers. E.P. Thompson, in a celebrated essay, talked about the 'task-orientation' as characteristic of the pre-industrial work as opposed to the work-by-clock regime in an industrial setting and the attempts by the factory owners to teach discipline to the workers.[1] Many other historians also found the early workers resisting the imposition of industrial work regime. T.S. Ashton, writing about the eighteen-century workers, stated: 'It would be wrong to imagine that what the ordinary man sought above all was continuity of work. . . . It is true that the workers resented the imposition of unemployment. . . . But leisure, at times of their own choice, stood high on their scale of preference.' [2]

David Landes concurs with this view and states that the English workers of that period 'were accustomed to work at their own pace, to take their rest and distraction . . . as and when they pleased'.[3]

This view about an easy-going, indisciplined workforce was countered by some other historians. Mark Harrison found that 'a very disciplined, formalized, surprisingly regular and long working week had existed in England since at least the mid-eighteenth century'. He further added that any irregularity or unceratainty in this respect 'stemmed not from the endemic idleness of the workforce but from the vagaries of the economy; the same continued to be true during the nineteenth century'.[4] Thomas Smith, in a study of the time discipline in Japan found that the Japanese peasantry had a surprisingly modern sense of time.[5]

Jonathan Parry, in the Indian context, questioned the notion of the shift from the task-orientation to clock-orientation and concluded that, 'Significant numbers of industrial workers in certain niches of the labour market appear to be no less leisured than Sahlins's proverbially leisured hunter-gatherers.'[6] But then Parry's focus was on the workers of a public sector enterprise where it was nobody's interest to enforce rigorous discipline and whose employees were, in author's words, 'a notoriously leisured segment of the Indian labour force'.[7]

The situation was quite different in the Bombay mills. Here there was no security of employment and the workers could be hired and fired on the free will of the management and the jobbers. It was in the interests of the owners and the managers to enforce the time-discipline and to create a workforce more amenable to the requirements of the industry. But, as has been discussed earlier in detail,[8] the imposition of time-discipline in Bombay mills was notoriously haphazard, inconsistent and varied from one mill to another and caused great hardships to the workers. In fact, it can also be said that the millowners and managers were not much concerned about imposing a rigorous time-discipline in their concerns. They were content with working the mills for inordinately long hours and leave the actual training and disciplining to the jobbers. They were loath to invest in a system of proper discipline or in the infrastructure which would create a settled and disciplined workforce. The demand for keeping regular hours with proper breaks and holidays came from the ranks of the workers, the jobbers, the social workers, and the critical observers of the industry.

Right since 1879, there are records of a section of workers raising the issue of long and uncoordinated hours of work in the mills and demanding legislation to set things right. In December 1879, a memorial was submitted to the government signed by 578 workers demanding a working day of 9 hours and a weekly holiday.[9] In 1884, when it became known that a Factory Commission was appointed, some of the workers took the initiative in holding a meeting and presented their demands before the Commission. The demands presented by the agitators called for a proper time-discipline. They demanded that the 'work in the mills should commence at 6.30 (a.m.) and cease at sunset', that 'all millhands must be allowed one complete day of rest every Sunday', and 'half an hour's recess be allowed them at noon every day'.[10] The workers speaking before the Commission of 1885 clearly stated that 'We want the mill to open and close at *fixed times*',[11] and that 'If there was one definite time for all the people to take their meals it would be much better.'[12] They averred that it would be both in the interests of the industry as well as the workers to have fixed working time: 'Our object is to have more definite times, and I think if this was done we should do our work better and give more satisfaction to our employers.'[13]

When the Indian Factory Commission of 1890 was appointed the workers again held such meetings and presented their demands which included a working day of fixed hours.[14] The Commission turned down this plea on the grounds that the state should not interfere in the working hours of adult males and that the 'operatives as a body are satisfied with the present hours of work—daylight to dusk'.[15] This was despite the fact that all the adult male workers responding to the related questions of the Commission stated that they would like to have fixed hours of work. Besides this, they also demanded a weekly holiday and half-an-hour of mid-day break for lunch.[16]

But nothing came out of it. The working hours remained as haphazard as ever. In fact, with the introduction of electric lights in certain mills in the 1890s and in the majority of mills in 1900s, the situation got worse. The work-time became more varied and irregular than it had hitherto been. T.M. Nair, in his note of dissent in the Report of the IFLC, wrote:

> Out of 20 cotton textile mills in Bombay, whose exact working were ascertained by the Commission, one mill worked day and night with changing shifts. Of the remaining 19 only 8 had fixed hours of working all the year round, and all of them worked 13 hours or more everyday, exclusive of the midday interval, while one of them worked 14 hours a day. The 11 other mills, although some of them were fitted with electric lights had changing hours in summer and winter. In summer they all worked between 13 and 14 hours, while in winter their hours came down to between 11 and 12½.[17]

The admonitions administered by the press or the authorities and some of the millowners themselves had no effects. Even the BMOA was helpless to enforce discipline in its ranks. Finally, it was the resistance by the workers culminating in the rioting which put a brake on this and imposed some amount of self-regulation. The IFLC, in the course of its investigations, found that 'while many of the workers were undoubtedly in favour of the long hour day a very large number were strongly opposed to it'.[18] T.M. Nair, the dissenting member, however, noted that the 'workers are practically unanimous in asking for a legislative restriction of their hours of labour'.[19] The Commission also conceded that: 'the great mass of the workers in textile mills would welcome any measure calculated to prevent their being worked excessive hours in future. . . . and we found them, with few exceptions, strongly opposed to the practice of working excessive hours, and in favour of interference by Government to prevent it'.[20]

The colonial state, on its part, was half hearted in either devising the rules or implementing them. In the ultimate analysis, it is the resistance and protests by the workers which worked, to some extent, in the direction of some sort of self-regulation.

The situation, however, did not improve much. The work-by-clock was just one component of the industrial life that the workers had to endure and adjust to. The inordinately long hours, the newness and incomprehensibility of work, bad ventilation, insanitary conditions both at the workplace and at home were other factors which worked on the bodies and minds of the workers.

The reactions and the resistance of the workers to hardships of industrial life were expressed in a variety of ways. There initial reaction was to go to some other mill or for some other work or to leave the work altogether and go home. However, if the villages were the places where they could have comfortably stayed, such large numbers would not have come to the city in the first place. In fact, the village was the last resort. Other ways to mitigate the pressures of work were to take unpermitted leaves either due to illness or for some other work. They had much to lose on this count as two days' pay was cut for one day's unpermitted leave. As there were no weekly holidays in the mills until 1891, most of the leaves they took would have marked them absent. Moreover, there were chances of harsher actions like dismissals. But the working conditions were such that the workers were forced to resort to this and, in a certain sense, it underlined their resistance to the industrial system, as it operated in Bombay. Although the functioning of the mills was not much affected, these absences inconvenienced the employers to a certain extent.

The IFLC stated that the 'Indian operative is fond of change; he prefers to wander from mill to mill rather than remain settled'.[21] The figure of absenteeism given by the employers before the Factory Commission of 1885 varied from 4.5 per cent to 14 per cent. In 1889, one official estimated the figure of average daily absenteeism to be 12 per cent and, according to Morris, the average daily absenteeism for the pre-War years was from 8 to 15 per cent.[22] S.D. Mehta asserts that the same figure for the pre-War period was about 50 per cent. But, as Morris rightly points out, this figure is too high to be a relevant one.[23] In a survey conducted by the Bombay Labour Office in August 1923, this figure was stated to be 11.2 per cent. For men, it was recorded at 9.7 per cent, while for women it was 16 per cent.[24] In October 1926, the ITB found it to be 12.25 per cent, while another survey conducted in July 1926 had put it at 8.97 per cent.[25] The BMOA, in its written statement before the ITB, quoted the figures for June 1926 at 11.13 per cent.[26] The actual level must have been higher because the weavers used to provide their own substitutes and, therefore, could remain absent without being marked as such. Only when they failed to provide substitutes were they marked absent.

If we take the qualitative evidences into account we find confirmation for this state of affairs. Almost all the employers testifying before the Factory Commission of 1885 stated that the attendance was quite irregular. Even N.M. Lokhanday, representing the workers' side, talked about the 'irregularity in attendance which is very remarkable at present'. Most of the witnesses said that the workers leave for their homes for two or three months in two or three years. H.B. Warden, the manager of the Victoria Mill, said that 'the hands went home after 12 to 18 months in the mill'.[27] E.C. Madan of Hongkong Mill said that, 'Unlike English operatives, they (the Indian workers) do not work continuously for a number of years. They generally go to their homes in the country for a rest, or to attend to cultivation of their lands.'[28] C.N. Wadia provided quatitative support to his statement: 'The hands went away for a month each year. . . . Out of 3,000 hands from 250 to 300 are always away.'[29] This view was supported by Nair who was sympathetic to the workers and wanted the government to legislate for them. In his note of dissent he recorded that 'the figures of the Carnatic Mill show that the hands left the mill in large numbers every month. Taking the year 1907 the lowest number that left any month was 264 in November and the highest 397 in May. The average for the whole year was 329 a month.'[30] The IFLC, therefore, concluded that the worker 'returns to his village for one month each year'.[31] N.M. Joshi, in his evidence before the ITB in 1926, conceded that the workers 'generally go once in a year or once in two years to their districts'.[32] The evidence given by the Girni Kamgar Mahamandal before the ITB supported this: 'Its (absenteeism's) percentage was highest immediately after pay day. Moreover, it is more marked amongst females than amongst men. Besides this monthly absenteeism, there is a kind of seasonal absenteeism when workers go to their villages for some weeks at a stretch.'[33]

Apart from this, other kinds of absenteeism were also reported. Findlay Shirras, the Director of the Bombay Labour Office, noted that 'after the payment of wages . . . the percentage of absentees in the mill rises considerably'.[34]

This did create problems in the organization of the industry. The ITB commented in its report that 'the efficiency of labour in Bombay is greatly reduced by the high percentage of absenteeism among the operatives'. Even though it had no financial implications for the owners, 'it seriously detracts from efficiency as the place of the absentee has to be taken by a casually recruited, and often inefficient substitute who is known as a "budli"'.[35]

It was, however, another kind of resistance practised daily at the workplace that proved to be a bigger irritant to the employers. It was what was termed as the 'idling habit' of the workers. Confronted with a situation where they were supposed to work extraordinarily long hours without holidays or easily sanctioned leaves, the workers developed their own method of coping with it. Initially, the complaints by the employers on this count were muted and infrequent. There were talks of workers taking their meals outside the allotted time and the supposed half-hour interval of lunch was said to be used 'rather for recreation than for meals'. It was reported that the workers do not take 'their meals at one and the same time. Some remain at work while others go; and when they have returned the others go'. The women workers were said to waste even 'more time than other work-people for various purposes during the working hours, such as smoking & c'.[36] A report on Bombay mills by John Robertson of Glasgow, given approvingly in the first report of the BMOA, was more critical of the inefficiency of the workers who were found to be wanting in 'skill and care'. The women were said to be particularly 'irregular and troublesome'.[37]

The percentage of workpeople who were found to be resting, 'loitering' and taking their meals during the work-time varied from 7 to 47 per cent according to the testimonies given by the employers before the Factory Commission of 1885.[38] Later on, the complaints became shriller in tone. It is interesting to note that more frequent references to this silent resistance by the workers occurred when the latter had also started to show more open defiance of authority in the form of strikes. The IFLC recorded numerous such complaints from the employers. H.R. Greaves of the Greaves Cotton and Company talked about the 'casual' attitude of the workers and said that the millowners 'anticipated labour troubles if they attempted to restrict the liberty of the Indian operatives' and stated that he had to 'employ 30 to 40 per cent more hands than ordinarily be required for mill purposes'.[39] Another employer spoke about the imperative of the owners 'to engage more hands than was necessary for the ordinary running of the mill'.[40] Speaking against the restriction of hours by law, Fazulbhoy Currimbhoy Ibrahim, the then vice-chairman of the BMOA, in a reversal of the logic, stated:

> Generally the actual working hours at present are 13, but about 15 per cent of the workmen are at all times found outside the mills, thus reducing their actual working hours from 13 to 11½. If twelve hours per day be enforced by law, the result would be a reduction in production, since the men will never give up their habit of resting, or loitering about the compound, thus reducing a 12 hours' day to one of 10.5 hours.[41]

Meyers, a mill manager, detailed the process:

> The mill-hands, although they work 13 hours at present, have every latitude for working as they like without any restrictions. From observations taken during the last 20 years, I find that no employee works more than two hours at a stretch, they go out in the mill compound when they like for smoking, drinking and natural purposes, and stop out from 15 to 30 minutes at a time. The doffer boys in all the departments of the mill, also the piecers in the ring and mule departments, as a rule go out after every doffing, which means on an average every 1.5 hours. Besides they take their meals during the working hours inside the mill, but never during the half hour stoppage.[42]

David Sassoon tried to further strengthen the case against the legal restriction of working hours by putting even lower figures and by visualizing the prospects of open resistance in case of intensification of work:

> Even when the engines work for 13 hours a day the operatives scarcely put in more than 8.5 or 9 hours of work. This being the case it will be readily seen that if the working hours are restricted by legislation, mill owners have to make up for lost ground by demanding steadier and more regular work, and more constant attention on the part of the operatives; and as these are not at all likely to agree to the new conditions, or to be able to put up with them, the result would lead to strikes amongst the mill-hands.[43]

Another mill representative said that the workers 'put 10 hours of work out of a 13 hours' day' and when he tried to put restrictions by issuing passes, they 'threatened to strike' forcing him to do away with this system.[44]

Such complaints from the employers are to be found all over the pages of the IFLC. They persisted even later on. C.N. Wadia, the agent of the Century Mill and the BMOA representative, said that 'the man, who is supposed to work in our mill for twelve hours never does work for 12 hours, but works eight hours, and remaining four hours he spends in the compound, sleeping or talking or amusing himself otherwise.' [45]

The colonial officials uncritically concurred with the views of the employers. The Textile Factories Labour Committee, 1906, concluded in its Report: 'No legislation can alter the nature and ingrained habits of Indian workers. They have been in the habit of leaving their work at odd and uncertain periods throughout the nominal working hours. They go into the mill compounds which generally speaking are large and open for taking food, smoking, bathing, drinking water, and necessary purposes.'[46]

The IFLC also reached the same conclusion. According to it, the Indian worker liked to work 'in a leisurely manner throughout . . . taking intervals of rest whenever he feels disinclined for further exertion'. On an average, the workers were said to take about two hours off during the working time. Whenever restrictions were imposed in the form of a limited number of passes, they resisted and threatened to strike forcing 'their employers to revert to the old arrangement where each man was allowed to come and go freely'. It estimated that due to 'these temporary absences during working hours, the complement of workers in an Indian textile factory is always from 10 to 15 per cent in excess of the number of hands actually required to man the machinery at any one time'.[47]

The official view maintained a surprising consistency on this issue. The IIC declared in its report that the 'mill-hands loiter away much of the time during which they are nominally at work'.[48] And it was emphasized by the RCL that there was a 'substantial difference between the nominal hours and the hours of actual work': 'In Bombay particularly, the visitor is struck by the large number of men who can be found outside the factory building at almost any hour of the day. Thus meals are generally taken, not during the statutory interval . . . but during the nominal working hours.'[49]

This phenomenon of passive resistance was expressed in other forms as well. The IFLC reported:

One of the main difficulties experienced at present, when unrest appears among the workers, is in ascertaining the cause of that unrest. Frequently no definite demands are formulated, no grievances are stated, no indication is given as to the cause of the discontent; the operatives simply leave the mill in a body, or more commonly they drop off one by one without explanation, and accept employment under more congenial conditions in other factories.[50]

The intolerable working conditions and the insecurity of employment prompted the workers to develop their own mechanism to cope with the situation which increasingly formed part of their resistance to the extractive mechanism instituted by the employers.

This daily resistance by the workers against the long hours of work, bad ventilation and insanitary conditions in the mills gave rise to one of the most potent, persistent and pervasive myths in the history of industrial relations in India—the myth of the indolent worker. It encapsulated within its framework most aspects of workers' existence and pervaded many levels of official and non-official thinking. Right from the beginning an Orientalist construction was effected which attributed these experiences as the formative aspects of the native character. In this view, the workers spread out their work not because the working hours were too long and the conditions of work intolerable, but because of their 'ingrained habit' and 'natural inclination'. Seen in this light, any voluntary or legal restrictions on the hours of labour and any improvement in the working conditions would do no good because the workers would not respond to that. In any situation, their 'idling' and 'loitering' habits would persist to dog the industry with inefficiency. Even when it was sometimes recognized that there was a connection between this behaviour and the intolerable conditions of work, this was not given much importance and was considered secondary to their 'natural' way of working.

It is difficult to say when exactly this myth, particularly with reference to the Bombay textile workers, originated but documents since 1874-5 had begun to record it. The language adopted an Orientalist hue. 'The work-people are in the *habit* of taking holidays', stated one mill representative,[51] as if it had nothing to do with long hours of work and almost total lack of permitted holidays in the industry. John Robertson of Glasgow, in his report on the working of the Bombay mills, talked glibly about the 'inferiority of the workers' in comparison with the Europeans without any reference to the differences in wages, management and the history of their development in both contexts.[52] The TFLC talked about the '*nature and ingrained habits* of Indian workers' which could not be changed by any legislative interference.[53] The IFLC had more details to offer on this count. It found the workers 'incapable of prolonged and intense effort' and with a 'natural inclination' to dilatoriness.[54] They were 'fond of change' and liked 'to wander from mill to mill rather than remain settled'.[55] At the same time, however, they were 'capable of remaining quiescent' even in intolerable conditions.[56]

The non-official view was equally enamoured by this explanation. The *ITJ* commented early on that the 'moral tone of the average millhand's character is . . . not a high one'. The writer was piqued because the workers applied for leave on some pretext or the other to get away from the forced misery of work.[57] It later spoke about 'the *constitutional aversion* of any cooly to routine and punctuality' which was said to hamper the mill work.[58] In 1914, it complained about the 'irregular and whimsical habit of the Bombay millhand' and berated the workers for their irrationality: 'The millhand does not seem to know his own mind; neither would he listen to the advice of those he has selected as guardians of his interests. He is often a perverse, obstinate fellow inclined to lean more towards disorder and idleness.'[59]

John Wallace, the then editor of the *ITJ*, declared before the IIC that 'our industrial population is notoriously inefficient'.[60] Even those sympathetic to the workers sometimes fell prey to such characterizations. Burnett-Hurst, who wrote in detail about the problems which the workers faced in their living and working, could not resist saying that the 'Pardeshi . . . is inclined to be lazy and rather turbulent', and the untouchables 'have filthy habits and live in squalor'.[61] Similarly, Kelman, who sympatheticlly detailed the travails of the women workers in the modern industry of India, characterized the Julahas as 'amongst the most riotous'.[62]

The stereotyping of the workers across various levels could be seen in the categorization of the millworkers into five types. This categorization was initially given by V.A. Talcherkar in 1905 during the heat of the controversy about the hours of work. Talcherkar, then a weaving master in the Gold Mohar Mill at Dadar, later became the President of the Kamgar Hitwardhak Sabha. The millworkers, according to him, could be divided into five types—the 'model hands', the '*budliwala*', the '*athawada*', the '*mowali*' and the '*dada*'. He provided the defining characteristics of each type. Thus the 'model hand' was 'steady, sober and regular in attendance' and 'a family man'. The '*budliwala*' or the substitute was the one 'who as a rule fights shy of fixed employment and works only temporarily in lieu of others'. The '*athawada*' or the seven-day man had the 'habit of working only seven days at a stretch'. The '*mowali*' was a 'bohemian . . . a gay man given to vice'. And the '*dada*' was a 'vagabond', a 'hooligan', 'lazy . . . but dangerous'.[63] The same categorization is repeated almost verbatim in Edwardes' official publication, *The Gazetteer of Bombay City and Island* (1909),[64] and, with minor changes, in Burnett-Hurst's non-official book, published in 1925.[65]

In none of these accounts was there any recognition of the fact that at least four of these types intermixed. The supposedly regular 'hands' could become irregular due to illness or some other pressing needs at home in the village and end up as a substitute (*budliwala*) or even as a seven-day man (*athawada*) later on. Or, conversely, the substitutes, on being given a regular job, could be transformed into a model worker. In fact, only a page earlier he describes a substitute as 'inefficient workers who shirk regular employment'. Burnett-Hurst talks about how a new worker starts as a substitute for anyone who was absent and 'His position and earnings are precarious until such time as he can secure a permanent post.'[66] As BTLU stated, 'The 'badlis' are not always inexperienced men. Most of them are such men as are unable to find a permanent job on return from their native places. Such men have to accept 'badli' jobs till they are able to secure permanent ones. Also men who have lost their jobs have to accept 'badli' in another mill. Very few of the 'badlis' are men new to their jobs'.[67]

Yet these stereotypes continued. Similarly, a large number of workers, who were described by many as 'lazy' and with 'loitering and idling habits' and prone to drinking and 'tomtoming', could as easily be categorized as '*mowalis*'. And, finally, the '*dada*' was taken out of the class of the workers altogether and described by the *Gazetteer* as a 'member of the vagabond and hooligan *tribe*'.[68] The employers also persistently complained about the deficient 'material and moral condition of our mill labourers',[69] their 'inefficiency'[70] and 'migratory habits'.[71]

The explanation generally offered for this supposed natural inefficiency of the workers was their rural origins. The IFLC stated that the 'claims of the village' were 'sufficiently powerful to recall him from the city life for a period which extends, on the average, to at least a month in each year'.[72] It sweepingly concluded that the 'habits of the Indian factory operative are determined by the fact that he is primarily an agriculturist or a labourer on the land'.[73] Similarly, C.N. Wadia, the chairman of the BMOA in 1918, asserted that 'Our operatives are agriculturists first and agriculturists last'.[74] This view was supported by the Industrial Disputes Committee which claimed that the workers 'came to

Bombay—as a rule without families—and work till they have funds enough to return to their villages'.[75] The RCL also stated that 'the great majority of those employed are at heart villagers'.[76] S.D. Mehta, the official historian of the cotton mills, characteristically summed up the situation by saying that the majority of the workers:

> . . . came from the classes which have a vested interest in agricultural land and other rural property and who, as a consequence, have only an unstable nexus with the towns of their migration. Only too often in the early decades a worker came to the mills, or for that matter to the city, to collect the cash required for adding an extra bit of land to his plot or for purchasing a new pair of bullocks. These wants satisfied, the men went back, probably never to return. . . . It was this state of affairs which led to the average working life of a worker in cotton factories being only 5 or 6 years as late as 1896.[77]

While the officials and the employers argued that it was the attachment to the villages and their unwillingness to work for long hours that were responsible for the workers remaining absent from work, or for their shirking work, those sympathetic to them thought otherwise. They put the blame on the working and living conditions which impaired the health of the workers forcing them to take long and unpermitted leaves. K.A. Keluskar, the Secretary of the Maratha Aikyechhoo Sabha, a welfare organization functioning among the workers, attributed this phenomenon entirely to the unbearable conditions of work.[78] Chavan, who hailed from Ratnagiri and had a large practice among the mill workers, remarked: 'One thing I have marked is that they do manage to prolong their lives by running down to their villages and it is only then that they are able to throw off even ordinary ailments.'[79]

N.G. Powar, the Honorary Secretary of Maratha Education Society, stated: 'The operatives usually went home once a year and this recruited their health. No mill-hand in Bombay possessed a house in this city.'[80] Sometimes, the pressure of the work became so much that a large number of workers even risked their jobs to go home. A.K. Leslie, a partner in the Greaves Cotton and Company, was surprised to find 'the number of people who applied for what is known as "leave altogether", or, in other words, resigned. These total no less than 2,158 and represent 38 per cent of the total number of people employed'.[81]

Even as late as 1926, the Girni Kamgar Mahamandal maintained that, 'a labourer looks upon Bombay only as an unavoidable but necessary evil to which he must submit for his living during the period in which he has nothing to depend upon in his village. This state of things is bound to continue as long as the conditions of living for labour in Bombay are not improved and labour does not come to look upon Bombay as its permanent residence.'[82]

The IFLC noted in passing that there was 'some casual connection' between the long hours of work and the 'the extent to which loitering occurs',[83] and the RCL conceded that 'it is impossible for the average operative to remain at work regularly through a 10-hour day either in a cotton mill or in any other factory. The unauthorised intervals are a form of self-defence against over-work'.[84] And T.M. Nair pithily summed up the situation:

> it is not an ingrained habit at all but only a manifestation of the adaptive capacity which all human beings possess more or less. Intense and concentrated labour in a cotton mill for 13 or 14 hours, day after day, week after week, and month after month is beyond the physical endurance of all human beings. And so when a mill operative . . . is put to work at a machine for a longer period than he can possibly endure, he has to adapt himself to that work in such a way that he can get through the work required of him with the least possible injury to himself. The labourer does not spread out the work over a long period of time, but finding himself compelled to work a long number of hours, reduces the intensity of labour as a safeguard to his own physical well-being. . . . A system more likely to bring about degradation of labour is impossible to conceive.[85]

While the employers were inconvenienced by the daily resistance of the workers, they were willing to put up with this and accommodate it in the routine working of the mills. The strikes, on the other hand, were considered as open defiance and treated accordingly.

Talking about the pre-War situation the Royal Commission on Indian Labour reported: 'Prior to the winter of 1918-19, a strike was a rare occurrence in Indian industry . . . to the majority of the industrial workers the use of strike was probably unknown.'[86]

This misunderstanding on the part of the Commission arose from its misconception about the nature of the workers' activities and protests. Unless some apparently permanent organization was floated, unless a proper record was maintained, it refused to recognize the workers' protests.

Several authors on the Indian labour movement have disagreed with this view.[87] But their objections are mainly of a technical nature. They have merely tried to show that strikes did occur even before the First World War. But they did not appreciate the real nature of the workers' protests. This is apparent in the way they periodize the phases of the labour history. R.K. Das, for example, divides the period of the historical growth of the 'labour organizations' into three phases: (a) The regulation period (1877-91), during which the hours, etc., of the factory labour were regulated; (b) The abolition period (1891-1918), during which the indentured and slave labour were abolished; and (c) The organization period (1918 onwards), when the trade unions began emerging.[88]

This periodization ignores the initiative of the workers and puts undue emphasis on the state action and formal trade unionism. Another scheme adopted by some authors divides the period into two phases—pre-War and post-War, and some treat the period until 1928 in the same phase.[89] It, however, again misses the problem of workers' agency and takes into account only the existence or non-existence of formal trade unions.

Is such periodization at all necessary? Taking congnizance of the fact that no Chinese wall can be erected between the supposedly distinct phases, because, after all, it is the activities of the former phase which leads to the later one, any such attempt may seem futile. Moreover, there is no linear progressive path; reverses occur quite frequently. In addition to this, the rapid turnover and constant renewal of the workforce from the migrants from the rural areas required perpetual re-learning of the experiences of previous resistance and struggles. In such circumstances, collective learning from and resistance to industrial experience was bound to often revert to the original block and a beginning had to be made from scratch. But, as the industry matured and more and more workers constantly experienced city lives, the collective learning and its dissemination both in the urban and rural areas (from where the workers came) became wider in scope. The new migrants did not need to know the details of the industrial experience firsthand. The learning might occur from the old hands who had returned to the villages either permanently owing to failing health or joblessness or from those who moved to-and-fro between the city and the country for various purposes and under different circumstances. This previously acquired knowledge would have helped the newcomers in coping with the industrial situation more efficiently than would have been the case for a complete novice. The later newcomers, therefore, were not total greenhorns as they were the inheritors of the collective wisdom drawn and forged from the previous experiences. The collectivities were emerging and getting wider and more organized not only within the framework of the industry but the city as a whole. The numerous caste, regional and community associations which were springing in the city at regular intervals and which were operating in the working-class neighbourhood also helped the workers to fight their industrial battles and sustain them more securely outside the mills. Seen in this light and taking a long-term view, the resistance of the workers roughly from 1875 to 1928 both inside the mills as well as from outside can be divided into three broad phases. It also seemed to coincide with the development of the industry, the various crises faced by it, and the responses of the employers both at the time of crisis and that of prosperity.

The first phase was from 1875 to the early 1890s during which there were isolated strikes and other forms of protests but nothing amounting to large collective actions. The second phase (covered by the present study) can be put from the early 1890s to 1918 when the strikes became more frequent involving more and more workers and even other forms of resistance became more self-conscious and enduring. The third phase was heralded with the general industrial strike of 1919, the first in the series of many such collective actions leading to the great general strikes of 1928-9.

Even in 1875, although the strikes might not be of 'frequent' occurrence, as Issac Alocock, the engineer in New Dhurumsey Poonjabhoy Mills, said,[90] they did take place, as J. Helm, the manager in the Bombay United Mill, admitted.[91] Another manager, Nusserwanjee Dadabhoy, said that the practice of keeping the wages of the workers in arrears was to prevent them from leaving 'without proper notice' and also from striking work.[92] On 15 June 1884, the *Rast Goftar* reported that the weavers of the Kurla Mill had struck work for the 'last whole week'. The employers, as usual, tried to put the blame on the 'instigators'. But the paper said that it was due to three genuine reasons. The first was that the workers were called on the day of their fortnightly rest to clean the machinery in which more than half a day was wasted. The second was that they were given only one ticket for the whole department of more than 75 workers for going out to pass water, etc. And the third was that the rents charged in the chawl leased in by the Mill were excessive and more than what was agreed upon.[93]

The strikes were not initiated by the male workers only. The women also resorted to them. *Din Bandhu* (26 January 1890) reported 'a recent strike by female mill-labourer in a certain cotton mill of Bombay'. It was on account of change in the hours of work without notice which caused inconvenience to them. They were finally subdued by the threat of 'criminal prosecution' by the employers. The paper commented: 'Now-a-days rich men can fabricate evidence and get any poor innocent man convicted in a court of justice and this trick is resorted to whenever mill-labourers in this part of the country strike work.'[94]

The fact that the workers could not expect much from the legal system was brought out by their evidence before the Factory Commission of 1890. All those workers who gave evidence said that the court's decisions were almost invariably in favour of the employers. One worker stated that the 'operatives are really afraid to go to court, because the mill-owners employ vakeels and oppose them with great persistence'.[95] So, in case of trouble, the workers generally preferred 'to forfeit their wages and go away'.[96]

Their grievances at the mill and the ineffective fight for their redressal made them turn to the government for help. *Din Bandhu* voiced their problems by saying that, 'If the mills in Bombay continue to be managed as at present, the mill-labourers will be totally ruined in a very short time.' It, therefore, appealed to the government to do something because the 'Indian mill-labourers . . . are not able to get their grievances redressed without the help of Government.'[97]

The government, on its part, had already appointed three commissions of enquiry by this time. The first was in 1875, the second in 1885 and the third in 1890. It was not their concern for the workers that made them do so, but the pressure from the Lancashire manufacturers who feared the competition from the Bombay mills thriving on much cheaper labour. Whatever the motives for the appointment of these commissions, they were never very wide in scope. The Act of 1881, enacted on the basis of the 1875 report, legislated for children and the Act of 1891 for women. The male workers were not given any legislative protection till 1911.

The provisions of these Acts did not mean much to the workers as they were either the prevailing practice (e.g. most of the women did not work more than 11 hours) or, as in case of ventilation, they were systematically evaded. However, it was at a different level that these commissions influenced the workers.

When they heard about the appointment of the Factory Commission in 1884, some of the workers took the initiative in holding meetings and presented their demands before the Commission. These meetings, although they must have received some support from N.M. Lokhanday, were organized mainly on the initiative of the workers themselves. One agitator, Narayan Surkoji, stated that, 'This Association (the Millhands'

Association of Lokhanday) has nothing to do with meetings we have been holding.'[98]

These meetings were held in the belief that the government was about to do something for their benefit. It was an independent response of the workers to the government's initiative. Lokhanday said in his evidence before the Commission that the 'agitation was voluntary and arose when the mill-hands found that a Commission was appointed to inquire into the matter'.[99] This was confirmed by the statement given by an agitator:

> We held the meeting because we knew that the Government was going to make some change in the law and we thought it would be well to represent our different troubles and grievances. If the Government had not been about to alter the law we should not have held any meetings.[100]

When the Commission of 1890 was appointed, the workers again held such meetings and presented their demands.[101] At a time when the workers were feeling the pressures of their work and also realizing the necessity of protest, the appointment of Factory Commissions provided some hope and stimulation for at least a section of workers to systematically think about themselves. During the course of holding meetings and presentation of their demands before the Commissions, many of them must have felt more conscious of their problems and rights. More important than the demand-list, however, was the collective formulation of their grievances.

In the 1890s, as discussed earlier,[102] the industry's growth was retarded by various factors. The millowners resorted to cuts in the wages of the workers to cope up with the depressed conditions. Now there was stiff resistance by the workers. N.M. Lokhanday, in the course of his evidence before the RCL, 1892, said, 'The strikes are of frequent occurrence in every one of the mills in this city. The chief cause is the reduction of wages on the day of payment without any previous intimation to workmen of the contemplated change. These strikes sometimes last for four days.'[103]

The strikes became so frequent that in December 1892, the *ITJ* was already referring to a 'strike mania' which had been 'prevalent lately in connection with the Bombay cotton mills'.[104] In September 1893, it again spoke about the 'strikes of workpeople' which 'continue in a regular fashion to interrupt work at several mills'.[105] In one month, from the middle of August to the middle of September, the workers of the David Sassoon Mills, the Alexandria Mills, the Indo-China Mills, the Bombay City Mills, the Wadia Mills and the New Great Eastern Mills had struck work. The total number of workers who had participated in these strikes was about 8,000 and many of them remained long on strike 'preferring to have their own terms'.[106]

The workers had started to realize their power to stop work and, although they did not always succeed, they at least exhibited enough perseverance to annoy their employers. The BMOA was much concerned that, 'During the past few months the owners of several mills had to contend with a series of strikes amongst their hands and these becoming so frequent and important, induced the Committee to give the matter serious consideration.'[107]

In its opinion, the situation was so serious that it could be dealt with only by refusing to employ the strikers of one mill in others.[108]

The alarm showed by the BMOA was not entirely unwarranted. The mood of the workpeople was such that even the appeals to the court were taking a different turn. The *ITJ* reported a case in which a mill worker filed a suit for the recovery of arrears in wages. The case was decided in favour of the owner. About four hundred workers who had struck work and gathered there to know the result were infuriated and when the mill manager, Perozshaw Jeejeebhoy, came out accompanied by some others, they 'pounced upon the manager . . . (who was) getting into his carriage and demanded the immediate payment of their wages, and threatened to molest him if he did not comply. The manager made an attempt to pacify the men, but they became very furious and some of the gang assaulted Mr. Perozshaw with sticks, inflicting a nasty cut on his forehead and dragged him about, and his turban fell off.'

Some policemen who were present tried to intervene but they were repulsed. An European constable with few others proved unequal to the task and it was only the arrival of two officers with a posse of policemen that could stop the workers from attacking the manager again. Five of them were arrested and others dispersed. The manager was escorted by the police to his residence.[109]

This incident revealed many of the situations which the workers faced and the way they reacted to them. Deprived of their wages on the pretexts which they knew nothing about, they appealed to the legal system where again they encountered an unknown and incomprehensible setting. Having failed there they felt even more frustrated and, in their desperation, they gave vent to their feelings in a violent manner. They were not dissuaded even by the intervention of the police and fought till they were forced to withdraw on the arrival of more policemen. This pattern was repeated in many instances in future.

The strikes continued on the matters of wages in the following years.[110] And it was probably the resistance offered by the workers to any attempt to reduce their wages that prevented the individual employers from complying with BMOA's instructions for a general reduction in wages. In 1894, the BMOA regretted that the proposals on the reduction of wages 'has made but little progress during the year', and despite BMOA's insistence, 'a large number of mills had still not returned the agreement embodying their willingness to abide by the proposal, personal interviews and frequent reminders having done little towards obtaining unanimous adhesion'.[111]

The advent of the plague created more problems for the industry. In 1896, it made its appearance in the Bombay city, first driving away the clerks in the mills, then the banias in the neighbourhood and finally a large number of workers. By the end of 1896 and the beginning of 1897 the situation was so bad that a lot of workers fled the city along with their families even at the risk of forfeiting their wages for the previous months. Some of the mills closed altogether but many kept working despite the warning given by industrial experts.[112]

Now the same epidemic which killed many workers and forced many more to leave the city, also brought to them the realization of their own strength—they could not so easily be dispensed with; their demands could not be dismissively brushed aside. In the words of the Factory Inspector, 'it has given rise, for the first time, in the industrial history of Bombay, to a Labour Question comparable to those of Europe'. It was because the 'residue of the regular hands . . . soon began to feel their power'.[113]

The Banias, who had hitherto provided credit to the workers, now fled. So the workers who remained could not get their daily necessaries on credit. In this situation they demanded that their wages be paid daily.

Till then the workers had received their wages monthly and that too in the middle or the end of the following month or, in many cases, almost six weeks later. This meant that the employers could keep their wages of more than a month out of which they could levy fines supposedly to maintain discipline. But now the workers demanded daily wages which they 'speedily got'. This was a surrender by the employers of their 'cherished "hold" over their hands'. The competition for skilled and trained workers increased enormously. To lure the workers the individual mills went on increasing the wages and bonus which were given to the workers on daily basis. In this situation, the loyalties to the mill or the employer, if any, were snapped completely. Even the authority of the jobbers crumbled. The Factory Inspector reported:

Mill jobbers would actually bid for labour at street corners. This of course meant very late attendance at the mills, for the reason that the operatives would attend the auctions to ascertain the prices ruling that day, and march off with the jobber who had the highest wage-limit allowed by the manager or the agent. The successful jobber was, however, not sure of his charge till he had them within the mill-gates as the chance meeting of a jobber from a rival mill with limit of an anna more would be sufficient to induce them to join the newcomer.[114]

Such competition for labour would obviously push up the wages of the workers.[115] But more important than the temporary increase in pay was the strength which the workers felt. This created in them a new sense of resistance to the arbitrary policies of the employers. When, due to return of the mass of workers, the labour market was again approaching normalcy the employers sought to withdraw the concessions which they had granted to workers. Some of them wanted to enforce the return to the previous times by 1 May 1897. But 'the temper of the men remained such that no mill dared to make the attempt unsupported'.[116] On 11 May 1897, the BMOA resolved that daily wages were to be discontinued from the first of June.[117] It, however, regretted that 'the resolution of 11th May . . . was not being entirely observed, it being alleged that the spirit of the agreement was being infringed'. It further stated that 'on 8th December . . . the Committee (of the BMOA) were led to believe that some mills still continue to pay daily wages to reelers', and 'since the close of this year (i.e. 1897) complaints were again made to the Association that the payment of daily wages was being resorted to by several mills'.[118]

The BMOA resolution was not implemented because of the resistance offered by the workers. When the workers came to know about the intention of the owners to return to the monthly wage-system, they struck work and demanded not only increased bonus but also the wages which they, in their hurry to leave Bombay, had forfeited six months ago. Both these demands were conceded.[119]

Similarly, when the weaving sheds were opened again (they were closed because the spindles had worked below usual capacity and there was not enough yarn), the employers tried to deprive the weavers of their bonus which was given to others on a daily basis. On this, the weavers struck work and 'these strikes assumed a more angry tone than those of a month before. A few blacklegs and spinners were assaulted, many were threatened and some windows were broken.' As a result, the 'weavers got their bonus. And everybody else's bonus was continued.'[120]

Ultimately, however, these concessions were withdrawn. By the middle and, in some cases, the end of 1898, a return to monthly payment was made, daily bonus was also taken back and though the female workers kept on getting daily wages for some more time, the earlier system was finally introduced even in their case.[121] Though the workers resisted, the overcrowded labour market filled again with jobless people gave them little opportunity for a prolonged resistance. Moreover, the employers were strongly in favour of a return to the old system. But, even after this, as the Factory Inspector noted, 'there remains in the chawls of Byculla and Parel a spirit of independence, not to say of unrest, which was unknown before. The immemorial trade unionism of caste and kinship and country has for the first time asserted itself and not without a measure of success.'[122]

These experiences, however, were not in vain. The workers had learnt the use of strikes as a weapon of protest. So, when in 1900-1, on the pretext of depression in the industry, the employers tried to cut wages, there were strikes all over. In most cases these strikes were resorted to at the departmental level or at the mill-level. But in one instance, about 20,000 workers from twenty mills in Parel struck work for ten days and won their demands.[123] This trend continued and the Factory Inspector reported for 1904:

> A strike of considerable dimension involving an important group of Bombay mills took place in the later part of the year. The cause was a dispute between the management and the workmen as regards wages. The former wished to reduce the rates of pay of the millhands proper and reelers. The operatives to whom the notice of this change was given simply struck work when it was attempted to bring the reduced rates into force. They professed their willingness to work 4 days a week but not accept any reduction in wages. Between 7 and 8 thousand people were involved in the strike which lasted about eleven days and was only terminated on considerable concessions being made to the operatives.[124]

These were only a few instances from the period when the use of strikes was becoming common. Our knowledge of these is limited because, as the Factory Inspector complained, 'Mill authorities are naturally not, as a rule, disposed to volunteer information affecting the interior working of their mills; so that only prolonged strikes become generally known.'[125]

By 1904, the industry had recovered from the earlier vicissitudes. The weaving section was expanded and the new units were generally composite ones. This way the industry endeavoured to tide over the crisis.

The Swadeshi, to a limited extent, also helped to create an environment which benefitted the mills. Besides this, the war between Japan and Russia temporarily minimized Japanese competition in the Chinese market. The cotton mills ushered in a prosperous period. Now the tendency was to work very long hours with the help of electric lights straining the workers to the utmost.

As we have seen earlier, the majority of workers resented this. On 24 September 1905, around ten to twelve thousand workers assembled at the Jain Dharmsthan at Chinchpoogly. A meeting under the presidency of Vithalrao Wandekar was held under the auspices of Maratha Aikyechhoo Sabha. A memorial was adopted demanding limiting the hours of work to twelve a day.[126]

Most of the workers who attended these meetings had boycotted work. In one instance, some of the workers of the Standard Mill wanted to come to the meeting and had applied for leave. The manager refused and warned them not to leave. But, even under this threat, about a hundred workers left their work and went to the meeting on 24 September 1905. They were dismissed and their wages forfeited. When they went to the Police Superintendent for assistance, he advised them to go to the court. They, however, adopted another method. On 7 October 1905, they stopped the vehicle of the manager on his way home and detained him there. He rushed to a nearby mill. The police was called and the strikers dispersed. Twelve men were charged and sentenced.[127]

But these memorials and small protests did not deter the millowners from working their mills for extremely long hours. Now the workers' frustrations took a different form. In October 1905, the workers resorted to large-scale strikes induced, as usual, with some amount of window-breaking. In some cases, for example, in the Phoenix Mill on 8 October, it took a more serious turn. Striking workers from some other mills arrived there and started throwing stones in order to bring the insiders out. The Police Superintendent, Walton, was called. On his arrival he advised the manager to stop the mill. When the workers of the Phoenix Mill were coming out, some of them were assaulted by those outside. Walton caught a few men. The other workers then became more agitated and broke into the time-keeper's office. Walton had to take refuge in the mill-building. The workers tore the time-keeper's records but did not touch the other properties. This, in a way, showed their particular resentment against the long hours of work. In the end, more policemen were called to disperse them.[128] Disturbances occurred in many mills and many had to be closed. Even by 12 October 1905, the

TOI reported that the 'situation in the mill district cause some anxiety'.[129] The Police Commissioner found the situation so bad that he warned the BMOA that 'under the circumstances he could not guarantee the safety of life and property unless there was uniformity in the hours of closing'.[130] Alarmed by these disturbances and pressurized by the public opinion, the BMOA finally passed a resolution asking for the limitation of the hours of work.[131]

The strikes on various issues—for more wages,[132] against the cleaning of machinery,[133] for the abolition of the pass-system[134]—continued. The IFLC admitted that the 'operatives fully understand the machinery of local strikes and have repeatedly forced the employers to comply with their demands in isolated cases'.[135] And the *ITJ* reported in July 1911 that, 'There is a spirit of independence abroad which renders the men less amenable to proper control.'[136]

By 1912, the strikes became so common that the BMOA complained about the workers 'organised in support of unjust demands' and 'their proneness to rush into strikes on the flimsiest of pretexts'.[137]

The intensity of strikes and the involvement of increasingly larger numbers of workers compelled the BMOA in 1913 to speak of 'a labour movement in this country'. Its then chairperson, Jehangir Bomanji Petit, stated, 'Indian labourers are now beginning to combine among themselves for the attainment of their common good and the removal of their common grievances; and I should not wonder if, before long, they are in a position to dictate terms to the capitalists as they are doing in Europe. Labour in this city has now commenced to realise the force of numbers and the power of combination.'[138]

Thus the increased frequency and prolonged duration of the strikes and the involvement of a greater number of workers was leading to a situation when strikes and solidarity at a wider level would be possible. However, it needed the intensified miseries of the War years, at a time when the capitalists were amassing wealth while the increasing prices forced the real wages of the workers down, to create the objective and subjective conditions for launching the struggle at a new pitch.

At the beginning of the War, the rumours about an impending German invasion and bombardment of the city created panic among the people. The banias fled and even 'the moneylenders converted their rupees into gold and departed to their homes'.[139] Many workers also left the city. In this situation, more than 20 mills were 'either working short time or closed altogether'.[140]

It was also the time for better market conditions for the textile mills. The millowners desperately wanted their mills to run. Even after the workers, who had left, returned and the rumours subsided, there remained a demand for labour, particularly for trained labour. So, when, owing to the increased prices of foodstuffs, strikes occurred for higher wages, the demands of the workers were conceded in 'almost every case . . . as the dearth of labour rendered it an easy matter for the work-people to find employment in other mills, who were ready enough to employ them on better terms'.[141]

Most of these strikes during the War years were 'settled in favour of the operatives'.[142] The employers also did not find much difficulty in doing so as they were earning huge profits.[143] During the months of September and October 1917, about 29 strikes occurred in the mills and the workers 'in almost all cases demanded 10 per cent increase in wages and in nearly every instance the strike was successful'.[144] In 1918, about 60 strikes took place 'for increased bonus to meet the cost of living (and) were mostly successful'.[145]

It was on this point of getting more wages to offset the cost of living that the workers' demands were getting concentrated now. The prices of the basic necessities of life had increased so much that all the workers were affected by this. This common demand combined with some success in frequent strikes during the War-years created a feeling of solidarity among them and a sense of strength *vis-ā-vis* their employers. The experience of protests and strikes tended to create the basis for a relatively swifter mobilization at the industrial level. Thus began the new phase in the history of industrial relations in Bombay bringing general strikes in its wake. It was not the formal trade unions but the general strikes which separated the post-War years from the pre-War ones. And it was not the educated, mass-oriented middle-class individuals who, by forming trade unions, changed the course of workers' struggles, but the workers themselves, who, by entering the arena of general strikes, created the conditions for a wider solidarity thereby facilitating the growth of trade unions.

The general strike of 1919 in the Bombay textile industry was a watershed. It was a link between the earlier forms of individual, departmental, mill-level and multi-mill-level strikes of the earlier period and the general industrial strikes of the later period. It is not that the earlier forms disappeared later on. But even they acquired a new poignancy and militancy and inspired a new cohesiveness among the participants. The scale and success of the 1919 strike heralded a new era in the history of industrial relations in Bombay which culminated in the great strike of 1928 which was unprecedented in scale and in the formation of workers' consciousness and remained so until 1982. The leaders and organizations operating in the mill areas until 1918 became more or less redundant after 1919 and a new phase of leadership and organizational initiatives became relevant after that. The workers in Bombay successfully resisted the employers' attempts to cut wages in the mid-1920s even while the employers in some other industrial centres like Ahmedabad managed to do so. The collective strength and consciousness of the workers in the 1920s were on a higher level and it was different from those of either the preceding or succeeding decades.

The strike started quietly without any indication of the reach and importance it was to acquire in the coming days.[146] The workers of the Century Mill, owned by the industrial magnate C.N. Wadia, struck work on 29 December 1918 demanding bonus and war allowance as it was given to the clerical staff of the mill, in addition to 25 per cent increase in wages. They approached H.B. Mandavale, a lawyer and supporter of Home Rule League, to write to the employers on their behalf. But the mill agents were adamant that there should not be any interference 'between the agents and their men'.[147] Instead it was proposed that the workers should join work and an arbitration panel consisting of C.N. Wadia and Lakhmidas Tairsee would look into their grievances. But this effort failed because the workers did not trust the employers, particularly in the light of the contemptuous treatment they received at the hands of J.G. Anderson, the European manager of the mill. The stalemate, therefore, continued for many days until, on the evening of 8 January 1919, they persuaded the workers of the neighbouring Textile Mill to join in. On the morning of the 9 January, although the Textile Mill had put on its machinery, the workers remained outside. When the workers from the Century Mill, after demonstrating before their mill, joined them, they all set off to persuade the workers of other nearby mills as well as those situated in Parel. They were soon successful in bringing the workers of many mills out including those of the Crown Mills, Dawn Mill, Globe Mill and the mills of the Currimbhoy Group. All this was done without much trouble because the workers inside those mills were willing to come out to join the strikers and the managers were keen to prevent the mill property from getting damaged.

This brought a large number of workers on to the street who now must have realized that a larger strike was within the range of immediate possibility. The gathering, therefore, branched out in two streams, the larger one moving towards the Delisle Road, Jacob Circle and Parel, where most of the mills were concentrated, and the smaller one going towards Dadar and Mahim. Similar tactics of persuasion and force were used to bring almost the entire industry to a standstill in a span of a few hours. Their purpose was generally achieved peacefully through talking, demonstrating and shouting. But sometimes, as in the case of Sun Mill, Finlay Mills, Sassoon Mills and Bombay Cotton and Dyeing Works, where the managers resisted, somewhat violent methods like throwing stones and brickbats were used to effect the strike. There was some destruction of property and occasional injuries to persons. But, by and large, the 'demonstrators were orderly and well-behaved'.[148] Even the *TOI*, which had generally adopted a disparaging tone towardes the strike, conceded the basically non-violent nature of the movement: 'In spite of the extensive area occupied by the strikers there was comparative quiet in the mill areas except for stone-throwing at intervals. Such incidents are inseparable from an organised movement of the nature which happened in Bombay on Thursday, but on the whole the attitude of the strikers was not such as to give anxiety.'[149]

By the afternoon of 9 January 1919, most of the 85 mills were closed and only those were working where either the strikers or news of the strike had not reached. The number of the strikers was roughly estimated to be from 100,000 to 120,000 and 'one could see knots of workmen gathered here and there in the whole mill district from Byculla to Mahim'.[150] By then the first general industrial strike on economic issues was a reality.

The relative ease and speed with which this mobilization took place owed to the deteriorating living conditions of the workers, their awareness of the fabulous prosperity of the industry, the experiences gained during the strikes of the War period, and the increasing realization of their power to successfully launch a strike.

The most important cause of the strike was the realization of common grievances. The prices of all essential commodities had risen enormously while the wages had lagged behind. One contemporary put the rise in the prices of the essential food items at 75 per cent 'by the lowest computation', and the rise in monthly rents from an average of Rs. 6 to that of Rs. 10.[151] The famine in the countryside and the cholera epidemic in the city further aggravated the situation because the workers not only had to send money home, but the expenditure on doctors, medicines and funerals in the city had gone up substantially. Their demand, therefore, was that they could be satisfied with the pre-War wages 'if the owners agreed to supply them with their daily necessities at the pre-War prices'.[152]

They knew that it was possible for the millowners to meet their demands as the mills were earning fabulous profits for about four years now.[153] There might also have been a deep feeling of injustice in the whole situation that the millowners were getting massively richer through the labour of the workers whose conditions were rapidly deteriorating.

The generalized formation of opinion and inter-personal and inter-group communications on these issues must also have helped in the swift mobilization. The success of many small and large strikes during the War years might have convinced the workers of the employers' ability to pay as well as their own power to achieve such a bargain. Moreover, the experiences gained and the difficulties endured in this period had created a general atmosphere among the workers in favour of bigger mobilization.

The strike lasted for about 20 days. It started on 9 January and it was only on 28 January that it was reported to have 'practically ended'.[154] Barring a few violent incidents, some of them provoked and caused by police intervention, it remained peaceful and workers' solidarity and resilience were noticeable factors. The strikers regularly went to their respective mills in the morning, but remained outside for some time before going back. Their resolve was slowly becoming firmer. They had realized that this strike was different from the previous ones and 'if by their conduct they allow it to fizzle out, they would be ruining the chance of a lifetime'.[155]

The BMOA and the individual millowners adopted a seemingly firm attitude, particularly in the initial phase of the strike. On 10 January, the BMOA notified that unless the workers resumed work 'the Committee will not take any notice whatsoever of any representations made by the workmen regarding their grievances'.[156] Even the individual millowners tried their own devices to break the strike by alternative display of toughness and promise of consideration. Many of the mills put on their machinery regularly in the morning throughout the strike period to lure some of the workers and break the resolve of the remaining. All these attempts were, however, unsuccessful. Later on the BMOA relented and promised 'sympathetic consideration' through notices put on all the mills. But even this failed to convince the workers who had been demanding that each mill should put written and signed notices stating that the demands had been granted.[157]

There were attempts from other quarters as well to convince the workers to join back. The Home Rule Leagues and the Kamgar Hitwardhak Sabha, the two most important organizations working in the mill areas, repeatedly tried to persuade the workers to resume work. On 10 January, in a meeting of workers, the Home Rulers advised 'the men to resume work and then make proper representations to their employers'.[158] The Kamgar Hitwardhak Sabha, on 11 January, also issued 'a printed circular' giving the same advice to the workers and assuring those who joined that they would 'not be molested by the rest of their fellows'.[159] The Sabha held many meetings and tried several times to convince the workers about the necessity to join work.[160] The government authorities led by the Governor and the Police Commissioner also tried to bring about a settlement and advised the workers to go back to their mills. On 15 January, the Police Commissioner, Vincent, addressed a meeting of workers and gave them this advice. Some of the strikers met the Governor three days later for the purpose of settlement where they were again given the same advice.

But all these attempts proved futile as the workers refused to join unless their demands were conceded beforehand because their previous experiences had made them wary of the verbal promises made by the employers and shown that the employers had reneged on their promises and victimized the workers. Therefore, they did not want to come out in the open and tried to present their demands through the channels of the middle-class leaders, government officials or even anonymously. Their only safeguard was the collective solidarity. The *Bombay Chronicle* reported:

> The men on the whole appear to be firm in their attitude and those who favour a return to work even without their demands being met are clearly in the minority and their number seems to have still further dwindled down, notwithstanding the belated efforts of the Kamgar Hitwardhak Sabha. Some of the strikers interviewed positively decline to believe in promises of "sympathetic consideration" and ask whether the treatment meted out to the GIP Railway men last year is not after all so old that they could forget its aftermath.[161]

The millowners sensed the mood of the workers and began to relent. They wanted a settlement which supposedly would not infringe on the discipline. The Police Commissioner, Vincent, provided the escape route. On 22 January, notices bearing Vincent's signature conceding the workers' demands were displayed in all the mills. But this was not considered sufficient by the workers who demanded that the signatures of the agents and managers should also be there on the notices. In addition to this, they demanded pay for the strike period. The latter demand was considered by the mill managers as 'subversive of all discipline' which would 'make the position of . . . managers . . . intolerable and risky, in fact that of a mere figure-head'.[162]

Ultimately, the workers joined without their demand for the strike pay being met. But the strike had been quite successful and brought a new sense of power among the workers and ushered in a new era in the history of industrial relations in Bombay.

Contemporary observers, particularly in the initial phase of general strikes and militant action by the workers immediately following the War, were vexed to find 'the capacity of the operatives to remain on strikes for considerable periods despite the lack of any visible organisation'.[163] The Government of Bombay, after the 1919 strike, though surprised at the apparent lack of leadership despite such a level of industrial protest, talked about the 'probability of some controlling organisation'.[164] Similarly, the *Bombay Chronicle* commented in 1924 that 'it is absurd to suppose that the men are lacking in leadership . . . it is clear that there is good sound leadership among them *somewhere*'.[165]

Attempts have been made to explain this phenomenon. Newman has underlined the role of the jobbers as the leaders of the workers: 'It was the jobber who, for the first sixty years of industry's existence, performed the welfare functions of trade unions, bargained with the employers and mobilised the workers in strikes.'[166]

On the other hand, Chandavarkar emphasizes the role of the mill districts in sustaining the movement. His opinion is that 'in Bombay it (the neighbourhood) provided an indispensable base for industrial action. . . . Without organization and action in the neighbourhood, it is doubtful whether the general strikes could have been sustained.'[167]

As discussed earlier, the jobbers did perform a certain level of leadership role at many junctures. They organized meetings, sent petitions, presented demands and represented the workers to various commissions of enquiries. Similarly, the neighbourhood provided the arena, particularly in the later period, where workers exchanged information, confabulated with each other, heard their well-wishers and potential leaders both from within their own ranks as well as from among the outsiders. It also served as the base for sustaining the strikes as it was here that credits in kind and cash were arranged and moral and material support of various sorts were given and received not only in times of conflicts and strikes but otherwise as well.

There is, however, one problem in attributing such a pivotal role to either the jobbers or the neighbourhood. The jobbers had been in existence almost since the beginning of the industry and the mill districts had also emerged since the 1890s. So why was it that the coordination of industry-wide strikes could be effected only after the War and not before it? This point leads us to an exploration of the workers' consciousness gradually forming itself around the demands related to their work in the mills and the growing realization of their common grievances and strength.

It is true that the relegation of powers of recruitment, training and discipline gave the jobbers an enormous authority over the workers. It was only to be expected because in a situation where the competition for relatively better-paid mill jobs was acute, the workers who got them through the agency of the jobber would be very grateful to him. In addition to this, the workers who were favoured by the jobbers could get better material and machinery thereby leading to an increase in wages. Alternatively, they could lose part of their wages through defective materials supplied to them, besides being marked for fines or dismissals. But the most important thing which tended to minimize the authority of the jobber at the workplace was the pressure of work. All the gratitude to a job-giver would be diluted when the strain of work on the body and mind of the worker reached beyond a certain point. Sometimes this also turned into antagonism. The *ITJ* reported about the difficulties faced by a throstle jobber. He, as a rule, exercised enormous power over the boys,

> . . . but when the rovings are bad and the frame does not spin well, their patience gets exhausted. And when they are still urged on by the doffer jobber, who always carries a cane and threatens pretty freely to use it, they frequently let him know that he cannot have it all his own way. They stay away after the mid-day interval and play in the streets, or go and work with their friends at a neighbouring mill where better cotton is used. It has not infrequently happened that nearly 30 per cent of the total number of piecers have gone away at a time under the above circumstances.[168]

At times of crisis, when the availability of labour was grossly inadequate, as during the outbreak of plague in 1896-7, the jobber's authority completely crumbled. Then, as we have discussed earlier, the workers went to any jobber who promised more payment on any given day.

The authority of the jobber was challenged not only by passive protests but also during the moments of conflict. The weavers, who were generally most active in strike-actions, were skilled workers and more in demand. This realization of their strength put them in a position from where they could defy the authority of both the jobbers and the employers. They were the ones who held out till the last during the 1919 strike.

The limitation of the jobber's authority over the workers was also exhibited when both the jobber-dominated bodies—earlier Lokhanday's Millhands' Association and later Bole's Kamgar Hitwardhak Sabha—not only failed to enrol many workers as members but also failed to influence them in moments of conflict. During the 1919 strike, despite its repeated attempts, the Sabha miserably failed to convince the workers to resume work. Even during the 1914-15, when the rumours about German invasion induced the workers to leave the city or stop work, the Sabha's efforts to dissuade them proved futile.

This is not to say that the jobbers did not have much authority. But the point which is made here is that the authority of the jobber, although extensive, broke at crucial moments due to the pressure of situation, economic or otherwise. At such moments, the jobber would either side with the workers or remain isolated. Some of these moments were sudden, violent and characterized by apparently erratic behaviour on the part of the workers. The *ITJ* related an incident in which the workers of a particular department in the New Great Eastern Mill suddenly left their work allegedly in sympathy with their jobber and assembled in the compound and adopted a 'threatening attitude' even after the jobber had left. On this the manager called the police. On being asked by the police officer 'as to what their grievances were and why they struck work, some of them replied that their wages had been cut off on account of their being absent, while the others stated that they had been fined by the manager'. When the manager asked them to resume work, they said that they wanted to see the agents. Then the agents came and tried to persuade them, but they 'commenced shouting, roaring, hurrahing'. Finally, the police dispersed them.[169]

The IDC emphasized certain features of the strike-actions in the mills. These were 'the frequency of strikes without notice', the 'absence of any clearly-defined grievances before striking', 'multiplicity' of demands, lack of any organization, and the 'increasing solidarity of the employers and employed'.[170]

The little leisure-time which the workers got between the working hours, along with the lack of proper negotiating channels, accounted for this apparent unpredictability in their behaviour, their irritated nature and occasional proneness to violence. Their hours of work extended up to 12, sometimes even 14 or 15, hours in a day. The remaining time was taken by other requirements and the necessity to get rest. So they hardly had time to organize in the neighbourhood or listen to the speeches of the leaders or even to hold extended talks among themselves to discuss the possibility of strikes. This constraint placed them in a situation in which not only their demands related to the problems at the workplace but the protests and strikes also had to be initiated there. Thus we find that most of the strike-actions in this period were not well thought out, nor were they conducted in a proper manner by giving notices, but were decided and initiated on the spur of the moment. Meetings and consultations were often held later, when the cessation of work had given them more collective time, and then a presentable demand-charter was formulated. Even the big strikes involving a large number of workers were generally not decided beforehand but were effected by the time-honoured method of throwing stones at mills and forcing the authorities to close down. Though the neighbourhood was important for supporting the strike, it was not the place where early mobilization took place, at least during this period.

This behaviour-pattern of the workers had been sometimes explained in terms of their supposedly pre-industrial mentality. Ravinder Kumar, analysing the general strike of 1919, characterized it 'as a species of a working class *jacquerie*' which 'exhibited all the features of a peasant uprising: complete spontaneity; an absence of class consciousness, class organisation and formal leadership; and finally, the expression of long standing grievances and pent up frustrations through a popular explosion'.[171]

Although this evaluation succinctly comprehends the apparent formlessness of the strike of 1919 in the beginning, it misses a few vital points. For one, even though their activities in the initial stages took unorganized forms, the workers were fully cognizant of their grievances. Second, as we have discussed in the preceding account, the strike was not particularly violent. The occasional violence which occurred was purposive and selective, not mindless and indiscriminate. Its purpose was to get the mills closed and achieve a full mobilization. Finally, there is no contradiction between spontaneity and consciousness. There can hardly be a movement without spontaneity and, in any case, the spontaneity of today is the accumulated consciousness of yesterdays. The cumulative experience of resistance and protests, combined with the generalized sufferings of the War-years, produced the first general strike. The strikes of the pre-War period could cover only a few mills at most, whereas the strikes of the post-War years could spread to all the mills. Spontaneity of the pre-War years was limited in scope; the spontaneity of the post-War period was realized at a much higher level. Spontaneity was not a static thing. It kept developing with the growth of consciousness among the workers. The commonality of demands was expressed through the unity of action. Thus in the years after the War the workers exhibited a sense of industrial solidarity which would prove very crucial for the general strikes in the 1920s.

However, this solidarity and the sense of class identity were limited in nature. Two very important groups—the women and the Dalits—were not fully integrated. The existence of separate enclaves of women's work and the discrimination against the Dalits were responsible for this situation. The women did strike work in many instances and they also supported the collective actions by other workers. But they were not actively engaged in larger actions of the period. On many occasions, even their demands were not taken into consideration. One worker- leader who participated in the workers' meetings held in 1884 to memorialize the FC, 1885 and the government said before the Commission: 'As regards the children of 9 years and below and the women we leave it to the option of the Government to deal with them.'[172] It was because, as another agitator pointed, 'There was no decision with regards women and children at the meeting; the question was not discussed.'[173]

The women also thought likewise. Although they followed the initiative taken by male workers, they, for the most part, did not participate in the meetings and demonstrations. Sakoo, the female overseer in the reeling department in the Colaba Mill, told the Commission: 'I know that there was a meeting of the operatives for the purpose of petitioning Government. We will do according to the wishes of those operatives who attended the meeting. I think it would be a good thing to have 4 Sundays in the month. The women have not joined the agitation; they were not asked.'

She further added that even if 'they (the women) had been asked they would not have gone; they did not wish to go'.[174]

Even as late as 1922, the women did not seem to have been integrated into the labour movement. In a meeting of women workers, Mrs D.G. Upson stated: '(We want to) make them (i.e., the women workers) strong enough to fight for themselves and their rights as men workers are doing successfully.'[175]

The Dalit workers, though they conducted and participated in strikes and other protests, experienced discrimination in their every-day working life and exclusion from better-paid jobs, particularly in the weaving department. These factors, along with their weak links with the countryside, made them less persevering in the course of a long strike, as was evident during the general strike of 1929.

NOTES

1. E.P. Thompson, 'Time, Work-Discipline and Industrial Capitalism', *Past and Present*, no. 38, December 1967.
2. T.S. Ashton, *An Economic History of England: The Eighteen Century* (London, 1972), pp. 203-4; quoted in Mark Harrison, 'The Ordering of the Urban Environment: Time, Work and the Occurrence of Crowds, 1790-1835', *Past and Present* (February, 1986), p. 137.
3. David S. Landes, *Revolution in Time: Clocks and the Making of the Modern World* (Cambridge, 1983), p. 229, quoted in Mark Harrison, 'The Ordering of the Urban Environment', p. 138.
4. Ibid., pp. 138-9.
5. Thomas C. Smith, 'Peasant Time and Factory Time in Japan', *Past and Present* (May 1986), pp. 165-97.
6. Jonathan P. Parry, 'Lords of Labour: Working and Shirking in Bhilai', in Parry, et al., eds., *Contributions to Indian Sociology*, vol. 33, nos. 1 and 2, January-August 1999, p. 110.
7. Ibid.
8. See Chapter 2, the section on 'Hours-of-Work'.
9. Bipan Chandra, *Economic Nationalism*, p. 328.
10. FC, 1885, p. 139. Also see the evidences of Raghoo Bhicaji, Genoo Babajee and Narayan Surkoji.
11. Ibid., evidence of N. Surkoji. Emphasis added.
12. Ibid., evidence of R. Bhicaji.
13. Ibid.
14. See IFC 1890, p. 11.
15. Ibid., pp. 10-11.
16. Ibid., evidences of various workers.
17. IFLC, I, p. 82.
18. Ibid., p. 7.
19. Ibid., p. 103.

20. Ibid., p. 31.
21. Ibid., p. 20.
22. Morris, *Industrial Labour Force*, p. 92.
23. Ibid., p. 92, fn. 28.
24. *Wages and Hours*, 1923, p. 8.
25. ITB, I, p. 134.
26. ITB, II, p. 138.
27. IFLC, II, p. 81.
28. Ibid., p. 133.
29. Ibid., p . 94.
30. IFLC, I, p. 89.
31. Ibid., p. 19.
32. ITB, III, p. 536.
33. Ibid., p. 562.
34. *Report of the Excise Committee, 1922-23*, vol. II, p. 38.
35. ITB, I, p. 134.
36. FC, 1875, p. 124; evidence of N. Dadabhoy, acting manager of the Morarjee Goculdass Spinning and Weaving Mill.
37. *Report of BMOA*, 1875-6, p. 74.
38. FC, 1885. See, for example, the responses to the question no. 64.
39. IFLC, II, p. 63.
40. Ibid., p. 65, evidence of Manmohandas Ramji.
41. Ibid., p. 66.
42. Ibid., p. 70.
43. Ibid., p. 76.
44. Ibid., p. 148.
45. IIC, IV, p. 10.
46. *Report of the Textile Factories Labour Committee*, 1906, p. 16.
47. IFLC, I, pp. 20-1
48. IIC, 1916-18, I, *Report*, p. 160.
49. RCL, 1929, *Report*, p. 41.
50. IFLC, I, p. 20.
51. FC, 1875, p. 124, evidence of S. Dhunjeebhoy of the Alliance Spinning Company. Emphasis added.
52. *Report of BMOA*, 1875-6, p. 74.
53. TFLC, 1906, p. 16. Emphasis added.
54. IFLC, I, pp. 20-21.
55. Ibid., p. 20.
56. Ibid., p. 19.
57. *ITJ*, 1890-1, p. 60.

58. *ITJ*, October 1893, p. 6. Emphasis added.
59. *ITJ*, October 1914, p. 1.
60. IIC, IV, p. 266.
61. Burnett-Hurst, *Labour and Housing*, pp. 13-14.
62. Kelman, *Labour in India*, p. 86.
63. *Indu Prakash*, 27 September 1905, in *RNP*, 30 September 1905.
64. *The Gazetteer of Bombay City and Island*, 1909, p. 208.
65. Burnett-Hurst, *Labour and Housing*, pp. 48-9.
66. Ibid., p. 47.
67. ITB, III, p. 471.
68. *The Gazeetter of Bombay City and Island, 1909*, p. 208. Emphasis added.
69. *Report of BMOA*, 1909, p. v.
70. ITB, II, p. 138.
71. Ibid., p. 139.
72. IFLC, I, pp. 18-19.
73. Ibid., p. 18.
74. *Report of BMOA*, 1918, p. xii.
75. *Report of the Industrial Disputes Committee*, 1922, p. 1.
76. RCL, I, *Report*, p. 12.
77. S.D. Mehta, 'Professor Morris on Textile Labour Supply', *Indian Economic Journal*, 1, 3, January 1954, p. 334; quoted in Morris, *Industrial Labour Force* , p. 84.
78. IFLC, II, p. 86.
79. Ibid., p. 123.
80. Ibid., p. 122.
81. Ibid., p. 60.
82. ITB, III, p. 562.
83. IFLC, I, pp. 20-1.
84. RCL, 1929, I, p. 41.
85. IFLC, I, p. 83.
86. RCL, 1929, I, p. 333.
87. For example, V.B. Karnik, *Strikes in India*; Sukomal Sen, *The Working Class of India*.
88. R.K. Das, *Factory Labour in India* (Berlin, 1923).
89. For example, Morris, *Industrial Labour Force*.
90. FC, 1875, p. 82.
91. Ibid., p. 24.
92. Ibid., p. 125.
93. Given in FC, 1885, p. 8.
94. *RNP*, 30 January 1890, p. 11.

95. IFC, 1890, p. 29, evidence of Balloo Atmaji.
96. Ibid., p. 25, evidence of Rama Gyanjee.
97. *RNP,* January 1890.
98. FC, 1885, evidence of Narayan Surkoji.
99. Ibid., evidence of N.M. Lokhanday.
100. Ibid., evidence of Narayan Surkoji.
101. See IFC, 1890, Appendix.
102. See Chapter 1.
103. Quoted in V.B. Karnik, *Strikes in India*, p. 6.
104. *ITJ*, December 1892, p. 64.
105. Ibid., September 1893, p. 237.
106. Ibid., p. 254.
107. *Report of BMOA*, 1893, p. 10.
108. Ibid.
109. *ITJ*, December 1892, p. 64.
110. See *ITJ*, for the years 1894 and 1895.
111. *Report of BMOA*, 1894, p. 11.
112. *AFR*, 1897, p. 7. The factory inspector wrote that the 'unanimous advice of the English managers, engineers and spinning masters was to close'.
113. Ibid.
114. *AFR*, 1897, p. 8.
115. Ibid., p. 8.
116. Ibid., p. 9.
117. *Report of BMOA*, 1897, p. 7.
118. Ibid.
119. *AFR*, 1897, p. 9.
120. Ibid.
121. Ibid., and *AFR*, 1898, pp. 6-7.
122. *AFR*, 1897, p. 9.
123. *ITJ*, June 1901, p. 235.
124. *AFR*, 1904, p. 2.
125. *AFR*, 1909, p. 2.
126. *TOI*, 25 September 1905.
127. *TOI*, 12 October 1905, p. 5.
128. *ITJ*, October 1905, p. 32; *TOI*, 10 October 1905.
129. *TOI*, 12 October 1905, p. 4.
130. *Report of BMOA*, 1905, p. 8.
131. Ibid.
132. See *ITJ*, 1909-10.

133. *ITJ*, April 1907, p. 221. Over 4,000 workers of the Maneckji Petit Mills struck work demanding that they should not be asked to clean the machinery on other working days but only on Saturdays.
134. IFLC, I, p. 20: 'Operatives have struck and forced their employers to give way when passes up to 15 per cent or even higher were granted; the workers demanded the abolition of the pass-out system.'
135. Ibid.
136. *ITJ*, July 1911, p. 351.
137. BMOA, 1912, p. iii.
138. BMOA, 1913, p. vii.
139. *ITJ*, September 1915, p. 370.
140. *ITJ*, October 1914, p. 1. The journal was led to comment about the work-people who 'showed a strange perversity of action despite the counsel of those who knew their interests'.
141. *AFR*, 1914, p. 5.
142. *AFR*, 1915, p. 4.
143. Century Mill, for example, made profits of Rs. 10.5 lakhs in 1917 and 22.5 lakhs in 1918 as against a profit of only Rs. 1.5 lakhs in 1914. *Bombay Chronicle*, 11 January, 1919, p. 7.
144. Burnett-Hurst, *Labour and Housing*, p. 146.
145. Ibid.
146. The following narration of the strike is based on the reports of the *Bombay Chronicle* (*BC*) and the *Times of India* (*TOI*) for the corresponding period.
147. *BC*, 10 January 1919, p. 8, in *LMI*, III, p. 107.
148. *BC*, 10 January 1919, p. 7.
149. *TOI*, 10 January 1919, p. 9, in *LMI*, III, p. 112.
150. *BC*, 10 January 1919, p. 7.
151. N.M. Joshi, in *BC*, 18 January 1919, p. 7.
152. *BC*, 14 January 1919, p. 7.
153. For example, the net profits of the Century Mill in 1918 was 22.5 lakhs on a total paid-up share capital of 18.5 lakhs. *BC*, 11 January 1919, p. 7.
154. *BC*, 28 January 1919, p. 8.
155. Ibid., 21 January 1919, p. 7.
156. Ibid., 11 January 1919, p. 9.
157. Ibid., 15 January 1919, p. 7.
158. Ibid., 11 January 1919, p. 9.
159. Ibid., 13 January 1919, p. 7.
160. See, for example, *BC*, 15, 20 and 21 January 1919.
161. *BC*, 14 January 1919, p. 7.
162. *TOI*, 24 January 1919, p. 10, in *LMI*, III, p. 149.

163. *Report of the Industrial Disputes Committee*, 1922, p. 2.
164. Quoted in R. Chandavarkar, 'Workers' Politics and Mill Districts in Bombay between the Wars', in *MAS*, March 1981, p. 603.
165. *BC*, 21 February 1924; quoted in ibid., p. 604. Emphasis added.
166. Newman, *Workers and Unions*, p. 4.
167. Chandavarkar, 'Workers' Politics and Mill Districts', p. 605.
168. *ITJ*, 1890-1, p. 91.
169. *ITJ*, March 1894, pp. 149-50.
170. IDC, *Report*, 1922, p. 2.
171. Ravinder Kumar, 'The Bombay Textile Strike, 1919', *IESHR*, vol. VIII, no. 1 (March 1971), p. 3.
172. FC, 1885, evidence of Raghoo Bhicaji.
173. Ibid., evidence of N. Surkoji.
174. Ibid., evidence of Sakoo.
175. *BC*, 6 March 1922.

CHAPTER 7

Conclusion

THE PROCESS OF identity-formation among the workers was shaped by various socio-cultural and political factors encompassing their inherited as well as acquired consciousness. The identities of caste, religion, language and region were carried by the rural folk seeking jobs over to the city. These were parts of their inherited baggage which had been handed over to them through generations and had defined their existence, outlook, attitude and behaviour until then. This does not mean, however, that these were static phenomena admitting no change. In the context of Maharashtra, these identities were constantly reshaped and redefined throughout the seventeenth and eighteenth centuries by the Bhakti movement and the battles and wars which the peasant armies and guerrillas had fought against the regional and central authorities. The whole array of Bhakti saints had sought to shape the religious and social outlook of the people at various levels.

Yet there was a certain stability in peasant society which was reflected in the relative fixity of status, position and attitudes following a generally predictable pattern. The impact of British rule proved to be destabilizing for Indian society, particularly in the urban situation. Here the social, political and economic changes were novel and rapid, various socio-political identities jostled with each other, sometimes in a symbiotic relationship and at other times conflicting and vying for supremacy. Bombay was a particularly pertinent example of this. During the nineteenth century, it underwent a reasonably fast economic and demographic growth. People from various economic, social and linguistic backgrounds thronged the city in pursuit of business and jobs. The sheer variety of people living in Bombay with their distinct language, dress, colour and occupation was quite noticeable by the end of the nineteenth century.

The cotton textile industry started in the 1850s and by the end of the century it had become prominent in the economy of the city. Depending on cheap labour and easy access to the raw material, the industry remained quite a profitable venture until the 1890s, despite the indifferent colonial government and a wary British textile industry which perceived it as a serious competitor. But, due to the policies of the government which were often influenced by its colonial imperatives and its pro-Manchester attitude and which were inimical to the growth of the industry, its position remained basically unstable because of its dependence on the export market in China. In the 1890s, a series of crises beginning with the colonial government's disturbing currency policy seriously undercut its competitive edge in the Chinese market for yarn. The availability of the foreign market remained uncertain while the home market was largely occupied by the goods from the British industry. The indifferent and pro-Manchester attitude of the colonial government left this newly emerging industry to fend for itself. Although it recovered by the turn of the century, the ups and downs continued till the beginning of the First World War which, by cutting down the imports, provided the opportunity for it to expand in the home market. It performed well until 1922 after which a long-term crisis began.

These uncertainties induced the industrialists to rely on the managing agents for the mobilization of capital and organization of production, and on the jobbers for procurement of labour and its management on the shop floor. No long-term solutions were devised. The reliance on the managing agents caused unnecessary overproduction as the agents were paid commission on the volume of production and the dependence on the jobbers resulted in the creation of an unstable and disorganized workforce.

There was no surety of jobs and the workers were worked for extremely long hours at relatively low payments. The working time varied from 12 to 15 hours in a day during this period. In the early phase the mills worked during the daylight. Although there was no uniformity of working time between the mills, the daylight imposed a natural restriction on the hours that the workers could be retained. But with the large-scale introduction of electric lights in the 1900s working time was prolonged inordinately, sometimes reaching up to more than 15 hours in a day. Later, with the passage of the Factory Act of 1911, the working time was reduced to 12 hours, but even this was more than the workers could endure. During the whole of this period, therefore, the workers had to spend 12 to 15 hours in the ill-ventilated, hot, damp and stuffy atmosphere inside the mills. The windows in the mills were kept closed for fear of the draught breaking the thread and other reasons and no alternative system was devised to get the workers a little fresh air. After working in this atmosphere for such long hours, the workers were exhausted both physically and mentally. To get some relief from the tiring and ceaseless monotony of their work, they resorted to drinking alcohol. By the first decade of the twentieth century the consumption of alcohol among the workers had become very common. While their health was already impaired due to the strenuous millwork and the intake of alcohol, their home surroundings also added their bit to the poor quality of life.

The rapid development of the mill-districts in the northern areas of the city where most of the mills were located and where the workers had moved *en masse* during the 1880s and 1890s created a lot of sanitary problems. The pace of the construction activities was so fast that the lethargic municipal authorities could not cope with it. The millowners and the government agencies did not do much to provide the workers with decent accommodation. The houses made by the private builders stood on damp grounds, on mud, near open sewage, on the garbage, any place where space was available. Although most of the buildings were single-storeyed, which made these areas less densely populated, the sanitary problems were not lessened by this. Open sewers, excreta and mud surrounded these houses. To these were added the mephitic exhalations from the nearby unreclaimed swamps. And since the rents were rising fast due to the rapid influx of people, and the rise in the wages were not commensurate with that, the workers had to take in additional lodgers leading to overcrowding in the living rooms. So the polluted atmosphere outside their homes was aggravated by the smoke from cooking inside, making the women workers doubly vulnerable.

This polluted atmosphere, along with their long hours in the equally polluted and hot mills and the intake of alcohol, weakened their bodies making them hosts to a variety of diseases. Cholera, small-pox, malaria, plague and many other diseases inflicted the workers along with the city's other poor inhabitants. Sometimes the situation became so bad that Bombay resembled a city of death. The death-rate in the Presidency, though quite high, was less than that of Bombay city. Here the death-rate was more than the birth-rate and the infant mortality rate was said to be the highest in the world.

To escape from this predicament, the workers individually and collectively went to their villages. The country home was their last resort. The visit to the countryside provided them with a better environment which somewhat improved their health. Moreover, the rural links were kept and nurtured because the city-jobs were often temporary and city-lives insecure. But since the villages could not provide them with extended work, they had to return to the city.

Although the villages were the last resort for the fatigued and broken, the workers did not take their situation lying down. They resisted the haphazard work-regime imposed on them by the employers and waged struggles for achieving proper living wages through the means of occasional absenteeism, daily resistance at the workplace and the strikes. Records of strikes exist since the mid-1870s, and by the 1890s the strikes, though small-scale, had become quite frequent. During the plague years this trend of protest was further advanced because the shortage of labour made the workers' position less vulnerable. And even if this realization of strength *vis-à-vis* the employers was short-lived due to the return of the workers from the countryside, these experiences strengthened and broadened their collectivities and were helpful in the later protests. In the next decades, through many ups and downs, this trend was strengthened and during the War years the strikes became more frequent, their duration longer and the collective feeling more pronounced. The experiences of the War years transformed the nature of their protests by bringing the entire mass of millworkers in an unprecedented show of class solidarity resulting in the general strike of 1919. But the class consciousness, i.e. a sense of solidarity among the co-workers and against the employers, was not the only consciousness existing among the workers, nor were their activities limited to this. In fact, their activities were various and their multiple consciousness was reflected in them.

The marginal and uprooted peasants who flocked to Bombay in search of jobs brought their old-world socio-cultural identities with them. These were rooted in their consciousness of caste, religion, region and language. In the city they stayed with their relations and the people from their own regions. In many cases, the old workers who visited their homes prompted their relations and neighbours to come to the city for jobs. These old workers also helped them in finding the jobs and accommodated and supported them until they managed to find some work. The process of finding jobs was difficult and retaining them was even more so. For this purpose, many formal and informal networks were established, used, activated and nurtured. Caste, kinship, region and language provided the most important social channels through which the job-seekers were brought, sustained and put on to the jobs in the city. These inherited identities proved to be extremely potent sustaining factors in the urban lives of the working masses. The workers from a particular caste, region and language tended to congregate in particular localities. These small collectivities gave them a sense of security and ease. They also helped to sustain them in times of adversities. These identities were maintained and strengthened through the endogamous marriages and continuing rural links.

In this way, the city environment, instead of eroding their old-world ties, reinforced and strengthened them further. But the process of reinforcement was not simple and unidirectional. The inherited identities were actively reshaped and remoulded. In the city, the terms of reference of these identities became wider. Therefore, the term 'Maratha' referred to a group of endogamous sub-castes from various regions of Maharashtra; the 'Bhaiyas' signified the Hindu migrants from north India, particularly the United Provinces; the 'depressed classes' denoted a wide group of untouchable castes. The cohesive caste identity which earlier belonged to the group of adjoining villages could now extend to the entire region or the state or even the whole country. The proliferation of caste-based associations in the mill areas and naming of various institutions including hospitals along caste and community lines attested to the fact that the urban environment had expanded the reach of the community and had turned a cultural phenomenon into a political one.

The city-life brought the workers in contact not only with people from their own caste and region but a variety of others as well. They interacted with middle-class educated persons professing various ideologies. These contacts with advocates of cow-protection, nationalists like Tilak and his followers, and later the trade unionists and the communists had their impact on the workers. These incipient communal, nationalist and leftist ideas were to be picked by the workers in the course of time.

The working-class crowds formed on innumerable occasions for various, sometimes contrasting purposes. Except for the nightly gatherings for singing *bhajans* and other songs, contemptuously described by some as 'tomtoming', the formation of crowds happened mostly, though not always, during working time because, particularly during the early period, it encapsulated almost the entire waking time. The workers, therefore, had to absent themselves, often without permission, to participate in public events. A significant portion of the crowd might, however, be composed of workers without jobs, the casually employed, the stragglers and destitutes living in the mill areas and, of course, the children. These crowds could be mobilized with considerable ease. In fact, the mill areas witnessed a constant happening of crowds. They formed for strikes and impromptu demonstrations against working conditions, for cow-protection rallies, for Ganapati and Shivaji festivals, on Holi, Diwali and Dushhera,[1] for participation in nationalist rallies and demonstrations, for temperance meetings. In fact, the working masses seemed to be available for any number of things one could think of. The crowds formed in so many ways, on so many occasions and for so many purposes that it is difficult to discern any clear pattern or to impute any fixed identities to the entire mass of workers. They were mobilized for the nationalist cause, but sometimes in opposition to it;[2] against the millowners, but sometimes in their favour; against the government, but sometimes for them. The frequency of these mobilizations was so high that it is difficult to pinpoint the identities around which many of these took place.

But the three biggest mobilizations during this period with clear political purposes took place around the identities of religious community, nation and class. The communal riots in 1893 witnessed the first major collective mobilization of workers on a sectarian issue. All the mills were forced to close and almost the entire mass of workers were mobilized along sectarian lines. The next occasion for such a massive mobilization of the workers was in 1908 on a nationalist issue when Tilak was arrested and convicted. There occurred a largely pre-mediated general strike in the mills for seven days and the workers' protest-demonstrations happened almost continuously in the mill areas. The third such mobilization took place in 1919 in the form of a general strike on economic issues which was the biggest, more integrative and the longest ever. The class identity of the workers made it successful and this identity was strengthened during the course of the strike and its aftermath.

Although these mobilizations occurred around distinctly different identities, there were certain similar patterns discernible among them. The complete mobilization in each case was effected through the method of throwing stones at individual mills forcing the management to close for fear of the loss of property, thus bringing the groups of workers out. Even during the protests against Tilak's conviction in 1908, when there were reports of the prior decision about strike, this method was adopted for mobilization. The rationality of such an action was sometimes rooted in avoiding victimization by the employers of the workers in their own mills. But there was another, more objective, reason behind it. The workers who worked such long hours did not have much time to discuss, organize and decide in the neighbourhood. Their actions, therefore, had to take place around the mills and later, when the forced strikes brought the entire mass of workers out, more meaningful discussion and action could take place.

Another characteristic of these mobilizations was the lack of visible leadership. On all the three occasions government authorities and commentators vaguely talked awhile about 'wire-pullers', 'ring-leaders' and 'mischief-makers' but failed to lay fingers on any individuals who could have played leadership roles and whom they could punish or with whom they could negotiate. In fact, the absence of any leadership in the modern sense was quite remarkable. The workers seemed to operate not only in a relatively autonomous domain but also in an arena where the self-conscious leaders did not have much of a role to play.

The third, but by no means less important, characteristic was that all these mobilizations, though of completely different nature and character, seemed to be based on the core consisting of the Maratha workers, who had wide links inside the city and some security of their rural links to fall back upon. A cohesiveness was also induced due to the newly emerging Maratha mass identity which was crucial both in the city and in the Presidency.[3] This core was big enough among the workers to effect a bigger mobilization. Thus, although the riots of 1893 was also against the minority Muslim workers, all the mills were forced to close and the masses of the workers were ranged on the Hindu side. Similarly, in 1908, although the Muslim workers were said to have resented the strikes and the consequent loss of their income, this never had any affect on the course of events. All the mills were forced to close and massive demonstrations occurred in mill areas and many of them led to violent confrontations with the police and military resulting in the loss of many lives. The Marathas from the Konkan region, who were preponderant among the millworkers, were said to be mainly responsible for this mobilization.[4] During the strike of 1919 also, although the Muslim weavers were among the most militant strikers, they were not significant enough to cause a general mobilization. The other groups like the 'Pardeshis', that is, Hindu workers from U.P. and the Dalit workers, although significant in number, could not bring about such mobilization. This mobilization was again based on this powerful group belonging to the 'Maratha-Kunbi caste cluster' with great mobilizational potential. Throughout they formed more than half of the total workforce. Over the years, as the weaving sections were added and expanded, many of them moved over to this better-paying department where they accounted for about 62 per cent of all the weavers. The weavers' capacity for mobilization and propensity for militancy were based on this regionally powerful group which was upwardly mobile in social and political contexts and had their rural connections largely intact to fall back upon in times of adversity. Without taking this group into account, no big mobilization was possible in the working-class areas. When this group was won over to the communists in the late 1920s, the latter became a big force to reckon with. S.H. Jhabvala, an important labour leader in Bombay, commented on this phenomenon: 'Labour activity in Bombay is largely Mahratta in its nature. The leaders must be conversant firstly with the Mahratta language, secondly with Mahratta habits of life and with a good deal of social outlook upon life that is Mahratta partly in its character.'[5]

However, even though the workers operated in a relatively autonomous domain with respect to some of the mobilizations and the moving force behind the bigger mobilizations was provided by the Maratha workers, the ideas were derived from many sources. Autonomy of action was guided by inter-connecting discourse. The ideologies behind the bigger mobilizations transcended parochial boundaries and sometimes assumed a pan-Indian character. The overarching identities woven around religious community, nation and class were based on the narrower identities, but the former also tended to subsume the latter in the course of time integrating increasingly more numbers around them.

NOTES

1. For workers' enthusiastic organization and participation in these festivals, see *ITJ*, November 1901 and March 1904.
2. For example, at the time of the move by some for presenting Willingdon with a memorial on the occasion of his retirement in December 1918, the workers were mobilized on the opposing sides—by those interested in presenting the memorial as well as by those opposing it. See, *BC*, 9 December 1918 and 12 December 1918. Also see, Newman, *Workers and Unions*, p. 95.
3. For details on this Maratha identity, see Rosalind O'Hanlon, *Caste, Conflict, and Ideology: Mahatma Jotirao Phule and Low Caste Protest in Nineteenth-Century Western India* (Cambridge, 1985), pp. 41-9.
4. S.M. Edwardes, *By-ways of Bombay*, p. 135; also, Edwardes, *The Bombay City Police*, p. 141.
5. Quoted in R. Chandavarkar, 'Workers' Politics and the Mill Districts', p. 646.

Appendices

Appendix I: Progress of Cotton Mills in the City and Island of Bombay, 1865-1919

Year	Number of Mills	Number of Spindles	Number of Looms	Average Daily Employment
1865	10	2,49,984	3,378	6,557
1866	10	2,74,371	3,251	6,733
1867	10	2,78,057	3,578	7,630
1868	10	2,82,644	3,643	7,715
1869	10	2,85,874	3,719	7,857
1870	10	2,90,920	4,090	8,103
1871	10	3,05,896	4,290	8,553
1872	11	3,14,396	4,302	8,816
1873	14	3,94,592	4,606	10,714
1874	15	4,62,151	5,713	11,398
1875	27	7,52,634	7,781	13,551
1876	29	8,16,830	8,041	–
1877	31	8,95,204	8,433	20,347
1878	32	9,55,344	10,266	26,942
1879	32	9,81,000	10,856	28,860
1880	32	9,87,676	10,856	29,417
1881	32	9,91,522	10,932	31,351
1882	36	10,56,004	11,274	31,801
1883	38	11,26,698	11,667	34,736
1884	43	12,51,726	11,985	36,071
1885	49	13,47,390	12,011	41,545
1886	50	13,88,773	12,068	44,111
1887	55	14,46,644	12,163	43,270
1888	61	14,57,015	12,752	47,789
1889	69	15,91,328	13,380	52,490
1890	70	18,95,660	13,785	59,139
1891	67	19,09,123	14,347	61,981
1892	68	19,34,716	14,900	65,087
1893	69	20,41,208	16,664	67,870
1894	69	20,27,374	18,265	70,553
1895	69	21,23,892	20,217	75,740
1896	71	21,86,323	21,335	78,455

(contd.)

Appendix I (contd.)

Year	Number of Mills	Number of Spindles	Number of Looms	Average Daily Employment
1897	75	21,87,425	21,287	69,530
1898	82	22,26,982	21,379	70,728
1899	82	24,10,861	22,209	77,169
1900	82	25,36,891	22,215	72,914
1901	81	25,71,092	22,414	82,162
1902	80	25,23,769	22,845	86,122
1903	80	25,33,382	23,125	86,913
1904	79	25,34,230	24,136	89,915
1905	81	25,60,916	28,073	92,924
1906	84	26,14,323	28,778	1,00,798
1907	85	26,13,483	31,982	98,101
1908	86	27,34,683	35,967	1,01,536
1909	89	28,00,345	39,264	1,05,751
1910	89	28,24,046	41,931	1,04,550
1911	87	28,90,590	42,467	1,04,500
1912	86	28,85,452	43,388	1,09,691
1913	90	29,25,966	45,250	1,10,033
1914	85	30,09,172	48,845	1,09,860
1915	86	29,94,367	51,846	1,11,924
1916	86	29,84,575	53,205	1,18,303
1917	87	29,33,715	57,921	1,25,713
1918	87	28,82,648	59,162	1,24,199
1919	85	29,34,476	60,778	1,26,368

SOURCE: *Indian Tariff Board, II*, pp. 69-70.

Appendix II: Accidents in the Town and Island of Bombay

Year	All the Factories				Cotton Mills Only			
	Fatal	Serious	Minor	Total	Fatal	Serious	Minor	Total
1892	5	72	525	602				
1893	5	33	639	677				
1894	11	24	712	747				
1895	11	32	765	808	9	24	656	689
1896	8	42	832	882	6	31	682	719
1897	11	51	770	832	9	37	681	727
1898	11	69	799	879	10	60	699	769
1901	16	32	1,237	1,285				
1902	16	24	1,113	1,153				
1903	11	30	1,111	1,152				
1904	7	29	1,022	1,058				
1905	11	41	996	1,048				
1906	6	53	976	1,035				
1907	13	87	1,028	1,128				
1908	15	83	908	1,008				
1909	10	52	1,034	1,096				
1911	12	23	1,014	1,049				

SOURCE: *Annual Reports of the Factory Inspector for the Presidency of Bombay.*

Appendix III: Variation in Population in Bombay City, 1872-1921

Section	1872	1881	1891	1901	1911	1921	Variation 1872-1921
Upper Colaba	3,348	2,867	4,335	3,956	1,557	293	-3,055
Lower Colaba	13,253	14,265	13,622	13,023	19,679	1,94,971	+6,244
Fort South	2,363	3,515	3,951	3,309	3,462	3,956	+1,593
Fort North	29,732	33,828	32,847	22,956	25,400	30,534	+,802
Esplanade	10,464	13,080	10,064	10,398	17,761	12,165	+1,701
Chakla	36,748	37,048	32,197	24,384	24,231	22,996	-13,752
Mandvi	35,100	42,351	37,295	31,402	33,202	38,517	+3,417
Umarkhadi	49,873	54,656	52,466	48,481	45,679	47,218	-2,655
Dongri	25,556	33,290	30,317	25,778	27,246	19,966	-5,590
Market	43,198	49,130	44,751	28,415	30,172	35,080	-8,118
Dhobi Talao	37,915	39,409	39,945	29,553	28,684	42,171	+4,256
Fanaswadi	20,760	23,218	24,069	16,354	27,403	30,105	+9,345
Bhuleshwar	36,029	38,106	38,363	30,229	36,459	36,422	-1,407
Kumbharwada	27,594	34,990	32,209	27,544	27,703	32,481	+4,887
Khara Talao	23,638	28,691	27,035	23,161	22,979	23,925	+287
Khetwadi	24,817	29,436	28,814	27,160	31,937	39,615	+14,798
Girgaum	21,234	35,319	26,999	14,866	30,779	36,003	+14,769
Chaupati	7,531	10,975	11,512	6,739	11,397	14,260	+6,729
Walkeshwar	7,741	11,303	12,990	10,563	10,640	17,188	+9,447
Mahalakshi	4,317	6,232	17,014	18,092	26,302	37,108	+32,791
Tardeo	–	20,281	18,980	20,958	27,758	31,933	+31,933
Kamathipura	46,996	28,455	29,203	26,706	36,751	44,585	-2,411
1st Nagpada	–	9,372	11,133	10,577	6,414	7,645	+7,645
2nd Nagpada	–	15,922	18,768	18,591	21,700	23,103	+23,103
Byculla	28,032	26,842	47,403	57,646	75,348	91,285	+63,253
Tadwadi	10,083	14,542	21,298	18,460	28,424	39,909	+29,826
Mazagaon	20,973	27,904	33,640	27,933	30,075	32,092	+11,119
Parel	13,773	18,560	28,740	33,390	45,474	59,534	+45,761
Sewri	4,460	5,555	6,063	9,294	19,067	27,124	+22,664
Sion	11,572	17,237	19,601	25,443	30,680	52,913	+41,341
Mahim	14,310	17,309	18,505	27,386	30,492	47,171	+32,861
Worli	10,042	14,621	25,493	45,588	89,611	1,18,045	+108,003
TOTAL	6,44,405	7,73,196	8,21,764	7,76,006	9,79,445	11,75,914	+5,31,509

SOURCE: *Various Census Reports and Tables.*

Appendix IV: Density of Population in Bombay (Number of Persons per Acre), 1881-1921

Section	1881	1891	1901	1911	1921
Upper Colaba	20	30	27	11	23
Lower Colaba	56	52	49	70	72
Fort South	27	30	25	26	31
Fort North	258	247	171	158	195
Esplanade	21	16	16	26	22
Chakla	726	624	473	470	489
Mandvi	261	227	191	202	206
Umarkhadi	526	498	460	434	469
Dongri	118	106	90	95	69
Market	556	502	319	339	412
Dhobi Talao	402	401	296	338	357
Fanaswadi	189	192	131	219	306
Bhuleshwar	508	506	399	481	471
Kumbharwada	778	699	598	602	737
Khara Talao	700	649	556	552	582
Khetwadi	175	169	159	188	256
Girgaum	206	217	119	247	320
Chaupati	100	103	60	102	131
Walkeshwar	21	24	19	20	31
Mahalakshmi	17	46	28	41	58
Tardeo	90	83	92	121	213
Kamathipura	438	442	404	556	714
1st Nagapada	323	376	357	218	260
2nd Nagpada	482	552	547	638	699
Byculla	29	51	113	147	161
Tadwadi	31	44	38	59	82
Mazagaon	49	59	45	41	34
Parel	17	26	60	82	107
Sewri	13	14	21	38	50
Sion	4	5	6	7	16
Mahim	19	10	21	24	32
Worli	10	17	25	49	53

SOURCE: *Various Census Reports and Tables.*

Appendix V: Number of Cotton Millworkers in Sections, 1872-1906

Section	1872	1881	1901	1906
Upper Colaba	–	6	6	13
Lower Colaba	174	666	837	942
Fort South	–	–	–	–
Fort North	4	66	99	–
Esplanade	5	83	81	114
Chakla	49	19	51	47
Mandvi	54	31	237	65
Umarkhadi	208	318	603	505
Dongri	89	558	659	331
Market	3	27	99	113
Dhobi Talao	51	278	124	145
Fanaswadi	18	94	118	100
Bhuleshwar	66	75	189	178
Kumbharwada	52	451	620	273
Khara Talao	57	188	359	2,352
Khetwadi	106	911	1,216	1,114
Girgaum	61	628	363	308
Chaupati	42	1,171	746	636
Walkeshwar	2	742	275	421
Mahalakshmi	16	1,192	4,172	5,571
Tardeo	–	3,008	1,859	3,090
Kamathipura	3,852	1,434	1,693	2,523
1st Nagpada	–	345	526	72
2nd Nagpada	–	479	964	868
Byculla	9	3,393	11,316	17,714
Tadwadi	–	1,716	2,765	5,063
Mazagaon	54	2,214	4,210	6,151
Parel	81	3,226	13,293	20,106
Sewri	–	239	2,474	4,854
Sion	3	870	3,113	6,591
Mahim	119	439	2,488	3,188
Worli	–	373	17,143	28,277
TOTAL	5,175	25,241	73,953	1,12,027

SOURCE: *Various Census Reports and Tables.*

Appendix VI: Births and Deaths in Bombay City, 1890-1919

Year	Births	Deaths	Birth-rate per 1,000 population	Death-rate per 1,000 population	Infant mortality (1 year and under)	Rate per 1,000 births registered
1890	15,568	20,534	–	26.55	–	–
1891	15,518	23,847	18.88	29.01	7,418	478.0
1892	15,485	26,518	18.84	32.26	7,763	501.3
1893	15,218	23,142	18.51	28.15	6.446	423.6
1894	15,058	27,339	18.32	33.25	7,451	494.8
1895	15,684	25,081	19.08	30.52	6,683	426.1
1896	15,890	33,451	19.33	40.71	7,273	457.6
1897	9,336	47,896	11.36	58.28	7,508	804.2
1898	10,784	51,961	13.12	63.23	6,279	582.3
1899	10,624	56,434	12.92	68.07	8,351	786.1
1900	12,688	79,350	15.43	96.55	13,492	1063.3
1901	13,520	59,495	17.42	76.56	7,768	574.5
1902	17,599	48,414	22.57	62.38	9,553	542.8
1903	16,375	50,513	21.10	65.09	8,718	532.3
1904	19,556	42,676	25.20	54.99	8,981	459.2
1905	19,141	47,762	24.66	61.54	10,664	557.1
1906	20,769	52,874	21.24	54.07	11,106	534.7
1907	19,535	38,687	19.97	39.56	8,276	423.6
1908	20,166	38,271	20.62	39.13	9,077	450.1
1909	19,839	34,878	20.28	35.56	8,030	404.7
1910	19,939	34,933	20.39	35.72	8,253	413.9
1911	21,376	34,961	21.82	35.69	8,120	379.8
1912	21,518	38,954	21.96	39.77	9,646	448.2
1913	19,644	31,806	20.05	32.47	7,488	381.1
1914	19,679	31,853	20.09	32.52	7,580	385.1
1915	20,052	23,681	20.47	24.17	6,602	329.2
1916	21,180	30,574	21.62	31.21	8,215	387.8
1917	21,651	33,390	22.10	34.09	8,870	409.6
1918	21,733	58,388	22.18	59.61	12,829	590.3
1919	20,730	68,610	21.15	70.04	13,534	652.9

SOURCE: *Annual Reports of the Municipal Commissioner for Bombay City and Island.*

Appendix VII: Births and Deaths in Bombay Presidency in British Registration Districts, 1890-1919

Year	Birth-rate/1,000 of population	Death-rate/1,000 of population	Infant mortality rate/ 1,000 of births
1890	38.97	28.18	153.48
1891	36.27	27.26	166.72
1892	34.57	32.52	187.67
1893	35.30	27.20	166.74
1894	35.08	32.26	185.75
1895	35.83	28.61	181.05
1896	36.76	31.69	176.44
1897	33.46	39.84	216.69
1898	30.94	29.16	171.00
1899	36.42	35.72	195.57
1900	26.87	70.07	313.33
1901	25.19	37.12	193.88
1902	34.16	39.04	196.32
1903	31.22	43.91	213.31
1904	35.09	41.39	194.54
1905	33.07	31.84	224.51
1906	33.84	35.06	220.39
1907	33.03	32.82	199.04
1908	35.72	27.15	185.57
1909	35.59	27.38	180.44
1910	37.32	30.30	202.77
1911	36.00	28.35	165.83
1912	34.97	34.88	218.70
1913	34.96	26.63	188.42
1914	37.43	29.48	–
1915	37.10	26.12	–
1916	35.98	33.32	–
1917	35.73	40.76	–
1918	31.61	88.05	–
1919	27.90	32.53	–

SOURCE: *Annual Reports of Sanitary Commissioner, Presidency of Bombay* and *Census of India, 1921*, IX.

Appendix VIII: Numbers of Deaths Among Weavers, Spinners and other Millworkers, 1890-1919

Year	Deaths from all causes	Deaths from phthisis
1890	123	–
1891	104	–
1892	133	–
1894	160	–
1895	126	–
1897	474	–
1900	413	641
1901	351	613
1902	230	308
1903	251	370
1904	2,268	358
1905	2,929	401
1906	3,430	534
1907	2,314	–
1908	2,056	–
1909	1,427	–
1910	1,465	–
1911	1,909	–
1912	1,898	–
1913	1,918	–
1914	2,033	–
1915	1,328	–
1916	2,215	–
1917	2,031	–
1919	7,227	–

SOURCES: *Annual Reports of the Municipal Commissioner for Bombay City and Island,* and IFLC, 1908, II, p. 43, Evidence of Dr. Turner, the Executive Health Officer, Bombay.

Bibliography

GOVERNMENT RECORDS

1. Government of India (National Archives of India, New Delhi)
   Home Department (Political).
   Home Department (Police).
2. Government of Bombay (Maharashtra State Archives, Bombay)
   General Department.
   Home Department.
   Judicial Department.

OFFICIAL PUBLICATIONS

Annual Administration Report of the Municipal Commissioner of Bombay, 1875-1920.

Annual Police Returns Showing the State of Crime in the Town and Island of Bombay, 1884-1920.

Annual Report of the Sanitary Commissioner for the Government of Bombay, 1875-1920.

Annual Report on the Working of the Indian Factories Act in the Bombay Presidency, 1893-1925.

Bombay Factory Commission, 1875 (Bombay, 1875).

Bombay Factory Commission, 1885 (Bombay, 1885).

Census of the City of Bombay taken on 21st February 1872 (Bombay, 1873).

Census of the City and Island of Bombay taken on 17 February, 1881, by T.S. Weir (Bombay, 1883).

Census of India, 1891, vol. VII, Bombay and its Feudatories, part I, Report (Bombay, 1892).

Census of India, 1901, vols. X and XI (Bombay, 1901).

Census of the Town and Island of Bombay, 1906 (Bombay, 1906).

Census of India, 1911, vol. VII, Bombay Presidency, part I, Report (Bombay, 1912).

Census of India, 1911, vols. VIII , Bombay, Town and Island, parts I and II, Report and Tables; and vol. X, part IV, History (Bombay, 1912).

Census of India, 1921, vol. IX, Cities of Bombay Presidency, parts I and II, Report and Tables (Bombay, 1922).

Census of India, 1921, vol. VIII, Bombay Presidency (Bombay, 1922).

Gazetteer of Bombay City and Island, 1909, vol. I, by S.M. Edwardes (Bombay, 1909).

Imperial Gazetteer of India, 1885, vol. 3, 2nd edn., by W.W. Hunter (London, 1885).

Imperial Gazetteer of India, 1908, vol. VIII, new edn. (Oxford, 1908).

Indian Industrial Commission, 1916-18, vols. I and IV (Calcutta, 1918).

Indian Tariff Board (Cotton Textile Industry Enquiry), vols. I, II and III (Calcutta, 1927).

Report of the Excise Committee appointed by the Government of Bombay, 1922-23, vol. I.

Indian Factory Commission, 1890, Report (Calcutta, 1890).

Indian Factory Labour Commission, 1908, Report and Evidences, 2 vols. (Simla, 1908).

Report of the Industrial Disputes Committee (Bombay, 1922).

Report of the Royal Commission on Labour in India, 1929 (HMSO, London, 1931).

Report of the Textile Factories Labour Committee, 1906.

Report of the Textile Labour Inquiry Committee, 1937-38, vol. II, Final Report (Bombay, 1938).

Report on an Enquiry into the Wages and Hours of Labour in the Cotton Mill Industry, May, 1921, by G. Findlay Shirras (Bombay, 1923).

Report on an Enquiry into the Wages and Hours of Labour in the Cotton Mill Industry in August 1923 (Bombay, 1925).

Report on an Investigation into the Causes of Malaria in Bombay and the Measures Necessary for its Control, 1911.

Report on the Native Newspapers in the Bombay Presidency.

Source Material for a History of the Freedom Movement in India, Government of Bombay, vol. II, 1885-1920 (Bombay, 1958).

NON-OFFICIAL PUBLICATIONS

Reports of the Bombay Millowners' Association, 1875-1925.

Labour Movement in India: Documents: 1891-1917, vol. II: Factories, edited by S.D. Punekar and R. Varickayil (Delhi, 1990).

Labour Movement in India: Documents: 1918-20, vol. III, edited by A.R. Desai, (Delhi, 1988).

NEWSPAPERS AND PERIODICALS

Bombay Chronicle

Bombay Gazette

Indian Textile Journal

Times of India

BOOKS AND ARTICLES

Amin, Shahid, 'Gandhi as Mahatma: Gorakhpur District, Eastern UP, 1921-2', in Ranajit Guha, ed., *Subaltern Studies, III* (Delhi, 1984).

Arnold, David, 'Industrial Violence in Colonial India', *Comparative Studies in Society and History*, vol. XIII, no. 2 (1980), pp. 243-55.

———'Touching the Body: Perspectives on the Indian Plague, 1896-1900', in R. Guha, ed., *Subaltern Studies, V* (Delhi, 1987), pp. 55-90.

Bagchi, A.K., *Private Investment in India, 1900-1939* (Cambridge, 1972, 1980).

———'Working Class Consciousness', *EPW*, vol. XXV, no. 30 (28 July 1990), PE54-PE60.

———'Workers and the Historians' Burden', in K.N. Panikkar, T.J. Byers and Utsa Patnaik, *The Making of History: Essays Presented to Irfan Habib* (Delhi, 2000).

Bayly, C.A., 'The Pre-History of "Communalism"? Religious Conflict in India, 1700-1860', *MAS*, vol. XIX, no. 2 (1985), pp. 177-203.

Bhattacharya, S., 'Cotton Mills and Spinning Wheels: Swadeshi and the Indian Capitalist Class, 1920-22', *EPW*, vol. XI, no. 47 (1976), 1828-34.

———'Capital and Labour in Bombay City, 1928-29', *EPW*, vol. XVI, nos. 42 and 43 (1981), pp. PE36-PE44.

———'The Colonial State, Capital and Labour: Bombay, 1919-31', in S. Bhattacharya and Romila Thapar, eds., *Situating Indian History* (Delhi, 1986), pp. 171-93.

———'Swaraj and the Kamgar: The Indian National Congress and the Bombay Working Class, 1919-31', in R. Sisson and S. Wolpert, eds., *Congress and Indian Nationalism: The Pre-Independence Phase* (Berkeley and Los Angeles, 1988), pp. 223-49.

Briggs, A. and J. Saville, eds., *Essays in Labour History* (London, 1960).

Burnett-Hurst, A.R., *Labour and Housing in Bombay: A Study in the Economic Condition of the Wage-Earning Classes of Bombay* (London, 1925).

Cashman, R.I., *The Myth of the Lokamanya: Tilak and Mass Politics in Maharashtra* (Berkeley and Los Angeles, 1975).

Chakrabarty, Dipesh, 'Communal Riots and Labour: Bengal Jute Mill Hands in the 1890s', *Occasional Paper no. 11*, October 1976, Centre for Studies in Social Sciences, Calcutta.

Chakrabarty, Dipesh and Ranajit Das Gupta, 'Some Aspects of Labour History of Bengal in the Nineteenth Century: Two Views', *Occasional Paper no. 40*, October 1981, CSSS, Calcutta.

Chakrabarty, Dipesh, *Rethinking Working-Class History: Bengal, 1890-1940* (Delhi, 1989).

Chandavarkar, R., 'Workers' Politics and Mill Districts in Bombay between the Wars', *MAS*, vol. XV, no. 3 (1981), pp. 603-47.

———*The Origins of Industrial Capitalism in India: Business Strategies and Working Classes in Bombay, 1900-1940* (Cambridge, 1994).

———*Imperial Power and Popular Politics: Class Resistance and the State in India, c. 1850-1950* (Cambridge, 1998).

———'Questions of Class: The General Strikes in Bombay, 1928-29', in Jonathan P. Parry, Jan Breman and Karin Kapadia, eds., *Contributions to Indian Sociology*, vol. 33, nos. 1 and 2 (January-August 1999), Special Issue: *The Worlds of Indian Industrial Labour.*

Chandra, Bipan, *The Rise and Growth of Economic Nationalism in India: Economic Policies of Indian National Leadership 1880-1905* (Delhi, 1966, 1991).

———*Communalism in Modern India* (Delhi, 1984).

Chicherov, A.I., 'Tilak's Trial and the Bombay Political Strike of 1908', in N.M. Goldberg and I.M. Reisner, eds., *Tilak and Struggle for Indian Freedom* (Delhi, 1966).

Das, R.K., *Factory Labour in India* (Berlin, 1923).

———*History of Indian Labour Legislation* (Calcutta, 1941).

Das Gupta, R., 'Factory Labour in Eastern India: Sources of Supply 1855-1946: Some Preliminary Findings', *IESHR*, vol. XII, no. 3 (1976).

———'Material Conditions and Behavioural Aspects of Calcutta Working Class, 1875-1899', Occasional Paper no. 22, January 1979, CSSS, Calcutta.

———*Labour and Working Class in Eastern India: Studies in Colonial History* (Calcutta, 1994).

De Haan, Arjan, 'Migrant Labour in Calcutta Jute Mills: Class, Instability and Control', in Peter Robb, ed., *Dalit Movements and the Meanings of Labour in India* (Delhi, 1993).

———'Migration in Eastern India: A Segmented Labour Market', *IESHR*, vol. XXXII, no. 1 (January-March 1995).

———'The *Badli* System in Industrial Labour Recruitment: Managers' and Workers' Strategies in Calcutta's Jute Industry', in Parry et al., eds., *Contributions to Indian Sociology*, vol. 33, nos. 1 and 2 (January-August 1999).

Dobbin, Christine, *Urban Leadership in Western India: Politics and Communities in Bombay City, 1840-85* (London, 1972).

Dwarkadas, Kanji, *Forty Five Years with Labour* (Bombay, 1962).

Edwardes, S.M., *The Rise of Bombay—A Retrospect* (Bombay, 1902).

———*By-Ways of Bombay* (Bombay, 1912).

———*The Bombay City Police: A Historical Sketch, 1672-1916* (Bombay, 1923).

Freitag, Sandria B., *Collective Action and Community: Public Arenas and the Emergence of Communalism in North India* (Delhi, 1990).

Ghosh, Parimal, 'Communalism and Colonial Labour: Experience of Calcutta Jute Mill Workers, 1880-1930', *EPW*, vol. XXV, no. 30 (28 July 1990).

Gopal, Ram, *Lokmanya Tilak: A Biography* (1956).

Gordon, L.A., 'Social and Economic Conditions of Bombay Workers on the Eve of the 1908 Strike', in N.M. Goldberg and I.M. Reisner, eds., *Tilak and Struggle for Indian Freedom* (Delhi, 1966).

Harrison, Mark, 'The Ordering of the Urban Environment: Time, Work and the Occurrence of Crowds, 1790-1835', *Past and Present* (February 1986).

Holmstrom, M., *Industry and Inequality: Towards a Social Anthropology of Indian Labour* (Cambridge, 1984).

Jones, Kenneth W., 'Religious Identity and the Indian Census', N.G. Barrier, ed., *The Census in British India: New Perspectives* (Delhi, 1987).

———*Socio-Religious Reform Movements in British India* (Cambridge, 1989).

Joshi, Chitra, 'Kanpur Textile Labour: Some Structural Features of Formative Years', *EPW*, November 1981.

———'Bonds of Community, Ties of Religion: Kanpur Textile Workers in the Early Twentieth Century', *IESHR*, vol. XXII, no. 3 (1985).

———'Hope and Despair: Textile Workers in Kanpur in 1937-38 and the 1990s', in Parry, et al., eds., Contributions to Indian Sociology, vol. 33, nos. 1 and 2 (January-August 1999).

Karmarkar, D.P., *Bal Gangadhar Tilak* (Bombay, 1956).

Karnik, V.B., *Strikes in India* (Bombay, 1967).

Kelman, J.H., *Labour in India: A Study of Conditions of Indian Women in Modern Industry* (London, New York, 1923).

Klein, I., 'Urban Development and Death: Bombay City, 1870-1914', *MAS*, vol. XX, no. 4, 1986.

———'Plague Policy and Popular Unrest in British India', *MAS*, vol. XXII, no. 4, 1988.

Kooiman, D., *Bombay Textile Labour: Managers, Trade Unionists and Officials, 1918-1939* (Delhi, 1989).

Kumar, Radha, 'Family and Factory: Women in the Bombay Cotton Textile Industry, 1919-39', *IESHR*, vol. XX, no. 1, March 1983.

———'City Lives: Workers' Housing and Rent in Bombay, 1911-47', *IESHR*, 25 July 1987.

Kumar, Ravinder, 'The Bombay Textile Strike, 1919', *IESHR*, vol. VIII, no. 1, 1971.

———'From Swaraj to Purna Swaraj: Nationalist Politics in the City of Bombay, 1920-32', in D.A. Low, ed., *Congress and the Raj: Facets of Indian Struggle*, London, 1977.

Kydd, J.C., *A History of Factory Legislation in India* (Calcutta, 1920).

McLane, John R., *Indian Nationalism and the Early Congress* (Princeton, 1977).

Masselos, J.C., *Towards Nationalism: Group Affiliations and the Politics of Public Associations in Nineteenth Century Western India* (Bombay, 1974).

———'Power in Bombay "Moholla", 1904-1915: An Initial Exploration into the World of the Indian Urban Muslim', South Asia, vol. VI (Dec. 1976).

———'Change and Custom in the Format of the Bombay Mohurrum during the Nineteenth and Twentieth Centuries', *South Asia*, n.s., vol. 5, no. 2 (1982), p. 57.

Mehta, M.M., *Structure of Cotton Mill Industry in India* (Allahabad, 1949).

Mehta, S.D., *The Cotton Mills of India, 1854-1954* (Bombay, 1954).

Morris, M.D., *The Emergence of an Industrial Labour Force in India: A Study of the Bombay Cotton Mills, 1854-1947* (Berkeley and Los Angeles, 1965).

———'The Growth of Large-Scale Industry to 1947', in Dharma Kumar, ed., *The Cambridge Economic History of India*, vol. II, *c. 1757-1970* (Cambridge, 1983).

Mukherji, K., 'Trends in Real Wages in Cotton Textile Mills in Bombay City and Island, from 1900 to 1951', *Artha Vijnana*, vol. I, no. 1 (1959).

Murphy, E.D., 'Class and community in India: the Madras Labour Union, 1918-21', *IESHR*, vol. XIV, no. 3 (July-September, 1977).

———*Unions in Conflict: A Comparative Study of Four South Indian Textile Centres, 1918-1939* (Delhi, 1981).

Nair, Janaki, 'Production Regimes, Cultural Processes: Industrial Labour in Mysore', *IESHR*, vol. XXX, no. 3 (July-September 1993).

———*Miners and Millhands: Work, Culture and Politics in Princely Mysore* (Delhi, 1998).

Newman, Richard, *Workers and Unions in Bombay, 1918-29: A Study of Organisation in the Cotton Mills* (Canberra, 1981).

O'Hanlon, Rosalind, *Caste, Conflict, and Ideology: Mahatma Jotirao Phule and Low Caste Protest in Nineteenth-Century Western India* (Cambridge, 1985).

Omvedt, Gail, *Dalits and the Democratic Revolution: Dr. Ambedkar and the Dalit Movement in Colonial India* (Delhi, 1994).

Pandey, Gyanendra, 'Rallying Round the Cow: Sectarian Strife in the Bhojpuri Region, c. 1888-1917', in R. Guha, ed., *Subaltern Studies, II* (Delhi, 1983).

———*The Construction of Communalism in Colonial North India* (Delhi, 1992).

———'The Prose of Otherness', in David Arnold and David Hardiman, eds., *Subaltern Studies*, VIII (Delhi, 1994),

Parry, Jonathan P., 'Lords of Labour: Working and Shirking in Bhilai', in Parry, et al., eds., *Contributions to Indian Sociology*, vol. 33, nos. 1 and 2 (January-August 1999).

Patel, Sujata, *The Making of Industrial Relations: The Ahmedabad Textile Industry, 1918-1939* (Delhi, 1987).

Robb, Peter, 'The Challenge of Gau Mata: British Policy and Religious Change in India, 1880-1916', *MAS*, vol. 20, no. 2 (1986).

Sarkar, Sumit, 'The Conditions and Nature of Subaltern Militancy: Bengal from Swadeshi to Non-Co-operation, c. 1905-22', in Ranajit Guha, ed., *Subaltern Studies*, III (Delhi, 1984).

Sen, Samita, 'At the Margins: Women Workers in the Bengal Jute Industry', in Parry, et al., eds., *Contributions to Indian Sociology*, vol. 33, nos. 1 and 2 (January-August 1999).

———*Women and Labour in Late Colonial India: The Bengal Jute Industry* (Cambridge, 1999).

Sen, Sukomal, *The Working Class of India: History of Emergence and Movement* (Calcutta, 1977).

Simeon, Dilip, *The Politics of Labour under Late Colonialism: Workers, Unions and the State in Chota Nagpur, 1928-1939* (Delhi, 1995).

———'Work and Resistance in Jharia Coalfield', in Parry et al., eds., *Contributions to Indian Sociology*, vol. 33, nos. 1 and 2 (January-August 1999).

Smith, Thomas C., 'Peasant Time and Factory Time in Japan', *Past and Present* (May 1986).

Tahmankar, D.V., *Lokmanya Tilak: Father of Indian Unrest and Maker of Modern India* (London, 1956).

Thompson, E.P., *The Making of the English Working Class* (Harmondsworth, New York, 1963, 1980).

———'Time, Work-Discipline and Industrial Capitalism', *Past and Present*, no. 38 (December 1967).

Upadhyay, S.B., 'Communalism and Working Class: Riot of 1893 in Bombay City', in *EPW*, vol. XXIV, no. 30 (29 July 1989).

———'Cotton Millworkers in Bombay, 1875 to 1918: Conditions of Work and Life', *EPW*, vol. XXV, no. 30 (28 July 1990).

Index